European Union Health Law

European Union Health Law

Fifth Edition

Herman Nys

This book was originally published as a monograph in the International Encyclopaedia of Laws/Medical Law.

Founding Editor: Roger Blanpain
General Editor: Frank Hendrickx
Volume Editor: Herman Nys; Associate Editor: Tom Goffin

Wolters Kluwer

Published by:
Kluwer Law International B.V.
PO Box 316
2400 AH Alphen aan den Rijn
The Netherlands
E-mail: lrs-sales@wolterskluwer.com
Website: www.wolterskluwer.com/en/solutions/kluwerlawinternational

Sold and distributed by:
Wolters Kluwer Legal & Regulatory U.S.
920 Links Avenue
Landisville, PA 17538
United States of America
E-mail: customer.service@wolterskluwer.com

ISBN 978-94-035-4728-2

e-Book: ISBN 978-94-035-4738-1
web-PDF: ISBN 978-94-035-4748-0

This title is available on www.kluwerlawonline.com

The Author

Emeritus Professor Dr Herman Nys (born on 20 January 1951) studied Law at K.U. Leuven, Belgium (1969–1974) and K.U. Nijmegen, Netherlands, (1974–1975). From 1975 to 1980, he worked as an assistant, specializing in Healthcare Law, at the Centre for Hospital Sciences in Leuven, where in 1980 he received his doctoral degree for his thesis on 'Legal Aspects of Health Care Planning'. From 1981 to 1989, he was affiliated with the law school in Leuven, first as Lecturer in Medical Law and since 1985 as an Associate Professor. He has been the Director of the Centre of Biomedical Ethics and Law in Leuven from 1989 until 2015. In 1992, he was appointed as a professor, and he retired on 1 October 2016.

Between 2000 and 2006, he was also Professor of International Health Law at the University of Maastricht, the Netherlands. Prof Nys is the author of numerous books and articles on medical law and healthcare policy. He is a member of the editorial boards of several learned journals and editor-in-chief of the *European Journal of Health Law.*

He was the co-founder and director (2008–2017) and is an honorary member (2022) of the European Association of Health Law and Vice-President of the World Association of Medical Law (2010–2012).

He is a member of the European Group of Ethics in Science and New Technologies (2022–2025).

The Author

Table of Contents

The Author 3

List of Abbreviations 19

General Introduction 21

§1. Medical Law and Health Law 21

§2. Medical Law and Health Law in the EU 22

§3. European Union Health Law or EU Health Law 23
I. EU Biomedical Law 23
II. EU Health Law 24

§4. The Contents of EU Health Law in This Monograph 26

Part I. Definitions 27

Chapter 1. Definition of Healthcare, Medical Care and Health Services in EU Law 27

§1. Are Healthcare and Medical Care Synonymous in EU Health Law? 27
I. Healthcare 27
II. Medical Care 28

§2. Health Services 33
I. Services to Assess, Maintain or Restore the State of Health of a Patient 33
II. Prescription, Dispensation and Provision of Medicinal Products and Medical Devices 36
A. Medicinal Product 38
B. Medical Device 38
C. Health Technology 39
III. Freedom of Member States to Determine Health Services 40
A. The Selling of Contact Lenses Is Not a Health Service 40
B. An Optician's Shop Is Not a Health Service 41
C. Pharmaceutical Activities Are Health Services 42

1. Health Services Include Pharmaceutical Services 42
2. All Pharmaceutical Services Are Health Services 42
D. Pharmacies Are Health Services 44
E. Dental Services Are Health Services 44
F. Day and Night Reception Centres for the Elderly 44
G. The Administration of Medication by a Nurse 48
H. Sports or Fitness Clubs Are Not Health Services 49
I. Cannabis-Based Medicinal Preparations 49

Chapter 2. The Concept of Health Professionals in EU Law 50

§1. Not Limited to Regulated Professions 50

§2. Medical, Allied and Pharmaceutical Professions 50

§3. Large Margin of Discretion for Member States to Determine a Medical or a Paramedical Profession 51
I. Opticians 51
II. Physiotherapy 52
A. General Observation 52
B. Physiotherapy and Disturbance Field Diagnostics (Method of Treatment Alternative to Traditional Medicine) 53
C. Physiotherapy and Osteopathy (Non-conventional Therapy) 56
D. Psychotherapy 59

Part II. Access and Pursuit of the Healthcare Professions 63

Chapter 1. The Mutual Recognition of Professional Qualifications 63

§1. Purpose 63

§2. Effects of Recognition 64

§3. The European Professional Card 64
I. Limited Implementation of European Professional Card for the Healthcare Professions 64
II. Application for an EPC and Creation of an Internal Market Information System File 65
III. Processing and Access to Data Regarding the EPC (Prohibition and Restriction of Activities) 65
IV. Verification of the Authenticity and Validity of an EPC by Third Parties 66

§4. Partial Access 66

§5. Proportionality Principle and Proportionality Test 69

Chapter 2. Free Provision of Services 72

§1. Principle of Free Provision of Services 72
I. No Restriction of Free Provision of Services 72
II. Subject to Professional Rules Directly Linked to Professional Qualifications 72
III. Exemption from Authorization by, Registration with or Membership of a Professional Organization 74

§2. Declaration to Be Made in Advance 74

§3. Use of the Professional Title of the Member State of Establishment 75

§4. Prior Check of Professional Qualifications 76

§5. Administrative Cooperation in the Event of Justified Doubts or Complaints 77

§6. Information to Be Given to the Recipients of the Service 77

Chapter 3. Freedom of Establishment Through Recognition on the Basis of Coordination of Minimum Training Conditions 78

§1. Doctors of Medicine 78
I. Principle of Automatic Recognition 78
II. (Admission to) Basic Medical Training 79
III. (Admission to) Specialist Medical Training 79
IV. Types of Specialist Medical Training 81
V. Specific Training in General Medical Practice 81
VI. Pursuit of the Professional Activities of General Practitioners 81

§2. Nurses Responsible for General Care 82
I. Principle of Automatic Recognition 82
II. Training of Nurses Responsible for General Care 82

§3. Dental Practitioners 84
I. Principle of Automatic Recognition 84
II. Basic Dental Training 84
III. Specialist Dental Training 86
IV. Pursuit of the Professional Activities of Dental Practitioners 86

§4. Midwives 87

I. The Training of Midwives 87
II. Procedures for the Automatic Recognition of Evidence of Formal Qualifications as a Midwife 88
III. Pursuit of the Professional Activities of a Midwife 88

§5. PHARMACISTS 89
I. Principle of Automatic Recognition 89
II. Training as a Pharmacist 89
III. Pursuit of the Professional Activities of a Pharmacist 90

Chapter 4. Freedom of Establishment Through the General System for the Recognition of Evidence of Training 91

Chapter 5. Common Provision on Establishment: Use of Professional Titles 92

Chapter 6. Detailed Rules for Pursuing the Profession 93

§1. KNOWLEDGE OF LANGUAGES 93

§2. USE OF ACADEMIC TITLES 95

§3. APPROVAL BY HEALTH INSURANCE FUNDS FOR DOCTORS AND DENTAL PRACTITIONERS 95

Chapter 7. Exchange of Information Regarding Disciplinary Action and Criminal Sanctions and Alert Mechanism 97

§1. EXCHANGE OF INFORMATION REGARDING DISCIPLINARY ACTION AND CRIMINAL SANCTIONS 97

§2. ALERT MECHANISM 97

Part III. The Practice of the Healthcare Professions 101

Chapter 1. The (Illegal) Practice of Medical Acts 101

§1. OSTEOPATHY 101

§2. EYE EXAMINATIONS 102

Chapter 2. Professional Rules of Conduct 104

§1. SINGLE-PRACTICE RULE 104

§2. ADVERTISING FOR MEDICAL SERVICES 107
I. Legal Prohibition of Advertising 107
II. Prohibition by National Disciplinary Rules 110

§3. MEDICAL FEES 112

Part IV. Patients' Rights in EU Law 115

Chapter 1. Who Is a Patient in EU Law? 115

Chapter 2. Patients' Rights in EU Law in General 118

§1. INTRODUCTION 118

§2. PATIENTS' RIGHTS IN THE CHARTER OF FUNDAMENTAL RIGHTS OF THE EU 119
I. Introduction 119
II. Free and Informed Consent (Article 3.1 and 3.2a Charter) 120
III. Right to Privacy and Right to Data Protection 122
IV. Right of Access to Preventive Healthcare and to Benefit from Medical Treatment 123

§3. PATIENTS' RIGHTS IN SECONDARY EU LAW 124
I. Right to Report Suspected Side Effects of Medicinal Products 124
II. Right to Report Suspected Adverse Reactions of Medicinal Products 125
III. Right to Receive Information Regarding Implantable Medical Devices on an Implant Card 125

§4. PATIENTS' RIGHTS IN EU SOFT LAW DOCUMENTS 126
I. Documents Approved by the European Parliament 126
A. European Charter on the Rights of the Patient 126
B. European Charter for Children in Hospital 128
II. The European Charter of Patients' Rights 129
A. Introductory Remarks 129
B. European Charter of Patients' Rights: Part One – Fundamental Rights 130
C. European Charter of Patients' Rights: Part Two – Fourteen Patients' Rights 131
1. Article 1 Right to Preventive Measures 131
2. Article 2 Right of Access 132
3. Article 3 Right to Information 132

4. Article 4 Right to Consent 132
5. Article 5 Right to Free Choice 132
6. Article 6 Right to Privacy and Confidentiality 133
7. Article 7 Right to Respect of Patients' Time 133
8. Article 8 Right to the Observance of Quality Standards 133
9. Article 9 Right to Safety 134
10. Article 10 Right to Innovation 134
11. Article 11 Right to Avoid Unnecessary Suffering and Pain 134
12. Article 12 Right to Personalized Treatment 134
13. Article 13 Right to Complain 134
14. Article 14 Right to Compensation 135
D. European Charter of Patients' Rights: Part Three – Rights of Active Citizenship 135
E. European Charter of Patients' Rights: Part Four – Guidelines for Implementing the Charter 135
III. Opinion on 'Patients' Rights of the European Economic and Social Committee 136
A. Introduction 136
B. Rights of Patients 138
1. Right to Information 138
2. Right to Free and Informed Consent 138
3. Right to Dignity 139
4. Other Individual Rights 139
C. Recommendations for Implementing Patients' Rights 139
D. Towards an Affirmation of Collective Rights 140
IV. Patient's Rights in the Interinstitutional Proclamation on the European Pillar of Social Rights 140

Chapter 3. Patients' Rights and the Cross-Border Healthcare Directive 142

§1. The Patients' Right to Healthcare 142
I. The Patients' Right to Healthcare 142
A. The Patients' Right to Receive Healthcare in Another Member State 142
B. The Special Case of Access to Organs for Transplantation 144

§2. Patients' Rights to Information 144
I. The Patients' Right to Information with Regard to Reimbursement 145
II. The Patients' Right to Information Regarding the Nature of Healthcare and the Circumstances in Which It Is Provided 145
A. Information on Request of the Patient by the NCP of the Member State of Treatment 145
1. Relevant Information on the Standards and Guidelines on Quality of Safety 146

2. Information on Supervision and Assessment of Healthcare Providers 147
3. Information on the Accessibility of Hospitals for Persons with Disabilities 147
4. Information on a Specific Provider's Right to Provide Services 147
5. Information on Patients' Rights, Complaints Procedures and Mechanisms for Seeking Remedies 148
6. Information on the Legal and Administrative Options Available to Settle Disputes, Including in the Event of Harm Arising from Cross-Border Healthcare 148
7. Information on NCP in Other Member States 149
8. Language in Which Information Is Provided by NCP 149

B. Information to Be Provided by Healthcare Providers 150

§3. THE PATIENTS' RIGHT TO HEALTHCARE THAT IS SAFE AND OF GOOD QUALITY 154

I. Healthcare Corresponding with National and Union Quality and Safety Standards 154

II. Quality and Safety as a Justification for Prior Authorization 155

A. The Treatment Presents a Particular Risk for the Patient or the Population 155

B. Serious and Specific Concerns Relating to the Quality or Safety of the Care Provided by a Healthcare Provider 156

III. Quality and Safety as a Justification to Refuse a Prior Authorization 158

A. The Patient Will Be Exposed to a Safety Risk 158

B. The General Public Will Be Exposed to a Substantial Safety Hazard 159

C. Concerns Regarding the Quality and Safety of the Care Provided by a Healthcare Provider 159

IV. Healthcare Within a Time Limit Which Is Medically Justifiable and Religious Beliefs 159

§4. THE PATIENTS' RIGHT TO COMPLAIN 160

§5. THE PATIENTS' RIGHT TO RECEIVE COMPENSATION FOR DAMAGES 160

§6. THE PATIENTS' RIGHT TO RESPECT OF PRIVATE LIFE 161

§7. THE PATIENTS' RIGHT TO A MEDICAL RECORD AND ACCESS TO IT 161

§8. THE PATIENTS' RIGHT TO RECOGNITION OF A PRESCRIPTION FOR A MEDICINAL PRODUCT 163

Part V. The Physician-Patient Relationship in Specific Terms in EU Law 165

Table of Contents

Chapter 1. Clinical Trials on Medicinal Products for Human Use 165

§1. Introduction 165

§2. Field of Application of the Clinical Trials Regulation 166

§3. The Protection of Subjects in Clinical Trials 167
I. Prior Authorization 168
II. General Provisions for the Protection of Subjects 172
A. General Principle 172
B. Proportionality Requirement (Balance Benefits-Risks) 172
C. Informed Consent 173
1. Express Informed Consent as a Rule 173
2. Implicit Informed Consent for Cluster Trials 175
3. Withdrawal of Informed Consent 176
D. Respect for the Rights to Physical and Mental Integrity, Privacy and Data Protection 176
E. As Little Pain, Discomfort, Fear and Any Other Foreseeable Risk 177
F. Medical Care under the Responsibility of an Appropriately Qualified Medical Doctor/Dental Practitioner 177
G. No Undue Influence 177
H. Protection of Subjects During the Clinical Trial 178
1. Conduct in Accordance with the Protocol and Good Clinical Practice Principles 178
2. Adequate Monitoring of the Conduct of the Clinical Trial 178
3. Qualified Investigator 178
4. Suitable Facilities 178
5. Notification of Serious Breaches of Safety and Rights of a Subject 178
6. No Costs to Be Borne by the Subject 179
I. Damage Compensation 179
J. Summary of the Results of the Clinical Trial Within One Year 179
III. Clinical Trials on Incapacitated Subjects 180
A. Incapacitated Subject 180
B. Informed Consent of the Legally Designated Representative 180
1. Basic Rule 180
2. Legally Designated Representative 181
3. Participation and Signature of the Subject 181
C. Information to Be Provided to the Incapacitated Person 181
D. Respect for the Explicit Wish to Refuse or Withdraw Consent 181
E. No Incentives or Financial Inducements 181
F. Clinical Trial Is Essential and No Alternative 182

G. Directly Related to the Medical Condition of the Subject 182
H. A Direct Benefit for the Subject … Or … 182
I. Some Benefit for the Population Represented by the Subject and Directly Related to the Life-Threatening or Debilitating Medical Condition from Which the Subject Suffers 182
J. Ethical Assessment on the Basis of Expertise in the Relevant Disease 183
IV. Clinical Trials on Minors 183
A. Basic Rule 184
B. Informed Consent 184
1. Informed Consent of the Legally Designated Representative 184
2. Participation of the Minor 184
3. Assent of the Minor 184
4. Informed Consent of the Minor When He Reaches the Age of Legal Competence 184
C. Information to Be Provided to the Minor 185
D. Explicit Wish to Refuse Is Respected 185
E. No Incentives or Financial Inducements 185
F. A Medical Condition That Only Occurs in Minors … Or … 185
G. … Essential to Validate Alternatives 185
H. Directly Related to the Medical Condition of the Minor or No Alternative but Minors 186
I. A Direct Benefit for the Minor … Or … 186
J. … Some Benefit for the Population Represented by the Minor 186
K. Ethical Assessment on the Basis of Paediatric Expertise 186
V. Clinical Trials on Pregnant or Breastfeeding Women 187
VI. Clinical Trials on Other Vulnerable Subjects 187
VII. Clinical Trials in Emergency Situations 188

Chapter 2. Clinical Investigations on Medical Devices 190

§1. Field of Application 190

§2. Conditions to Conduct a Clinical Investigation 191
I. Generally Applicable Conditions 191
A. Authorization 191
B. No Negative Opinion of an Ethics Committee 192
C. Sponsor Established in the EU 192
D. Proportionality Requirement (Balance Benefits-Risks) 192
E. Informed Consent of the Subject 193
F. Contact Details for Further Information 194
G. Respect for the Rights to Physical and Mental Integrity, to Privacy and to Data Protection 194

H. As Little Pain, Discomfort, Fear and Any Other Foreseeable Risk 194
I. Medical Care under the Responsibility of an Appropriately Qualified Medical Doctor/Dental Practitioner 194
J. No Undue Influence 194
K. The Investigational Device Conforms to the Applicable General Safety and Performance Requirements 195
L. Carried Out in Accordance with Recognized Ethical Principles 195
M. Qualified Investigator and Other Personnel 195
N. Suitable Facilities 195
O. Damage Compensation 195
II. Clinical Investigations on Incapacitated Subjects 196
III. Clinical Investigations on Minors 196
IV. Clinical Investigations on Pregnant or Breastfeeding Woman 197
V. Clinical Investigations on Other Vulnerable Subjects 198
VI. Clinical Investigations in Emergency Situations 198

Chapter 3. Performance Studies on In Vitro Diagnostic Medical Devices 200

§1. Field of Application 200

§2. Conditions to Conduct a Performance Study 201
I. General Requirements Regarding Performance Studies 201
II. Additional Requirements for Certain (Invasive) Performance Studies 201
III. Performance Studies on Incapacitated Subjects 203
IV. Performance Studies on Minors 203
V. Performance Studies on Pregnant or Breastfeeding Women 204
VI. Performance Studies on Other Vulnerable Subjects 204
VII. Performance Studies in Emergency Situations 204

Chapter 4. Non-interventional Post-Authorization Safety Studies 205

Chapter 5. Use of Human Embryos for Purposes of Scientific Research 206

Chapter 6. Genetic Testing 207

Chapter 7. The Processing of Data Concerning Health and Genetic Data 209

§1. FIELD OF APPLICATION 210

§2. PROCESSING OF DATA CONCERNING HEALTH AND GENETIC DATA 211
I. Prohibition of Processing of Data Concerning Health and Genetic Data 211
II. Derogation from the Prohibition on Processing of Data Regarding Health and Genetic Data 212
A. Compliance with the Principles Relating to Processing of Personal Data 212
B. One of the Following Justifications Applies 213
1. The Data Subject or the Holder of Parental Responsibility Has Given Explicit Consent 213
2. Necessity to Protect the Vital Interests of the Data Subject or of Another Natural Person 214
3. Necessary for Reasons of Substantial Public Interest 215
4. Necessary for Health-Related Purposes 215
5. Necessary for Reasons of Public Interest in the Area of Public Health 216
C. Comply with Member States Further Conditions 216
III. Rights of the Data Subject 217
A. The Right to the Protection of Personal Data 217
B. Information to Be Provided Where Personal Data Are Collected from the Data Subject 217
C. The Right of Access by the Data Subject 218
D. Right to Rectification 219
E. Restricted Right to Erasure of Personal Data Regarding Health or Genetic Data ('Right to Be Forgotten') 220
F. Right to Restriction of Processing 221
G. Restricted Right to Portability of Data Regarding Health or Genetic Data 222
H. Right Not to Be Subject to Automated Individual Decision-Making, Including Profiling 223
I. Right to Transparent Information and Communication Concerning Rights of the Data Subject 223
J. Right to Lodge a Complaint and to an Effective Judicial Remedy 224
K. Right to Be Represented 224
L. Right to Compensation and Liability 225
IV. Modalities for the Exercise of the Rights of the Data Subject 225
V. Data Protection by Design and by Default 226
VI. Communication of a Personal Data Breach to the Data Subject 226
VII. Data Protection Impact Assessment 227
VIII. Designation of a Data Protection Officer When Data Regarding Health or Genetic Data Are Processed on a Large Scale 227

§3. Scientific Research with Data Concerning Health or Genetic Data 228
I. Introduction 228
II. Research after Anonymization of the Data 229
III. Appropriate Safeguards for the Rights and Freedoms of the Data Subject 230
IV. Explicit Consent 230
V. Processing for Research Purposes Is in the Public Interest or Has a Legitimate Interest 231

§4. The European Health Data Space 231
I. Rights of Natural Persons and Access and Transmission of Personal Electronic Health Data for Primary Use 232
II. Access by Health Professionals 233

Chapter 8. Transplantation of Organs 234

Chapter 9. Clinical Use of Tissues and Cells of Human Origin for Human Application 237

Chapter 10. Rights of the Medical Examinee 239

§1. Rights of the Living Organ Donor 239

§2. Rights of the Living Donor of Tissue and Cells 241

§3. Rights of the Donor of Blood 242

Part VI. Beginning and End-of-Life Issues in EU Law 245

Chapter 1. Beginning of Life 245

§1. Definition of the Legal Term 'Person' or 'Individual' 245

§2. Protection of the Human Body 245

§3. Definition and Protection of the Human Embryo 246

§4. In Vitro Fertilization and the Beginning of a Pregnancy 248

§5. Gametes Donation for Reproduction 250

§6. Voluntary Termination of Pregnancy 251

§7. Forced Sterilization 253

Chapter 2. End of Life 255

§1. The Deceased Organ Donor 255

§2. The Deceased Cells and Tissue Donor 255

§3. Advance Directives 256

§4. Euthanasia 256

§5. Patients in a Vegetative State 257

Selected Bibliography 259

Index 269

List of Abbreviations

CJEU	Court of Justice of the European Union
COCOM	Commission Communautaire Commune de Bruxelles-Capital
CTR	Clinical Trial Regulation
ECA	European Court of Auditors
ECHR	European Convention on Human Rights
ECTS	European Credit Transfer and Accumulation System
EDPB	European Data Protection Board
EDPS	European Data Protection Supervisor
EEHRxF	European Electronic Health Record Exchange Format
EGE	European Group on Ethics in Science and New Technologies
EHDS	European Health Data Space
EPC	European Professional Card
EU	European Union
GDPR	General Data Protection Regulation
IMCO	Internal Market and Consumer Protection
IMI	Internal Market Information System
IVD MDR	In Vitro Diagnostic Medical Devices Regulation
MDR	Medical Devices Regulation
NCP	National Contact Point for Cross-Border Healthcare
OJ	Official Journal
SPUC	Society for the Protection of Unborn Children Ireland
TEU	Treaty on European Union
TFEU	Treaty on the Functioning of the European Union
VAT	Value-Added Tax
WHO	World Health Organization

List of Abbreviations

General Introduction

1. This supplement to the *International Encyclopaedia of Medical Law* is entitled 'European Union Health Law'. The choice of this title deserves a justification in more than one respect. First, because of the distinction made between 'medical law' and 'health law' in general. Second, because of the difference between 'medical law' and 'health law' when both terms are used in relation to the European Union (EU). Third, there is the most important question of whether there exists something that is called 'European Union Health Law'. In this regard, it is interesting to note that the COVID-19 pandemic (2020–) called for reinforced EU actions and laws and, as such, the creation of the European Health Union.[1]

§1. Medical Law and Health Law

2. When introducing the *International Encyclopaedia of Medical Law* in 1993, I wrote: 'The Encyclopaedia intends to cover medical law. Medical law does not respect the traditional compartments with which lawyers have become familiar, such as contracts, criminal law, family law and public law. Medical law cuts across all of these subjects and today may be regarded as a subject in its own right. Medical law is defined here as the law governing the interactions between doctors and patients. We also include the interactions of physicians with other healthcare providers and the healthcare system. Medical law may be considered as a part of health (care) law. In healthcare there is a large range of juridical relations in which a physician is not involved. This Encyclopaedia is deliberately limited to medical law, for reasons of limited space, comprehensiveness and mutual comparability.'

3. Today, I am still convinced that it was right not to treat the legal rules governing the organization and the financing of the healthcare system or pharmaceuticals and medical devices for the pragmatic reasons mentioned previously, nor the public health issues. But one cannot deny that since then, medical law and health law have come to be considered more or less synonymous. Or it might probably be correct to state that the concept of 'health law' is increasingly replacing the concept of 'medical law' to refer to a more or less comparable body of law, although in many

1. Answer given by Ms Kyriakides on behalf of the European Commission to a written Parliamentary question of L. Christoforou, Need to Introduce a Common EU Health Policy, 10 Nov. 2021, E-004311/2021; A.E. Schmidt et al., 'Cross-Border Healthcare Collaboration in Europe (2007–2017)', 126 *Health Policy* 1241–1247 (2022).

jurisdictions, medical law is still frequently used, either alone or in parallel with health law.[2] I agree with Hervey and McHale that 'health law has not superseded medical law'.[3] And I also agree with both authors that 'across Europe there is an observable trend towards the terminology of health law rather than medical law'.[4] In other words, health law is often also used in a less broad sense than medical law had been used (and to the extent that it is still used, still has). In that regard, the *International Encyclopaedia of Medical Law* could, without misleading readers, be called the *International Encyclopaedia of Health Law* in many jurisdictions.

§2. Medical Law and Health Law in the EU

4. Medical law is a concept that has been used in the Member States of the EU even long before the Union existed. In many Member States, health law is now also used, either replacing medical law or in parallel with it. In other words, in terms of national law, both medical law and/or health law are used. This is totally different when we deal with EU law. The parallel use of medical law and health law to describe a more or less comparable body of law or even the replacement of medical law by health law is unknown in the EU. The body of law that is generally considered medical law and/or health law in the national law of the Member States has, to my knowledge, never been considered medical law in European law but from the very beginning as health (care) law. For this reason, it is justified to use 'health law' instead of 'medical law' in this monograph in the *International Encyclopaedia of Medical Law*. I am aware that the European Union Health Law is also used in a wider sense. De Ruijter uses the term 'health law' and not 'healthcare law' or 'medical law' 'as these terms refer more particularly to the regulation of healthcare arrangements rather than public health, whereas the term "health law" here is taken to encompass both the regulation of public health and healthcare'. This author defines health law 'loosely as legal rules that regulate the provision of health care and the protection of human health'.[5]

5. Let us now turn to the question: Does 'European Union Health Law' exist?

2. *See* on this H. Nys, 'Medical Law and Health Law: From Co-existence to Symbiosis? in Health Legislation at the Dawn of the XXIst Century', 49 *International Digest of Health Legislation, Special Issue* 1–18 (1998).
3. T.K. Hervey & J.V. McHale, *European Union Health Law: Themes and Implications* 16 (Cambridge: Cambridge University Press 2015).
4. *Ibid.*, 17.
5. A. de Ruijter, *EU Health Law and Policy: The Expansion of EU Power in Public Health and Health Care* 8 and note 50 (Oxford University Press 2019).

§3. European Union Health Law or EU Health Law

6. Until recently, EU health law was considered non-existent. If there existed something, then it was the 'European Union *and* health law'[6] (the so-called and approach).[7] Have we reached now the stage of 'the solidification of the European Union health law and policy?'[8]

I. EU Biomedical Law

7. In 2011, Hennette-Vauchez discovered the 'emergence of a body of biomedical law at the EU level' and concluded that 'such a body of law now exists'.[9] She called it 'EU biomedical law'. According to Hennette-Vauchez, 'this emerging body of law is very diverse and heterogeneous and thus rather grudging to traditional academic taxonomies'.[10] One might question whether one can speak of a 'body of law' in this context. Rather, it still seems to be 'a patchwork of legal provisions'.[11] Moreover, instead of EU health law, Hennette-Vauchez uses the expression 'EU biomedical law'. Whether this biomedical law belongs to a larger body of law called EU health law remains unclear, but it probably does. According to Hennette-Vauchez, some norms of this EU biomedical law directly aim at biomedical issues: most of the directives and regulations in the field, such as the directives on the protection of

---

6. T.K. Hervey & J.V. McHale, *Health Law and the European Union* (Cambridge University Press 2004). Still in 2008, 'at the European level, there is not much health law that really can be considered European although there is a growing body of European law that is relevant to health care', S. Gevers, 'Health Law in Europe: From the Present to the Future', 15 *European Journal of Health Law* 261 (2008). This article was one of the keynote addresses at the Founding Conference of the European Association of Health Law, 10–11 Apr. 2008, Edinburgh, Scotland. Note that the name of this Association is not, Association of European (Union) Health Law. *See* on the founding of this Association also G. Laurie, 'Editorial. The European Association of Health Law: Addressing Unmet Needs in Policy, Practice and Research', 15 *European Journal of Health Law* 251–259 (2008) and H.D.C. Roscam Abbing, 'Editorial. Founding a European Association for Health Law: The Rationale', 13 *European Journal of Health Law* 203–207 (2006), stressing that 'it is difficult to imagine health law today without its international (European) dimension' (at p. 205) and that 'new developments in medical science and technology will continuously give rise to different, more complicated legal issues, requiring an appropriate European answer' (at p. 206).
7. T.K. Hervey, 'Telling Stories about European Union Health Law: The Emergence of a New Field of Law', 15 *Comparative European Politics* 352 (2017); already in 1994 H. Leenen predicted that 'European health law will become a new branch of health law', H.J.J. Leenen, 'Editorial. The European Journal of Health Law: A New Publication', 1 *European Journal of Health Law* 1 (1994). Note that the title of the Journal is not: Journal of European (Union) Health Law. According to Carmi, the title of the new journal symbolized 'the change which occurred during the last decade or two as health law occupies the position of medical law'; *see* A. Carmi, 'Editorial. Health-Law Towards the 21st Century', 1 *European Journal of Health Law* 225 (1994). In this way he missed however the point made by Leenen: European (Union) law as a new branch of health law.
8. A. de Ruijter, 'Mapping the Institutional Consolidation of EU Human Health Expertise', 15 *Comparative European Politics* 371 (2017).
9. S. Hennette-Vauchez, 'Biomedicine and EU Law: Unlikely Encounters?', 38 *Legal Issues of Economic Integration* 9 (2011).
10. *Ibid.*
11. *Supra* n. 7, 353.

biomedical inventions,[12] clinical trials,[13] blood,[14] tissue[15] and organ[16] quality and safety products. She also includes a number of so-called soft law acts, such as resolutions adopted by the European Parliament regarding in vitro embryos, cloning and trade in oocytes.[17] Other parts of this EU biomedical law only indirectly deal with biomedical issues, such as the EU's research policy as defined in the five-year-long framework programmes or patent law.[18]

8. In the second part of her article, Hennette-Vauchez confronts the question 'of what has in fact bridged EU law and biomedicine?' In order to answer this question, an in-depth analysis of EU biomedical law has been carried out which led to the very interesting hypothesis 'according to which ethics (*bio*ethics) have played an instrumental role in the emergence and contemporary development of biomedical law at the level of the EU. At different stages and under different guises, the injection of "ethics" in the normative process has been the condition of possibility of EU biomedical law'.[19] In other words: 'ethics would provide some grandeur to EU (biomedical law)'.[20] The approach of Hennette-Vauchez is a very interesting one, but it is confronted with its own limitations. She demonstrates convincingly that bioethics functions as a bridge between EU law and biomedical issues, but in doing so, she has implicitly limited EU health law to such issues. EU health law can and should be approached in a much broader sense.

II. EU Health Law

9. Hervey starts from the assumption that EU health law should be seen as a distinct field of law or at least of legal enquiry and then deals with the question: 'how did it come into being?'[21] Or, in the wordings of Hennette-Vauchez: what is the 'condition of possibility' of EU health law? In the latter's opinion, it is bioethics. Hervey takes another, also broader approach: 'EU health law has been narrated into existence' by three key groups of narrators: the legislature, the courts and the academy.[22] The practical mechanisms of narration used by each of these three differ. The textual changes to legal provisions are important elements of the story. Hervey gives as an example the text of early EU food labelling legislation that only referred to the internal market as its rationale and aim, while more recent EU food legislation is understood as promoting public health through reducing obesity as part of EU

12. Directive 98/44/EU of 6 Jul. 1998, *OJ* 1988, L 213.
13. Directive 2001/20/EU of 4 Apr. 2001, *OJ* 2001, L 121/34.
14. Directive 2002/98/EU of 27 Jan. 2003, *OJ* 2003, L 33/30.
15. Directive 2004/23/EU of 31 Mar. 2004, *OJ* 2004, L 102/48.
16. Directive 2010/45/EU of 7 Jul. 2010, *OJ* 2010, L 207/14.
17. *Supra* n. 9.
18. *Ibid.*, 9–10.
19. *Ibid.*, 13.
20. *Ibid.*, 27; *see* however *supra* n. 3, 18: 'there is danger in assuming that medical or health law is predicated upon ethics, as this may be true in some areas but is not the case across the board'.
21. *Supra* n. 7, 353.
22. *Ibid.*, 354.

health law.[23] And 'the Patients' Rights Directive is more explicitly expressed as falling within an entity which is understood as EU health law'.[24] The role of the Court of Justice of the European Union (CJEU) as a narrator is also exemplified through the Patients' Rights Directive: 'even before it came into force formally, [it] resulted in the CJEU "seeing" or "reading", and then "retelling", its jurisprudence on free movement of patients in a different way from the way it recounts that jurisprudence in "ordinary" internal market law'.[25] And finally, 'concrete material expressions of EU health law in the academy (Chair in EU health law; programmes in EU health law) would be the most convincing form of evidence for the argument made in this article'.[26]

10. Hervey then distinguishes the three processes through which EU health law has been narrated. First is the process of discerning and articulating principles and themes. Examples are the EU's Council *Conclusions on Common Values and Principles in European Health Systems* adopted in 2006, endorsed by the European Commission in 2007 and the European Parliament in 2008. These Common Values and Principles 'are a credible expression of the principles and themes of EU health law'. Another example is the EU's human rights instruments.[27] It seems that de Ruijter takes a more nuanced stance in this regard: 'The language of this statement of Common Values (referring to "values" rather than principles of EU law) suggests that it is not intended to constitute a statement of general principles of EU law that are on equal footing with fundamental rights. However, in combination with particular EU fundamental rights it could be argued that the Common Values may help shape the *interpretation* of fundamental rights in the context of EU health law. At the very least, the 2006 Common Values represent an indication of the baseline principles that are common to the Member States, and in that regard they can also at least be taken into consideration in the European Union legislative process, though this is not legally required.'[28] The second process mentioned by Hervey is the expression of EU health law as structurally coherent. She admits that not every area of health law is significantly covered by EU health law and that there are some areas of health law where EU law is of no or only very little relevance, such as end-of-life decision-making.[29] Nevertheless, 'much of the substantive content of health law *is* covered by EU health law, and increasingly so … the trajectory has reached a stage of sufficient structural coherence to evidence the existence of EU health law'.[30] The third and final process is in understanding EU health law as a distinctive body of law: 'EU health law is no longer understood as comprised of a series of unrelated exceptions to free trade rules, but rather as a distinctive legal area, with

23. *Ibid.*, 355.
24. *Ibid.*
25. *Ibid.*, 356.
26. *Ibid.*
27. *Ibid.*, 358.
28. *Supra* n. 5, 188.
29. *See also* T.K. Hervey, 'Reflecting on Supporting Health Systems in Europe: Added Value of EU Actions', 10 *Health Economics, Policy and Law* 487 (2015).
30. *Supra* n. 7, 361–362.

its own underlying principles and structural coherence.'[31] The CJEU has played an important role in this process by articulating 'the idea that health systems occupy a distinctive position in internal market law … to the extent that that position can be said to be part of the principles or structural coherence of EU health law'.[32] In the future also, European competition law might become an important, although maybe uninvited, element in the development of EU health law.[33]

§4. THE CONTENTS OF EU HEALTH LAW IN THIS MONOGRAPH

11. What is EU health law about, and more specifically, what are the contents of this monograph on EU health law, having regard that it is part of the *International Encyclopaedia of Medical Law*? A significant area of EU health law concerns pharmaceuticals and medical devices. Given that those subjects are not treated in the country-wise monographs in this Encyclopaedia, neither is it here. The same holds true for EU public health law, where the literature is divided on whether it is included in EU health law or not.[34]

---

31. *Ibid.*, 362.
32. *Ibid.*, 363.
33. A.J.B. Morton, 'European Health Care Systems and the Emerging Influence of European Union Competition Policy', 46 *Journal of Health Politics, Policy and Law* 467–486 (2021).
34. *Supra* n. 3, 54 and n. 5.

Part I. Definitions

Chapter 1. Definition of Healthcare, Medical Care and Health Services in EU Law

§1. Are Healthcare and Medical Care Synonymous in EU Health Law?

I. Healthcare

12. Article 3a of Directive 2011/24/EU of the European Parliament and the Council of 9 March 2011 on the application of patients' rights in cross-border healthcare (The Cross-Border Healthcare Directive)[35] contains the following definition of 'healthcare': 'health services provided by health professionals to patients to assess, maintain or restore their state of health, including the prescription, dispensation and provision of medicinal products and medical devices'. As a consequence, the scope of the Cross-Border Healthcare Directive is 'relatively broad'.[36] According to Recital 7 in the Preamble, the Directive respects and is without prejudice to the freedom of each Member State to decide what type of healthcare it considers appropriate. No provision of this Directive should be interpreted in such a way as to undermine the fundamental ethical choices of Member States. In light of this, the European Commission does not intend to bring forward a proposal for reimbursement of the costs of terminating a pregnancy anywhere in the EU.[37]

13. In this definition of healthcare, two categories of services can be distinguished: on the one hand, health services to patients to assess, maintain or restore their state of health and on the other hand, the prescription, dispensation and provision of medicinal products and medical devices.

35. *OJ* 2011, L 88/45.
36. *Supra* n. 5, 157.
37. Answer given by Ms Kyriakides on behalf of the European Commission to a written Parliamentary question of L. Miller et al., The Situation of Women in Poland and Reimbursement of the Costs of Terminating a Pregnancy in Strictly-Defined Cases Anywhere in the EU, 2 Feb. 2021, E-005773/2020.

II. Medical Care

14. According to Advocate General Kokott, 'medical care' has 'undoubtedly its own meaning in Community law'.[38] The Advocate General made this remark in the context of a preliminary ruling concerning the interpretation of Article 13A, 1c of the Sixth Council Directive 77/388/EEC of 17 May 1997 on the harmonization of the laws of the Member States relating to turnover taxes.[39] Meanwhile, this Directive has been repealed and replaced by Council Directive 2006/112/EC of 28 November 2006 on the common system of Value-Added Tax (VAT) Directive.[40] Article 132.1c of the VAT Directive contains the fundamental rule for exempting transactions related to medical care. It is formulated in exactly the same way as its predecessor and thus may be interpreted in the same way.[41]

Also, Article 13A, 1b of the Sixth Council Directive made a reference to 'medical care'. It has been replaced by Article 132.1b of the VAT Directive. Neither the Sixth Council Directive nor the VAT Directive holds definitions of 'medical care'. The meaning of 'medical care' has been the subject of analysis by the CJEU in a number of cases.[42] It is clear from this case law that the expression 'medical care' under Article 132.1b also covers any medical care referred to in Article 132.1c. The CJEU has repeatedly stated that the criterion for drawing a clear distinction between the two exemptions is less the nature of the service than the place where it is provided.[43] In other words, both concepts of medical care are synonymous. The difference between them is the place of supply: inside or outside a hospital.[44]

15. Article 13A, 1b and 1c of the Sixth Directive provided the following: 'Without prejudice to other Community provisions, Member States shall exempt the following under conditions which they shall lay down for the purpose of ensuring the correct and straightforward application of such exemptions and of preventing any possible evasion, avoidance or abuse: (b) hospital and medical care and closely related activities undertaken by bodies governed by public law, by hospitals, centres for medical treatment of diagnosis and other duly recognised establishments of a similar nature [and] (c) the provision of medical care in the exercise of the medical and paramedical professions as defined by the Member State concerned.'[45] Note that it is up to the Member States to define (the exercise of) the medical and paramedical professions (*see* paragraph 74).

---

38. Opinion AG Kokott in *Solleveld*, C-443/04, ECLI:EU:C:2005:788, para. 19.
39. *OJ* 1997, L 145/1.
40. *OJ* 2006, L 347/1.
41. R. Pahlsson, 'The VAT Exemption for Health Care: The EU Law and Its Impact on Swedish Law', *Nordic Tax Journal* 20 (2015); CJEU, *Peters*, C-700/17, ECLI:EU:C:2019:753, para. 18.
42. *Ibid.*, 21, footnote 15.
43. CJEU, *Kügler*, C-141/00, ECLI:EU:C:2002:473, para. 36; Opinion AG Sharpston in *Klinikum Dortmund*, C-366/12, ECLI:EU:C:2013:618, para. 33.
44. *Supra* n. 40, 27 and para. 21.
45. *See* the exact wording in Art. 132.1b and c: 'Member States shall exempt the following transactions: (b) hospital and medical care and closely related activities undertaken by bodies governed by public law, or under social conditions comparable with those applicable to bodies governed by private law, by hospitals, centres for medical treatment of diagnosis and other duly recognised establishments of

16. In a preliminary reference, the *Landesgericht St. Pölten* (Austria) asked the CJEU whether a genetic investigation carried out by a court-appointed medical expert in the context of a paternity dispute fell within the scope of the exemption provided for by Article 13A, 1c of the Sixth Council Directive.[46] All the governments which had intervened proposed that the question be answered in the affirmative.[47]

17. The Austrian Government observed that the medical services which gave rise to the dispute are different from 'normal' medical services in two respects: first, the expert in this case provided her services on the instructions of the court rather than in the context of a contractual relationship as is normally the case; second, her work was limited to establishing a technical fact, pure and simple, and had no connection with the provision of medical care or treatment. In relation to the first point, in particular, the Austrian Government also submitted that the fact that an expert is instructed by a court does not alter in any way the substance of the services he provides and that, consequently, there is no reason to treat such services any differently from 'ordinary' medical services. As far as the second point is concerned, namely the absence of any functional connection between providing expert opinion and curing sickness, the Austrian Government maintained that the Directive should be interpreted as meaning that investigatory work done by an expert at the request of a court (such as the conduct of laboratory tests) which is necessary for resolving a dispute should also be regarded as medical care for the purpose of applying for the exemption from VAT. The fact that such services are not connected with medical treatment is irrelevant in this specific context.[48]

18. Also, the Dutch Government maintained that medical work requested by a court should be regarded in the same way as the provision of medical care because the concept of medical care covers all activities performed in the exercise of the medical and paramedical professions, and thus also experts' investigations.[49]

19. The United Kingdom Government approached the question in two ways. It first queried whether paternity examinations fall within the scope of 'medical care' and expressed the opinion that medical care ought to cover every type of activity that requires medical expertise, the reason being that Article 13 of the Sixth Directive gives a very broad definition of the work carried out in the medical profession. On that premise, it asserted that medical care includes not only patient care but also all activities in areas which are not closely connected with protecting or restoring health, such as the preparation of reports on the general state of health of patients, family planning, sterilization and cosmetic surgery. The common factor in all these activities is that they require particular medical knowledge and skill. The United

a similar nature [and] (c) the provision of medical care in the exercise of the medical and paramedical professions as defined by the Member State concerned.'.

46. CJEU, *D. v. W.*, C-384/98, ECLI:EU:C:2000:444.
47. Opinion AG Saggio in *D. v. W.*, Case C-384/98, ECLI:EU:C:2000:55, para. 8.
48. *Ibid.*
49. *Ibid.*, para. 9.

Kingdom Government reinforced that point by asserting that referring to the purpose to which services are directed would be to use an ambiguous criterion that would be difficult to apply. For example, a person could be given the same blood test either for the purpose of identifying an illness or in the context of a paternity dispute; the medical service could be identical in both cases, although the applicable tax treatment would be different.[50]

20. Unlike the intervening States, the Commission maintained that the question should be answered in the negative. It reached this conclusion on the basis of the assumption that the exemption at issue concerns exclusively medical services which consist of providing individuals with medical care or medical treatment. Investigations intended solely to establish paternity do not fall within that description and consequently cannot benefit from exemption from VAT.[51]

21. Advocate General Saggio started his opinion by referring to the purpose of the VAT exemption for medical care, namely to reduce the cost of activities which are in the public interest, such as 'services provided by doctors or paramedics such as dental technicians'.[52] For that reason, the term 'medical care' needs, according to the Court, not to be interpreted strictly.[53] Does this mean that medical services which are not linked to the prevention, diagnosis or treatment of illness, like a genetic test designed solely to establish paternity, are also medical care? According to the Advocate General, the literal wording of Article 13A, 1c gives it to be understood that the exemption does not cover this last category of services. With the exception of the Italian version which uses *prestazioni mediche* (medical services), all the other versions refer in a quite explicit way exclusively to the provision of services in relation to the health of persons. Hence, he concluded that the exemption 'is centred on the therapeutic function of the medical care', and he concluded that medical services consisting of genetic tests to establish paternity are not medical care in the sense of Article 13A, 1c.[54]

22. In its judgment, the CJEU confirmed that 'apart from the Italian version, all the versions of Article 13A, 1c refer only to medical care concerning the health of persons. It should be pointed out, in particular, that the German, French, Finnish and Swedish versions use the concept of therapeutic treatment or of care provided to the person. Clearly, therefore, the concept of "provision of medical care" does not lend itself to an interpretation which includes medical interventions carried out for a purpose other than that of diagnosing, treating and, in so far as possible, curing disease of health disorders'.[55] On another occasion, the CJEU stated that this article applies to services outside hospitals and similar establishments and 'within the framework of a confidential relationship between the patient and the person providing the care,

50. *Ibid.*, para. 10.
51. *Ibid.*, para. 11.
52. *Ibid.*, para. 12.
53. CJEU, *Dornier,* C-45/01, ECLI:EU:C:2003:595, para. 48.
54. *Supra* n. 47, paras 13–16.
55. *Supra* n. 44, paras 17–18; *supra* n. 40, para. 38.

a relationship which is normally established in the consulting room of that person'.[56] However, this does not mean that the exemption under Article 132(1)(c) of Directive 2006/112 only applies to the provision of medical care within the framework of a confidential relationship between the person providing the care and the person being treated. The existence of a confidential relationship between the patient and the person providing the care was raised by the Court in *Kügler* in order to highlight the difference between the two exemptions under Article 13(A)(1)(b) and (c) of the Sixth Directive as regards the place where the services must be supplied, illustrating the framework within which the services under Article 13(A)(1)(c) of that Directive are generally provided. It follows that the exemption from VAT is not subject to the condition that the medical care in question is supplied within the framework of a confidential relationship between the patient and the person providing the care, which is the case when the medical care is provided by a specialist in clinical chemistry and laboratory diagnosis.[57] Also, services provided by phone that consist of giving advice regarding health and diseases may be considered medical care on the condition that they have a therapeutic purpose.[58] The therapeutic aim is larger than to cure: activities whose direct purpose is not to cure but is merely preventive do constitute activities with a therapeutic aim which are to be regarded as involving the provision of medical care.[59] Article 132(1)(b) of Directive 2006/112 must be interpreted as meaning that an activity consisting of compiling an individual file, including the user's clinical record, which entitles the user to purchase 'traditional thermal cure' medical care within a spa establishment, is liable to come within the exemption from VAT provided for in that provision as an activity closely related to medical care, where those files set out data relating to the user's state of health, planned and prescribed medical care as well as the manner in which that care is to be administered which must be consulted for the provision of care and to achieve the therapeutic objectives pursued.[60]

23. In other cases, the CJEU added: 'it follows that medical services effected for the purpose of protecting, or maintaining or of restoring human health benefit from the exemption under Article 13A.1b and 1c of the Sixth Directive'.[61] This definition reflects very much the first part of the definition of healthcare in Article 3a of the Cross-Border Healthcare Directive: 'health services provided to patients to assess, maintain or restore their state of health' (*see* paragraph 12). The main difference is that this part of the definition refers to assessment (diagnosis) instead of protection, as in the definition of the CJEU. Protection implies preventive measures. However, this is rather a practical than a principle difference: in the context of cross-border healthcare, preventive care is, in most cases, not really an issue. Although there is

56. *Supra* n. 43, para. 35.
57. CJEU, *Peters*, C-700/17, ECLI:EU:C:2019:753, paras 36, 39 and 42.
58. CJEU, *X-GmbH*, C-48/19, ECLI:EU:C:2020:169, para. 34.
59. Opinion AG Stix-Hackl in *Unterpertinger*, Case C-212/01, ECLI:EU:C:2003:59, para. 72; CJEU, *Unterpertinger*, Case C-212/01, ECLI:EU:C:2003:625, para. 40 in the same sense; CJEU, *d'Ambrumenil*, Case C-307/01, ECLI:EU:C:2003:627, para. 58; CJEU, *L.u.p.*, Case C-106/05, ECLI:EU:C:2006:380, para. 29.
60. CJEU, *Autoridade Tributária e Aduaneira*, Case C-513/20, ECLI:EU:C:2022:18, para. 42.
61. CJEU, *Unterpertinger*, Case C-212/01, ECLI:EU:C:2003:625, paras 40 and 41.

no evidence that this part of the definition of healthcare in Article 3a of the Cross-Border Healthcare Directive has been inspired by the case law of the CJEU, it nevertheless may be concluded that healthcare and medical care are synonymous in EU law to the extent that healthcare consists of services to assess, maintain or restore the state of health of the patient.

24. According to Article 1.3a of the Cross-Border Healthcare Directive, this Directive is not applicable to 'services in the field of long-term care the purpose of which is to support people in need of assistance in carrying out routine, everyday tasks'. However, cross-border long-term care does exist.[62] The exclusion of long-term care has been linked to the fear of high costs for the State of affiliation.[63] For chronically ill persons, who often suffer from more than one disease, it may be difficult to draw the line between healthcare and social care. From an older person's perspective, this is especially worrying.[64] Recital 14[65] in the Preamble to the Directive is not very helpful in answering the question of what the nature of this kind of service exactly is. It states: 'more specifically, this Directive should not apply to those long-term care services deemed necessary in order to enable the person in need of care to live as full and self-determined a life as possible. Thus, this Directive should not apply, for example, to long-term care services provided by home care services, in assisted living facilities and in residential homes or housing ("nursing homes")'. Given the explicit exclusion, one might be inclined to consider these services as healthcare services because, otherwise, there would be no need to exclude them. The exclusion in Article 1.3b (allocation of and access to organs for the purpose of organ transplants) and in Article 1.3c (public vaccination programmes against infectious diseases) supports this reasoning because both are generally considered as healthcare. According to de Ruijter, vaccination programmes have been excluded because the 'EU has no formal powers to create vaccination strategies'.[66] This point of view has been confirmed by the European Commission: 'The responsibility for vaccination lies with Member States, and this also applies for decision making on whether COVID-19 vaccination should be mandatory or not,

62. G. Berki, *Free Movement of Patients in the EU. A Patient's Perspective* 13 n. 75 (Intersentia 2018).
63. S. Devetzi & J. McHale, 'Health and Long-Term Care Benefits and the Proposed Revised Coordination Regulation: A Brave New World or Much Ado about Nothing?', 22 *European Journal of Social Security* 186 (2020).
64. M. Axmin, *Access to Cross-Border Healthcare for Older Persons in the European Union* 191 (Lund University 2020).
65. According to Hervey and McHale, 'The Recitals of a measure of EU Law do not have any binding effect, and only represent a form of soft law. However this does not necessarily mean that Recitals do not have any effect. In particular, when the content of a Recital is reflected in a binding provision, the Recital can be used as the basis for interpretation of the binding provision', *see supra* n. 3, 355, footnote 62. *See also* CJEU, *European Citizens' Initiative One of Us,* C-418/18 P, ECLI:EU:C:2019:1113 para. 76: 'The preamble to an EU act has no binding legal force and cannot be relied on as a ground either for derogating from the actual provisions of the act in question or for interpreting those provisions in a manner that is clearly contrary to their wording.'
66. *Supra* n. 5, 181.

and for which population groups.'[67] It is for Member States to ensure the respect of fundamental rights in accordance with their international human rights obligations and constitutional traditions.[68]

25. However, the case law of the CJEU regarding the concept of medical care in the VAT Directives points to another direction. According to the CJEU, the exemption in Article 13A, 1c of the Sixth Directive 'applies to the care of a therapeutic nature by a company running an outpatient service under which care, including home care, is provided by qualified nursing staff, to the exclusion of the provision of general care and domestic help'.[69] It follows from this that services in the field of long-term care, the purpose of which is to support people in need of assistance in carrying out routine, everyday tasks, are no medical care or healthcare according to EU law.

§2. Health Services

I. Services to Assess, Maintain or Restore the State of Health of a Patient

26. The Cross-Border Healthcare Directive does not define 'health services'. According to the definition in Article 3a, healthcare is always a service, not a good. It is a service provided by at least one health professional. The same service provided by someone who is not a health professional is not a health service according to this definition. However, not every service provided by a health professional is a health service or healthcare. The service has to be delivered to a patient 'to assess, maintain or restore the state of health'. Euthanasia (if legal at all, *see* paragraph 661) cannot be considered a health service according to this definition because euthanasia does not aim to assess, maintain or restore a patient's state of health. Also, an autopsy or the removal of an organ from a living or dead person is not a health service according to this definition.

27. No definition of 'state of health' is currently given in EU law. Neither is there an 'authoritative legal text that defines human health' in the EU.[70]

28. The definition of medical care in the case law of the CJEU may offer some guidance to understand this part of the definition of healthcare in Article 3a of the Cross-Border Healthcare Directive.

---

67. Answer given by Ms Kyriakides on behalf of the European Commission to a written Parliamentary question of K. Papadakis, Ending the suspension of health workers, 4 Aug. 2022, E-002068/2022.
68. Answer given by Ms Kyriakides on behalf of the European Commission to a written Parliamentary question of I. Lagos, Persecution by the Greek government of unvaccinated health workers, 8 Nov. 2022, E-002928/2022.
69. *Supra* n. 43, para. 41.
70. *Supra* n. 5, 55.

29. Genetic tests purely to determine paternity are no healthcare in EU law.[71] In a later case, Advocate General Stix-Hackl wondered what particular factor causes the service of establishing paternity to fall outside the exemption in Article 13A, 1c of the Sixth Directive. Some regard as critical the fact that establishing paternity has nothing to do with the health of any person. That approach differentiates between a medical act whose object is purely to establish certain biological characteristics and one whose object is to ascertain a person's state of health. However, such a distinction, based on the type of medical act, should be rejected. It is, for example, conceivable that a test which the CJEU found not to qualify as medical care might be necessary to establish whether a person is suitable as an organ donor. If the distinction according to the type of medical act was to be made, this test, too, would fall outside the exemption, even though it clearly forms part of, or is a prerequisite to, the provision of medical care. The same would be true of ascertaining a person's blood group which also involves determining a biological characteristic by scientific tests and has no bearing per se on any person's state of health.

30. Thus, neither the nature of the medical intervention nor its centrality in terms of the functions of the medical profession is decisive; as the Court's case law on the words 'provision of medical care' in Article 13A, 1c makes clear, the crucial issue is, rather, the aim of the medical intervention, being a therapeutic one.[72] From the foregoing followed that the Court excluded establishing the genetic affinity of individuals from the scope of Article 13A, 1c of the Sixth Directive, not because the object of that test was to ascertain a person's biological characteristics rather than their state of health, but because the medical procedure, in that case, served a purpose that was other than therapeutic, namely the drawing up of an expert opinion.[73]

31. Also, because of the lack of a therapeutic aim, services provided by private stem cell banks through the collection, transportation, analysis and storage of umbilical cord blood from newborn children are not medical care.[74]

32. The CJEU also held that plastic surgery is tax-exempt only if the principle of therapeutic purpose is fulfilled and provided that the need is assessed by professionals. It is the medical or therapeutic expertise that determines whether a supply has the required therapeutic purpose.[75] Cosmetic treatments are healthcare since such treatments are not limited to services which promote well-being, such as relaxing massages or waxing, but can take the form of actual surgical operations, such as the re-modelling of part of the face or the body.[76]

---

71. *Supra* n. 46.
72. *Supra* n. 57, paras 60–66.
73. *Ibid.*, para. 76.
74. CJEU, *CopyGene,* Case C-262/08, ECLI:EU:C:2010:328, para. 36; CJEU, *Future Health Technologies,* Case C-86/09, ECLI:EU:C:2010:224, paras 36–40 and para. 43.
75. CJEU, *PFC Clinic,* Case C-91/12, ECLI:EU:C:2010:198, paras 34–35; *supra* n. 38, 25.
76. Opinion AG Bot in *Corporacion Dermoest ética SA,* Case C-500/06, ECLI:EU:C:2008:62, paras 103–104 (not a VAT case).

33. If the context in which a medical service is effected enables it to be established that its principal purpose is not the protection, including the maintenance or restoration, of health but rather the provision of advice required prior to taking a decision with legal consequences, the exemption under Article 13A, 1c does not apply to the service.[77]

34. Where a service consists of making an expert medical report, it is clear that, although the performance of that service solicits the medical skills of the provider and may involve activities which are typical of the medical profession, such as the physical examination of the patient or the analysis of his medical history, the principal purpose of such a service is not the protection, including the maintenance or restoration, of the health of the person to whom the report relates. Such a service, whose purpose is to provide a reply to questions set out in the request for the report, is effected in order to enable a third party to take a decision which has legal consequences for the person concerned or other persons. While it is true that an expert medical report may also be requested by the person concerned and may indirectly contribute to the protection of the health of such a person by detecting a new problem or by correcting a previous diagnosis, the principal purpose pursued by every service of that type remains that of fulfilling a legal or contractual condition in another's decision-making process. Such a service cannot benefit from the exemption under Article 13A, 1c.[78]

35. Where fitness certificates are required by a third party as a condition precedent to the exercise by the person concerned of a particular professional activity or the practice of certain activities requiring a sound physical condition, the principal purpose of the service effected by the doctor is to provide the third party with a necessary element for taking a decision. Such medical services are not intended principally to protect the health of the persons who wish to carry on certain activities and cannot, therefore, be exempt under Article 13A, 1c. Nonetheless, where the purpose of a certificate relating to physical fitness is to make clear to a third party that a person's state of health imposes limitations on certain activities or requires that they are carried on under particular conditions, the protection of the health of the person concerned may be regarded as the principal purpose of that service. Therefore, the exemption under Article 13A, 1c may apply to such a service.[79]

36. Where medical examinations and the taking of blood or other bodily samples are carried out with the aim of enabling an employer to take decisions on the recruitment of, or on the duties to be performed by, a worker or to enable an insurance company to fix the premium to be paid by an insured person, the services in question are intended principally to provide that employer or that insurance company with evidence on which to take its decision. Such services do not, therefore, come within the meaning of 'provision of medical care' exempted under Article 13A, 1c. By contrast, regular medical checks at the behest of certain employers and certain

---

77. *Supra* n. 57, para. 42.
78. *Ibid.*, para. 43; CJEU, *d'Ambrumenil*, Case C-307/01, ECLI:EU:C:2003:627, para. 61.
79. *Ibid.*, paras 64 and 65.

insurance companies may satisfy the conditions for exemption under Article 13A, 1c, provided that such checks are intended principally to enable the prevention or detection of illness or the monitoring of the health of workers or insured persons. The fact that such medical checks take place at a third party's request and may also serve the employers' or insurance companies' own interests does not preclude health protection being regarded as the principal aim of such checks.[80]

37. Psychotherapeutic treatment is medical care. The term 'medical care' in Article 13A, 1b of the Sixth Directive must be interpreted as covering all provision of medical care envisaged in letter (c) of the same provision, including services provided by persons who are not doctors but who provide paramedical services, such as psychotherapeutic treatment given by qualified psychologists.[81]

II. Prescription, Dispensation and Provision of Medicinal Products and Medical Devices

38. The definition of 'healthcare' in Article 3a of the Cross-Border Healthcare Directive contains an important enlargement of health services (and healthcare) by including the prescription, dispensation and provision of medicinal products and medical devices.

39. Prescription means, according to Article 3k, 'a prescription for a medicinal product or for a medical device issued by a member of a regulated health profession within the meaning of Article 3.1a of Directive 2005/36/EC, who is legally entitled to do so in the Member State in which the prescription is issued' (physicians but in some jurisdictions also nurses, midwives, physician-assistants, etc.). Accordingly, such prescription can also be subsumed under the first category of health services. Article 3k does not precise whether the name of the patient for whom the medicinal product or the medical device is prescribed has to be mentioned in the prescription.[82] In a request for a preliminary ruling, the referring Court (the Budapest Administrative and Labour Court, Hungary) asked the CJEU whether Article 3k and Article 11.1 of the Cross-Border Healthcare Directive and the principle of freedom to provide services must be interpreted as precluding the legislation of a Member State under which medicinal products cannot be dispensed on the basis of order forms that do not contain the name of the patient concerned if they were issued by a doctor authorized to practise only in a different Member State. Article 11 deals with the recognition of prescriptions issued in another Member State. Article 11.1. provides that if a medicinal product is authorized to be marketed on their territory, in accordance with Directive 2001/83/EC or Regulation (EC) No. 726/2004, Member States have to ensure that prescriptions issued for such a product in another Member State for a named patient can be dispensed on their territory in compliance with their national legislation in force and that any restrictions on recognition of

80. *Ibid.*, paras 66 and 67.
81. *Supra* n. 53, paras 21 and 50.
82. CJEU, *VIPA Kereskedelmi és Szolgáltató Kft*, Case C-222/18, ECLI:EU:C:2019:751, para. 35.

individual prescriptions are in principle prohibited. According to Advocate General Bot, the issues raised by the referring Court concerned, among others, the requirement in Article 11.1. that a prescription must have been issued for a 'named patient': 'the doubt seems to arise when a comparison is made of the wording of that Article in Hungarian, which states that the prescription must be "nominative"'. The doubts raised by the referring court could, however, be settled without difficulty by analysing the wording of Article 11.1. in other language versions, and the objectives that the Directive pursues. Most of the other language versions of Article 11.1. that the Advocate General had been able to check (i.e., to say, the Spanish, German, English, Italian and Polish versions) state that the prescription must be intended for a named patient or a given, specific or particular patient.[83] The CJEU confirmed that all language versions, except the Portuguese and the Hungarian, require explicitly that the prescription is destined for a named patient or an equivalent, such as a particular or concrete patient.[84] The wording of Article 11.1. also concurs with the objective of the Directive, which is to lay down the conditions under which a patient can go to a different Member State to receive safe, high-quality healthcare. Those conditions include the recognition of prescriptions issued in a different Member State. In those circumstances, it was clear, according to the Advocate General, that so-called order forms for medicinal products, which, by definition, are not for named patients, do not serve the same purpose. Order forms, therefore, fall outside the scope of the Cross-Border Healthcare Directive.[85]

40. According to the CJEU, Article 3k and Article 11(1) must be interpreted as not precluding legislation of a Member State under which it is not permissible for a pharmacy in that Member State to dispense prescription-only medicinal products on the basis of an order form where that order form has been issued by a healthcare professional authorized to prescribe medicinal products and to exercise his or her activity in another Member State, whereas such dispensing of those products is permitted where that order form has been issued by a healthcare professional authorized to exercise his or her activity in the first Member State, bearing in mind that, under that legislation, such order forms do not contain the name of the patient concerned. Articles 35 and 36 of the Treaty on the Functioning of the European Union (TFEU) must be interpreted as not precluding such legislation of a Member State, in so far as that legislation is justified by the objective of protecting human health and human life, is appropriate for securing the attainment of that objective and does not go beyond what is necessary to attain it, which is for the national court to determine.[86]

41. No definition of 'dispensation' and 'provision' is given in the Cross-Border Healthcare Directive. The difference between both notions is not very clear, the more so because in some language versions of the Directive, this distinction is not

83. Opinion AG Bot in *VIPA Kereskedelmi és Szolgáltató Kft*, Case C-222/18, ECLI:EU:C:2019:482, para. 37 and paras 46–48. This is also the case in the Dutch version (*bepaalde patiënt*) and the French version (*patient nommément désigné*).
84. *Supra* n. 80, para. 38.
85. *Ibid.*, paras 49–50; *supra* n. 81, para. 39.
86. CJEU, *VIPA*, Case C-222/18, ECLI:EU:C: 2019:751, para. 83.

made. The Dutch version, for example, only uses the notion *verstrekken* that apparently covers both dispensation and provision.[87]

A. *Medicinal Product*

42. A 'medicinal product' means a medicinal product as defined by Directive 2001/83/EC of the European Parliament and the Council of 6 November 2001 on the Community code relating to medicinal products for human use[88] (Article 3i of the Cross-Border Healthcare Directive). Article 1.2 of Directive 2001/83/EC defines 'medicinal product' as '(a) any substance or combination of substances presented as having properties for treating or preventing disease in human beings; or (b) any substance or combination of substances which may be used in or administered to human beings either with a view to restoring, correcting or modifying physiological functions by exerting a pharmacological, immunological or metabolic action, or to making a medical diagnosis'.

43. Although medicinal products are not ordinary products in view of their effects on human health, they none the less constitute goods for the purpose of Article 28 EC, that is to say, products which can be valued in money and which are capable, as such, of forming the subject of commercial transaction.

B. *Medical Device*

44. A 'medical device' means a medical device as defined by Article 1.2a of Directive 90/385/EEC of 20 June 1990 on the approximation of the laws of the Member States relating to implantable medical devices,[89] Article 1.2a of Directive 93/42/EEC of 14 June 1993 concerning medical devices[90] or Article 1.2a of Directive 98/79/EC of 27 October 1998 of the European Parliament and of the Council on in vitro diagnostic medical devices[91] (Article 3j Cross-Border Healthcare Directive). Those three Directives define a medical device as 'any instrument, apparatus, appliance, software, material or other article, whether used alone or in combination, including the software intended by its manufacturer to be used specifically for diagnostic and/or therapeutic purposes and necessary for its proper application, intended by the manufacturer to be used for human beings for the purpose of: diagnosis, prevention, monitoring, treatment or alleviation of disease, diagnosis, monitoring, treatment, alleviation of or compensation for an injury or handicap, investigation, replacement or modification of the anatomy or of a physiological process, control of conception and which does not achieve its principal intended action in or on the

---

87. Also the German version (*Abgabe* and *Bereitstellung*) and the French version (*la délivrance* and *la fourniture*) make this distinction but still then the difference remains unclear.
88. *OJ* 2001, L 311.
89. *OJ* 1990, L 189.
90. *OJ* 1993, L 169.
91. *OJ* 1998, L 331.

human body by pharmacological, immunological or metabolic means, but which may be assisted in its function by such means'.

45. Directives 90/385/EEC and 93/42/EEC are repealed by Regulation EU 2017/745 of the European Parliament and of the Council of 5 April 2017 on medical devices, amending Directive 2001/83/EC, Regulation (EC) No. 178/2002 and Regulation (EC) No. 1223/2009 and repealing Council Directives 90/385 and 93/42/EEC.[92] Regulation EU 2017/45 has been amended by Regulation EU 2020/561 of 23 April 2020 as regards the date of application of certain of its provisions (delay of application until 26 May 2021).[93] Article 2.1 of Regulation EU 2017/745 defines 'medical device' as follows: 'any instrument, apparatus, appliance, software, implant, reagent, material or other article intended by the manufacturer to be used, alone or in combination, for human beings for one or more of the following specific medical purposes: diagnosis, prevention, monitoring, prediction, prognosis, treatment or alleviation of disease; diagnosis, monitoring, treatment, alleviation of, or compensation for, an injury or disability; investigation, replacement or modification of the anatomy or of a physiological or pathological process or state; providing information by means of in vitro examination of specimens derived from the human body, including organ, blood and tissue donations, and which does not achieve its principal intended action by pharmacological, immunological or metabolic means, in or on the human body, but which may be assisted in its function by such means. The following products shall also be deemed to be medical devices: devices for the control or support of conception; products specifically intended for the cleaning, disinfection or sterilisation of devices as referred to in Article 1(4) and of those referred to in the first paragraph of this point'. Article 1(4) refers to active devices. Article 2(1) of Regulation (EU) 2017/746 of the European Parliament and of the Council of 5 April 2017 on in vitro diagnostic medical devices and repealing Directive 98/79 EC and Commission Decision 2010/22[94] refers to this definition of medical device.

46. In the case of medical devices, the extent to which the healthcare professional is under an obligation to inform and advise is reduced compared to his obligation in case of medicinal products, in view of the difference in terms of risk.[95]

C. Health Technology

47. Article 31 of the Cross-Border Healthcare Directive defines 'health technology' as follows: 'a medicinal product, a medical device or medical and surgical procedures as well as measures for disease prevention, diagnosis or treatment used in

92. *OJ* 2017, L 117/1.
93. *OJ* 2020, L 130/18.
94. *OJ* 2017, L 117/176; *see* on this, H.D.C. Roscam Abbing, 'Editorial. New EU Rules for in Vitro Diagnostic Genetic Tests, a First Step in the Right Direction', 15 *European Journal of Health Law* 121–133 (2017).
95. Opinion AG Mengozzi, in *Ker-Optika*, Case C-108/09, ECLI:EU:C:2010:341, para. 76.

healthcare'. Article 2(4) of Regulation (EU) 2021/2282 of the European Parliament and the European Commission of 15 December 2021 on Health Technology Assessment and amending Directive 2011/24/EU has confirmed this definition.[96] This Regulation shall apply from 12 January 2025 (Article 36.2).[97]

III. Freedom of Member States to Determine Health Services

48. Member States are not entirely free to determine whether services are health services.

A. *The Selling of Contact Lenses Is Not a Health Service*

49. In *Ker-Optika,* a Hungarian tribunal submitted to the CJEU, among others, the following question for a preliminary ruling: 'Does the sale of contact lenses constitute medical advice requiring the physical examination of a patient and thus not fall within the scope of the Directive on electronic commerce?'[98] According to Recital 18 in the Preamble to this Directive, 'activities which by their very nature cannot be carried out at a distance and by electronic means, such as the statutory auditing of company accounts or medical advice requiring the physical examination of a patient are not information society services'. In his opinion, the Advocate General made it first clear that 'if, under the Hungarian legislation, the sale of contact lenses constitutes a health service [this] is, in any event, only a purely national classification'.[99] He concluded with regard to the question submitted to the CJEU that 'the question whether the sale of contact lenses is medical advice requiring the physical presence of the patient, for the purposes of Recital 18 is irrelevant'.[100]

According to the CJEU, however, if medical advice requiring a physical examination of a customer is inseparable from the selling of contact lenses, the fact that such advice is required means that such selling does not, ultimately, fall within the scope of the Directive on Electronic Commerce.[101] In other words, in that case, the selling of contact lenses[102] had to be considered a health service. However, the CJEU continued that physical examination is not inseparable from the selling of contact lenses. It can be carried out independently of the act of sale, and the sale

96. *OJ* 2021, L 458/1-32; G. Ernst & K. Stöger, 'Give Due Consideration … Some Thoughts on Member States' Obligations Under Article 13 of the HTA Regulation', 31 *European Journal of Health Law* 171–186 (2024).

97. J. Wested, 'The New Regulation of Health Technology Assessment', 6 *European Pharmaceutical Law Review* 122–126 (2022).

98. *Supra* n. 93, para. 27. The Directive on Electronic Commerce is the Directive 2000/31/EC of the European Parliament and of the Council of 8 Jun. 2000 on certain legal aspects of information society services, in particular electronic commerce, in the Internal Market, *OJ* 2000, L 178, 1.

99. *Supra* n. 93, para. 43.

100. *Ibid.*, para. 51.

101. CJEU, *Ker-Optika*, Case C-108/09, ECLI:EU:C:2010:725, para. 34.

102. Contact lenses are to be classified as medical devices; *see* Opinion AG Sharpston, in *Laboratoires Lyocentre*, Case C-109/12, ECLI:EU:C:2013:253, para. 43.

can be effected, even at a distance, on the basis of a prescription made by the ophthalmologist who has previously examined the customer. Consequently, it must be held that it is possible to separate the selling of contact lenses from the obtaining of medical advice which requires the physical examination of a patient and on which the sale may be dependent.[103]

B. An Optician's Shop Is Not a Health Service

50. Although the selling of contact lenses is not a health service, 'the sale of such lenses, even if ophthalmologists are responsible for prescribing them, cannot be regarded as a commercial activity like any other, since the vendor must be able to provide users with information on the use and care of lenses'.[104] However, the establishment and the operation of an optician's shop may not be subjected to an authorization that can only be granted to a recognized optician who is a natural person and who holds at least 50% of the company's share capital and participates at least to that extent in the profits and the losses of the company.[105] In other words, the operation of an optician's shop cannot be considered a health service.

51. In this respect, it is interesting to cite the opinion of Advocate General Colomer in *Commission v. Greece.* In this case, the European Commission sought a declaration by the CJEU that Greece, by the conditions it had imposed on both natural and legal persons for authorization to operate opticians' shops in its territory, had failed to fulfil its obligations under Articles 43 EC and 48 EC. One of these conditions was that each optician, as a natural person, cannot run more than one shop. According to the Greek Government, the contested legislation sought to preserve the personal relationship of trust in the context of the sale of opticians' goods and to ensure the absolute liability of the qualified optician, who is, in turn, the owner of the business.[106] According to the Advocate General, however, 'there are two spheres of relationship in the shops, one internal and the other external. The first comprises ownership – which includes, for example, the premises or room in which it is situated, the list of customers, the goods or trade name –, the labour links with the employees and, particularly relevant to the problem presented by these proceedings, proprietorship – which is not the same as ownership, with which it is connected through various legal forms –, as well as administration and management. The second comprises relations with third parties, particularly with suppliers and, of interest in this case, with buyers, customers or, if you prefer, patients. The Greek legislation confuses these two profiles. In the field of internal relations, it prohibits a qualified optician from setting up more than one shop, justifying the measure on grounds of an external nature, basically on the special personal relationship of trust with the customer and the optician's unlimited liability. If it distinguished between them, there would be less serious consequences for Community freedom, because

103. *Supra* n. 98, paras 37–40.
104. CJEU, *LPO*, Case C-271/92, ECLI:EU:C:1993:214, para. 11.
105. CJEU, *Commission v. Greece*, Case C-140/03, ECLI:EU:C:2005:242.
106. Opinion AG Colomer, in *Commission v. Greece*, Case C-140/03, ECLI:EU:C:2004:777, para. 29.

the establishment of several shops would not be contrary to the requirement that qualified staff should do the dispensing and also attend to the customers'.[107] The external sphere of relations coincides with the provision of health services, while the internal sphere does not.

C. Pharmaceutical Activities Are Health Services

1. Health Services Include Pharmaceutical Services

52. The definition of healthcare in the Cross-Border Healthcare Directive is potentially a very broad one but 'is not always obvious'.[108] Moreover, one should also have regard to Article 2.2f of Directive 2006/123/EC of the European Parliament and of the Council of 12 December 2006 on services in the internal market (the Services Directive).[109] This article excludes 'healthcare services' from its field of application but does not contain a definition of that notion. It provides for the following: 'This Directive shall not apply to healthcare services whether or not they are provided via healthcare facilities and regardless of the ways in which they are organised and financed at national level or whether they are public or private.' Recital 22 in the Preamble to the Services Directive reiterates the exclusion and makes a remarkable distinction between healthcare and pharmaceutical services: 'The exclusion of healthcare from the scope of this Directive should cover healthcare and pharmaceutical services provided by health professionals to patients to assess, maintain or restore their state of health where those activities are reserved to a regulated health profession in the Member State in which the services are provided.' This may give the impression that pharmaceutical services are not health services. However, pharmaceutical services are clearly covered by the definition of healthcare in the Cross-Border Healthcare Directive (*see* paragraph 12). It is beyond discussion that the supply of medicinal products is a health service.

2. All Pharmaceutical Services Are Health Services

53. Does this, however, mean that all pharmaceutical activities are health services? In *ApothekerKammer des Saarlandes*, the national court asked whether Articles 43 EC and 48 EC preclude national legislation, such as that at issue in the main actions, which prevents persons not having the status of a pharmacist from owning and operating pharmacies. In his opinion, Advocate General Bot made reference to those who hold the view that a distinction must be drawn between aspects relating to the operation, management or administration of pharmacies (the internal aspect of pharmaceutical activity) and those relating to contact with third parties

---

107. *Ibid.*, paras 34–36.
108. R. Zahn, 'The Regulation of Healthcare in the European Union: Member States' Discretion or a Widening of EU Law?', 51 *Femarbel and Ottica New Line, Common Market Law Review* 1521 (2014).
109. *OJ* 2006, L 376.

(the external aspects of pharmaceutical activity) (*see* paragraph 51). The need to be a professionally qualified pharmacist is, according to this point of view, justified in respect of the latter aspects, but not the former, because the requirement to protect public health concerns only the external aspect of pharmaceutical activity, that is to say, the aspect relating to contact with third parties and, more specifically, with suppliers and patients and not the internal aspects.[110] In other words, the internal aspects, such as ownership, administration and management of a pharmacy, are not health services, while the external aspects are health services.

54. The Advocate General, however, was not persuaded by the argument that it is necessary to draw that distinction[111] and more fundamentally considered the distinction as 'artificial'.[112] He took the view that the requirement that the person who has economic control of the pharmacy and, as such, determines its commercial policy should be a pharmacist is in accordance with Article 43 EC.[113] He rejected the argument that the reasoning followed by the Court in *Commission v. Greece* in respect of the operation of an optician's shops should be applied to pharmacies since medicinal products can have a more serious impact on health than optical products and, if improperly used, may even cause the death of those who take them.[114]

55. According to the CJEU, a Member State may take the view that, unlike the case of a pharmacy operated by a pharmacist, the operation of a pharmacy by a non-pharmacist may represent a risk to public health, in particular to the reliability and quality of the supply of medicinal products at the retail level.[115] The Court explicitly stated that this conclusion is not called into question by its judgment in *Commission v. Greece*. Given the particular nature of medicinal products and the medicinal product market, the Court's findings in that case cannot be transposed to the field of retail supply of medicinal products. Unlike optical products, medicinal products prescribed or used for therapeutic reasons may none the less prove seriously harmful to health if they are consumed unnecessarily or incorrectly, without the consumer being in a position to realize that when they are administered. Furthermore, a medically unjustified sale of medicinal products leads to a waste of public financial resources which is not comparable to that resulting from unjustified sales of optical products.[116] In other words, all 'activities in the pharmacy field'[117] are closely related, and all of them can be considered in national law as healthcare services without violating EU law.

110. Opinion AG Bot, in *ApothekerKammer des Saarlandes*, Case C-171/07, ECLI:EU:C:2008:729, para. 45.
111. *Ibid.*, para. 49.
112. *Ibid.*, para. 73.
113. *Ibid.*, para. 77.
114. *Ibid.*, paras 83–89.
115. CJEU, *ApothekerKammer des Saarlandes*, Case C-171/07, ECLI:EU:C:2009:316, para. 40.
116. *Ibid.*, paras 59–60.
117. *Ibid.*, para. 20.

D. *Pharmacies Are Health Services*

56. Also, pharmacies are health services. According to the CJEU in *ApothekerKammer des Saarlandes*, 'Member States [have the power] to adopt, in particular, provisions to govern the organisation of health services such as pharmacies.'[118] In the same sense, the CJEU in *Blanco Perez* stated that 'organisation of health services such as pharmacies'[119] and the Advocate General in this case stated that 'although pharmacies are commercial undertakings, they also represent part of the health system … just as other health services'.[120]

E. *Dental Services Are Health Services*

57. Although under the Austrian legislation, a 'group dental practice' is not a health institution, Advocate General Bot in *Hartlauer* considered that an outpatient dental clinic (which is a health institution under the Austrian legislation) and a group dental practice are likely to carry out their activities on the same market.[121] Also, for the CJEU, it was obvious that the premises and equipment of dental group practices and those of outpatient dental clinics may have comparable features and that, in many cases, the patient will not notice any difference between them. Moreover, dental group practices generally offer the same medical services as outpatient dental clinics and are subject to the same market conditions. They may, therefore, have a similar impact on the medical services market. In those circumstances, the CJEU concluded that the national legislation at issue in the main proceedings did not pursue its stated objectives in a consistent and systematic manner, since it did not make the setting up of dental group practices to a system of prior authorization, as is the case with new outpatient dental clinics.[122] In other words, national authorities are not completely free to label some services as health services and not others when both are legally comparable.

F. *Day and Night Reception Centres for the Elderly*

58. In *Femarbel*,[123] the CJEU had to interpret the concept of 'healthcare services' and how this relates to 'social services'. While all healthcare services are excluded without any exception from the Services Directive,[124] only social services

118. *Ibid.*, para. 18.
119. CJEU, *Blanco Perez*, Case C-570/07, ECLI:EU:C:2010:300, para. 43.
120. Opinion AG Poiares Maduro in *Blanco Perez*, Case C-570/07, ECLI:EU:C:2009, para. 8.
121. Opinion AG Bot in *Hartlauer*, Case C-169/07, ECLI:EU:C:2008:478, paras 114 and 117.
122. CJEU, *Hartlauer*, Case C-169/07, ECLI:EU:C:2009:141, paras 58–63.
123. CJEU, *Femarbel*, Case C-57/12, ECLI:EU:C:2013:517; 20 *European Journal of Health Law* 499–504 (2013).
124. Emergency medical services as healthcare services are excluded from the scope of application of the Services Directive. *See* answer given by Ms Bienkowska on behalf of the Commission on 31 Jan. 2018 to a Parliamentary question of B. Bedtsen and C. Schaldemose on 9 Oct. 2017, E-006310-17. The Commission has adopted Commission Delegated Regulation (EU) 2023/4441 to

relating to housing, childcare and support of families and persons permanently or temporarily in need which are provided by the State, by providers mandated by the State or by charities recognized as such by the State are excluded in Article 2.2j of that Directive of its application. Other social services fall under the Services Directive; thus, the distinction between healthcare services and social services is not academic.

59. The *Femarbel* judgment was delivered after a reference for a preliminary ruling from the Belgian Constitutional Court. *Femarbel* (Belgian federation of private retirement homes) is a sectoral body that represents the interests of private establishments providing reception and accommodation facilities for the elderly. *Femarbel* brought an action before the Belgian Council of State in respect of the decision of the 'Commission communautaire commune de Bruxelles-Capital' (COCOM) of 3 December 2009, laying down rules relating to approvals for centres for the elderly.[125] This decision was based on Articles 11–19 of COCOM's Order of 28 April 2008,[126] requiring to obtain prior approval from COCOM before being brought into service on the grounds that such establishments offer healthcare services which should be regulated. *Femarbel* sought the annulment of the 2009 decision alleging the unconstitutionality of the 2008 Order. The Belgian Council of State referred an issue of unconstitutionality to the Belgian Constitutional Court, expressing various doubts concerning the compatibility with the Belgian Constitution of the Brussels rules. In the context of these proceedings, the Belgian Constitutional Court questioned the compatibility of the aforementioned Brussels legislation with EU law, specifically the Services Directive. In light of the particular characteristics of the centres at issue, the Belgian Constitutional Court referred the following question to the CJEU for a preliminary ruling: 'Must the healthcare services referred to in Article 2.2f and the social services referred to in Article 2.2j of the Services Directive be interpreted in such a way as to exclude from the scope of the Service Directive day reception centres in so far as they provide assistance and care appropriate to the loss of independence of old people, and night reception centres in so far as they provide health assistance and care that cannot be given to old people by their close relatives on a continuous basis?'

60. *Femarbel*, the European Commission and the Netherlands argued that the exclusion of healthcare services did not apply to day reception and night reception

---

ensure effective access to emergency services through emergency communications via the single EU emergency number, 112 (*OJ L* 65, 2 Feb. 2023). The continuity of access to emergency services, which may include cross-border cooperation, is the responsibility of the Member States. Cross-border cooperation in emergency call centres should therefore be voluntarily organized by the Member States themselves; *see* Answer given by Ms Kyriakides on behalf of the European Commission on a written Parliamentary question of T. Metz and Ch. Goerens, Access to healthcare and emergency services in cross-border territories (case of Alzette-Belval, Luxembourg/France), 14 Jun. 2023, E-001173/2023.

125. *Moniteur belge* 17 Dec. 2009.

126. Order of 28 Apr. 2008 concerning facilities receiving or accommodating the elderly, *Moniteur belge* 16 May 2008.

centres for the elderly. They took the view that, as their main activity is not the provision of healthcare services, reception centres should be regarded as falling within the Services Directive. The Brussels authorities emphasized the similarities between day and night reception centres and centres providing a higher level of care or those that are purely medical, leading them to the conclusion that day reception and night reception centres are 'healthcare services' and, as such, fall outside the ambit of the Services Directive.

61. In his opinion, Advocate General Cruz Vallanon began with an interpretation of 'healthcare facilities' in Article 2.2f of the Services Directive and the already cited Recital 22 in the Preamble to this Directive (*see* paragraph 52) and the definition of healthcare in Article 3a of the Cross-Border Healthcare Directive (*see* paragraph 52). The description given in Recital 22 is further developed in the *Handbook on the Implementation of the Services Directive*, a document approved by the Commission in 2007 that has no legal value but is nevertheless illustrative. In reference to Article 2.2f, the Handbook points out that it means that 'services which are not provided to a patient … are not covered by this exclusion' and that 'moreover, the exclusion does not cover activities which are not designed to maintain, assess or restore patients' state of health'. Furthermore, the Handbook goes on to say, 'the exclusion of health services only covers activities which are reserved to a regulated health profession in the Member State where the service is provided'.[127] The Advocate General then emphasized that the health professional must have a central part to play and be at a key stage in the provision of the service. In other words, simply providing medical supervision or introducing a certification procedure without affecting the substance or quality of the service does not automatically render it a 'healthcare service'.[128]

62. At this point, the Advocate General turned to the case under discussion and differentiated between day reception and night reception centres for the elderly. With respect to day reception centres, Article 2(e) of the contested Order defines these as centres established within, or in connection with, a retirement home, which offers 'reception facilities, during the day, to elderly people living at home'. At the centre, elderly people receive 'assistance and care appropriate to their loss of independence'. Comparing the type of care given in such centres with that provided in a different type of centre that is provided for under the Order, namely 'care centres', it can be seen that the former is intended for elderly people with a lesser degree of loss of independence, while the intended users of the latter are persons with severe disabilities. Likewise, the defining feature of the specific services that day reception centres are charged with providing, as described by *Femarbel*, is not that they are medical in nature (in contrast to those known as care centres) but their function of receiving elderly people and providing social interaction and basic supervision.[129]

---

127. Opinion AG Cruz Vallanon in *Femarbel*, Case C-57/12, ECLI:EU:C:2013:171, para. 22.
128. *Ibid.*, para. 26.
129. *Ibid.*, paras 29 and 30.

63. Turning his attention to night reception centres, the Advocate General noted important differences on account of their being open at night. First of all, the dual system of 'care centres' and 'reception centres' that exists in the case of day centres does not seem to exist here, so it may be assumed that night 'reception' centres also fulfil the role of care centres. In fact, Article 190 of the contested Order provides that facilities (including night reception centres) must have 'sufficient nursing, care and paramedic staff to ensure continuous supervision and treatment of elderly people'. Nevertheless, the fact that qualified healthcare staff are in continuous attendance does not, in principle, mean that the centre as a whole is specifically medical in nature. There is a permanent presence of this type of staff as those using the centre will only require their services occasionally. The primary function of the night reception centre is not to provide a medical service but to enable elderly people to rest. As the Commission had correctly pointed out, the fact that a healthcare service exists as part of a package of activities carried out by a centre does not automatically make the centre a provider of healthcare services. The decision as to how to classify an economic activity that might be established in a Member State must be taken on the basis of an *overall* assessment of its functions, particularly its most characteristic functions.[130]

64. In the light of the foregoing, the Advocate General took the view that, with regard, first of all, to day reception centres, these do not constitute centres for the provision of 'healthcare services' within the meaning of Article 2.2f of the Services Directive. Both the nature of the services provided and the type of staff that provides them suggest that the healthcare function is not predominant and that the presence of healthcare staff is not such as to make it a healthcare service. However, the case of night reception centres may be different. But if the particular characteristics of the night centres do not amount to more than occasional or incidental medical care, the conclusion must be the same.[131]

65. 'In a very short judgment',[132] the CJEU adopted a similar approach to that of the Advocate General. The Court explored at the outset the constituent elements of the concepts 'healthcare services' and 'social services'. Referring to the wording of Article 2.2f of the Services Directive, it pointed out that the concept of 'healthcare services' adopted by the EU legislature is rather broad in that it includes services to human health, whether or not they are provided via healthcare facilities and regardless of the ways in which they are organized and financed at national level or whether they are public or private.[133] The Court also noted that as stated in Recital 22 in the Preamble, the exclusion of healthcare services from the scope of that Directive should cover 'healthcare and pharmaceutical services provided by health professionals to patients to assess, maintain or restore their state of health where those activities are reserved to a regulated health profession in the Member State in

130. *Ibid.*, paras 31–34.
131. *Ibid.*, paras 35–36.
132. *Supra* n. 106, 1528.
133. *Supra* n. 121, para. 35.

which the services are provided'.[134] And it went on as follows: 'That is, incidentally, reflected in Directive 2011/24, Article 3a of which defines "healthcare" as "health services provided by health professionals to patients to assess, maintain or restore their state of health, including the prescription, dispensation and provision of medicinal products and medical devices".'[135] Lastly, that broad interpretation of the concept of 'healthcare services', and therefore of the extent of the exclusion of those services from the scope of Directive 2006/123, is supported by the analysis of the scheme laid down by that Directive. In that respect, the CJEU pointed out that, as is clear from Recital 7 in the Preamble to the Services Directive, that Directive establishes a general legal framework which benefits a wide variety of services while taking into account the distinctive features of each type of activity and its system of regulation, as well as other general interest objectives, including public health. It follows that the EU legislature expressly sought to ensure the respect of the balance between, on the one hand, the objective of eliminating obstacles to freedom of establishment of service providers and the free movement of services and, on the other hand, the need to safeguard the specific characteristics of certain sensitive activities, in particular those linked to the protection of human health.[136]

66. The CJEU left it to the Belgian Constitutional Court to verify whether the care activities carried out in daycare centres, such as the distribution and administration by a nurse of medication prescribed by the attending physician, and in night-care centres, such as the care provided by the care staff or paramedical staff of the care home concerned, are genuinely intended to maintain or restore the state of health of elderly persons, are provided by a health professional and constitute a principal part of the services provided by those centres.[137]

67. Looking back to the definition of healthcare in Article 3a of the Cross-Border Healthcare Directive, it is interesting that the Court seems to have added a new element: In order to be healthcare services, healthcare has to be a principal part of the services delivered. However, it can also be regarded as tautologous.

G. The Administration of Medication by a Nurse

68. In his opinion in *Femarbel,* Advocate General Cruz Vallanon stated that the defining feature of the specific services that day reception centres are charged with providing is not that they are medical in nature (in contrast to those known as care centres), but their function of receiving elderly people and providing social interaction and basic supervision (*see* paragraph 62). This statement is followed by the following intriguing sentence: 'although the Order of 24 April 2008 does stipulate the attendance of a nurse, this requirement is so that medication prescribed by a doctor can be administered when necessary'. The Advocate General rightly suggests

134. *Ibid*., para. 36.
135. *Ibid*., para. 37.
136. *Ibid*., paras 38 and 39.
137. *Ibid*., para. 41.

here that the obligatory attendance of a nurse does not result in a day reception centre providing healthcare services. The attendance of a nurse is only provided for in order to administer medication prescribed by a doctor when necessary. Does the Advocate General also suggest that the administration of medication by a nurse is not a health service? Probably not, because that would be remarkable in light of the definition of healthcare in Article 3a of the Cross-Border Healthcare Directive that refers to the 'dispensation' and 'provision' of medicinal products and medical devices (*see* paragraph 12) and also because in some Member States (e.g., in Belgium) the administration of medication prescribed by a physician by a nurse is considered to be a health service. But also the CJEU has sowed some doubts in this respect by leaving it to the Belgian Constitutional Court to verify whether the care activities carried out in daycare centres, such as the distribution and administration by a nurse of medication prescribed by the attending physician, are genuinely intended to maintain or restore the state of health of elderly persons.[138]

H. Sports or Fitness Clubs Are Not Health Services

69. It is clear, according to Advocate General Cruz Vallanon in *Femarbel,* that 'healthcare services' as defined in EU Law mainly comprise assessing, maintaining or restoring a person's health. Where the activity consists of providing various services, some of which do not have those characteristics, it is necessary to look at the activity's principal service. That is why, as noted in the *Handbook on the Implementation of the Services Directive* (*see* paragraph 61), a sports or fitness club would not be deemed 'healthcare services', even though some of its services clearly focus on assessing, maintaining or restoring health.[139] In *Femarbel*, the CJEU also noted that healthcare services cover activities 'directly and strictly linked to the state of human health and therefore does not concern services which are designed to enhance well-being or provide relaxation, such as sports or fitness clubs'.[140]

I. Cannabis-Based Medicinal Preparations

70. Member States may allow patients access to cannabis-based medicinal preparations for their citizens. The Commission is aware of the deviating opinions of Member States on the subject. The Commission has no plans to propose further harmonization within the EU legal framework as there is currently no prospect of agreement on a common approach at the EU level.[141]

138. *Ibid.*
139. *Supra* n. 125, para. 24.
140. *Supra* n. 121, para. 36.
141. Answer given by Ms Kyriakides on behalf of the European Commission to a written Parliamentary question of S. Kouloglou, Violations of fundamental EU principles and lack of an EU framework for medical cannabis is forcing patients to turn to the black market, 19 Feb. 2024, E-003533/2023.

Chapter 2. The Concept of Health Professionals in EU Law

§1. Not Limited to Regulated Professions

71. According to the definition of healthcare in Article 3a of the Cross-Border Healthcare Directive and the CJEU's decision in *Femarbel*, the services have to be provided by 'health professionals' in order to qualify as healthcare. Article 3f of the Directive contains the following definition: 'health professional' means 'a doctor of medicine, a nurse responsible for general care, a dental practitioner, a midwife or a pharmacist within the meaning of Directive 2005/36/EC or another professional exercising activities in the healthcare sector which are restricted to a regulated profession as defined in Article 3.1a of Directive 2005/36/EC, or a person considered to be a health professional according to the legislation of the Member State of treatment'.

72. According to the *Handbook on the Implementation of the Services Directive*, 'the exclusion of health services only covers activities which are reserved to a regulated health profession in the Member State where the service is provided'.[142] But Advocate General Cruz Vallanon has rightly remarked that the Services Directive does not specify the type of qualification to be held by such professionals and that this is merely a matter of examining each specific situation. If the profession is regulated, then the relevant legal provisions will confirm that it is a healthcare profession. If, however, the profession is not regulated, it will be necessary to take into account the occupational group in the relevant Member State and the services provided by it, which will require a specific analysis of the activities carried out by the professional.[143]

§2. Medical, Allied and Pharmaceutical Professions

73. Article 53.2. TFEU refers to 'the medical and allied and pharmaceutical professions' without giving a detailed explanation of what professions these three categories exactly include. The Dutch,[144] French,[145] Italian[146] and Spanish[147] language versions of this article learn that 'allied' professions are the so-called paramedical professions.

74. Article 53.2. TFEU is a copy of Article 57, paragraph 3 Treaty and reads in full as follows: 'In the case of the medical and allied and pharmaceutical professions, the progressive abolition of restrictions shall be dependent upon coordination of the conditions for their exercise in the various Member States.' In *Bertini*, the

142. *Supra* n. 117, para. 22.
143. *Ibid.*, para. 25.
144. *Geneeskundige, paramedische en farmaceutische beroepen.*
145. *Les professions médicales, paramédicales et pharmaceutiques.*
146. *Le professioni mediche, paramediche e farmaceutiche.*
147. *Les profesiones medicas, paramédicas y farmaceuticas.*

CJEU decided: 'In that respect it is sufficient to point out that neither Article 3 (c) nor Article 57 (3) of the Treaty requires the Member States to modify the provisions applicable within their territories to their own nationals regarding the exercise of the medical professions. Such obligations could only arise from directives adopted by the Council to coordinate the relevant national rules.'[148]

§3. Large Margin of Discretion for Member States to Determine a Medical or a Paramedical Profession

75. Also, Article 3f of the Cross-Border Healthcare Directive, that defines professional health, leaves it almost entirely to the Member States to determine what a medical or paramedical professional is. In that sense, this Directive confirms Article 13A, 1c of the Sixth Directive that left it to the Member States to define the exercise of the medical and the paramedical professions. According to Advocate General Bot, it is not clear whether the phrase 'as defined by the Member States' relates only to medical and paramedical professions or to the expression 'the exercise of the medical and paramedical professions' as a whole. A definition of a profession as medical or paramedical would be incomplete if it simply laid down abstract requirements setting out the qualifications which those intending to carry on a particular medical profession must possess without also stipulating which activities fall within that profession. Not all medical and paramedical professional qualifications provide preparation for every type of care. It is obvious, for example, that a physiotherapist does not have the training required to perform a surgical intervention. The discretion which the Member States have to define medical and paramedical professions, therefore, also includes the power to define the activities which a particular profession qualifies an individual to perform.[149]

I. Opticians

76. This large margin of discretion of the Member States has been confirmed by the CJEU in *Ottica. Ottica New Line* – an optician's office – objected to a decision taken by a local government in a Sicilian town which permitted a rival optician to establish an optician's shop in its territory. This decision infringed a regional law that only allowed for new optician's shops that met the criteria of minimal inhabitants and distance. According to the judge in first instance, these limitations violated EU law. The judge in appeal referred three questions for a preliminary ruling to the CJEU. In these questions, the Services Directive was not expressly mentioned. Without going into an exhaustive analysis of that Directive in this case, in his opinion, Advocate General Jääskinen observed that, in Italy, the profession of optician is a regulated profession within the meaning of Directive 2005/36/EC.[150]

---

148. CJEU, *Bertini,* Case C-98/85, ECLI:EU:C:1986:246, para. 11.
149. Opinion AG Kokott in *Solleveld* and *van den Hout-van Eijnsbergen*, Joint Cases C-443/04 and C-444/04, ECLI:EU:C:2005:788, paras 51 and 55.
150. Opinion AG Jääskinen in *Ottica New Line*, Case C-539/11, ECLI:EU:C:2013:41, paras 28–29.

Interestingly, he later on also noted 'that the case-law of the Court does not place the profession of optician on the same footing as health professions in the strict sense'.[151] In its judgment, the CJEU noted briefly that the Services Directive 'is not applicable in the present case, even though it governs the freedom of establishment of providers from other Member States and it is alluded to by the referring court. It is apparent from Article 2.2f of Directive 2006/123, read in the light of Recital 22 in the Preamble thereto, that this Directive does not apply to healthcare services provided by health professionals to patients to assess, maintain or restore their state of health where those activities are reserved to a regulated health profession in the Member State in which the services are provided. First, the Court has already held that the intervention of opticians was likely to limit certain health risks and thus ensures the protection of public health. Second, the referring court points out that the opticians at issue in the main proceedings not only supply, check and adjust devices to correct sight defects, but may also themselves correct sight defects by using corrective visual devices or acting to prevent eye problems. As noted by the Advocate General in paragraphs 20 and 21 of his opinion, an optician who is authorised to conduct eye tests, to measure visual acuity, to define and check the ocular correction needed, to detect eye problems and to treat defects of vision using corrective optical devices, to advise customers in that regard and to refer them to an ophthalmic specialist is exercising an activity encompassed by the protection of public health. By contrast, opticians who carry out technical activities, such as assembling frames and repairing spectacles, and who sell products which do not, strictly speaking, form part of the treatment of visual problems, such as non-prescription sunglasses or spectacle care products, exercise a commercial activity which is not associated with the protection of public health. Moreover, the referring court points out that the activity of optician is a regulated profession in Italy. In those circumstances, pursuant to Article 2.2f of Directive 2006/123, the activities of the opticians at issue in the main proceedings are excluded from the scope of that Directive'.[152] As Zahn has rightly observed, the Member States have a wide margin of discretion in the regulation of (ancillary) healthcare providers.[153] This makes the notion of 'healthcare professional' in the definition of healthcare in Article 3a of the Cross-Border Healthcare Directive potentially very broad.

II. Physiotherapy

A. General Observation

77. According to the CJEU, the profession of physiotherapist and, accordingly, that of any type of masseur do not fall within the sector of medical professions, in the strict sense, but within the paramedical sector. The services supplied by a medical masseur-hydrotherapist consist merely of the implementation of a therapy prescribed to the patient not by that masseur but by a doctor. It is that doctor whom the

---

151. *Ibid.*, para. 56.
152. CJEU, *Ottica New Line*, Case C-539/11, ECLI:EU:C:2013:591, paras 17–22.
153. *Supra* n. 108, 1530.

patient sees first and that doctor who then indicates to the masseur what is to be done as regards the technical execution of the therapy. Thus, the medical masseur-hydrotherapist is not chosen directly by the patient and does not act on his instructions but is designated by and acts in close liaison with a representative of the medical profession, depending on and cooperating with each other.[154]

B. Physiotherapy and Disturbance Field Diagnostics (Method of Treatment Alternative to Traditional Medicine)

78. In *Solleveld,*[155] a reference for a preliminary ruling concerning the interpretation of Article 13A, 1c of the Sixth Directive (*see* paragraphs 14 et seq.) from the Netherlands Supreme Court was judged by the CJEU. Mr Solleveld was a physiotherapist registered as such in the Register established by the Dutch BIG Law (the Law regulating access to and pursuit of the health professions).[156] In addition to his 'classical' physiotherapy activities, Mr Solleveld carried out so-called disturbance field diagnostics, in respect of which he completed additional specific training in Germany. As Mr Solleveld did not pay any VAT on services in connection with his activities in the area of disturbance field diagnostics, notices of additional assessment were sent to him in respect of the period 1 January 1994–31 December 2000. The objections which he had made to those notices were rejected by the Inspector. The rejection was based, in particular, on the opinion of the Inspector of Public Health, according to whom disturbance field diagnostics does not fall within the area of expertise of a physiotherapist. The Amsterdam Regional Court of Appeal dismissed the action brought by Mr Solleveld against the decision to reject his objections on the ground, in essence, that the medical care in question could not be regarded as having been provided in his capacity as a physiotherapist. Mr Solleveld appealed to the Netherlands Supreme Court against this judgment. In its order for reference, that Court, after having observed that the medical care in question is not provided by Mr Solleveld in his professional capacity within the meaning of the BIG Law, was uncertain as to whether it should nevertheless be exempted from VAT, since, first, its purpose is, from a subjective point of view, to contribute to the medical treatment of the patient and, second, it is apparent from the facts established by the Regional Court that, in 40% of cases, Mr Solleveld's patients are referred to him by a doctor in medicine or a dentist, and most insurance companies reimburse the cost of the treatment, at least when the patients have taken out additional insurance covering medical practices other than those coming within the scope of traditional medicine. Under these circumstances, the Netherlands Supreme Court decided to refer a question to the CJEU for a preliminary ruling.

154. CJEU, *Nasiopoulos*, Case C-575/11, ECLI:EU:C:2013:430, paras 28–29.
155. CJEU, *Solleveld* and *van den Hout-van Eijnsbergen,* joint Cases C-443/04 and C-444/04, ECLI-:EU:C:2006:257.
156. *See* H. Nys, *Medical Law in the Netherlands* 39–44 (Alphen aan den Rijn: Kluwer Law International 4 ed. 2023).

79. By its question, the referring court asked, according to the CJEU in substance, whether the exemption from VAT laid down by Article 13A, 1c of the Sixth Directive applied to treatments carried out by a physiotherapist outside the context of the exercise of the medical and paramedical professions as defined by the Dutch legislation. According to a literal interpretation of Article 13A, 1c, the practitioner must satisfy two conditions to benefit from the exemption laid down in that provision, which are, first, that he must provide 'medical care' and, second, that this must be carried out 'in the exercise of the medical and paramedical professions as defined by the Member State concerned'.

80. With regard to the first condition, the CJEU considered that 'it is common ground that the treatments given by the applicant in the main proceedings constitute medical care within the meaning of that provision, since those treatments are carried out for the purpose of diagnosing, treating and, in so far as possible, curing diseases or health disorders, thus pursuing a therapeutic aim'.[157] According to Advocate General Kokott, 'that fact was not called into question even in the case of Mr. *Solleveld*, notwithstanding that disturbance field diagnostics constitutes a method of treatment alternative to traditional medicine'.[158]

81. With regard to the second condition, the CJEU considered that it was apparent from the orders for reference that although the treatments in question were given by a service provider belonging to a paramedical profession, they did not come within the areas of expertise of that profession, as defined by the said legislation.[159]

82. According to the CJEU, from the previous, it followed that by its question, the referring court asked in substance whether the Member States may exclude certain specific medical care activities from the definition of paramedical professions. In that respect, it was clear, according to the CJEU, from the wording of Article 13A, 1c, that that provision did not itself define the concept of 'paramedical professions' but referred instead to the definition adopted by the national legislation of the Member States. Under these circumstances, it is for each Member State to define, in its own domestic law, the paramedical professions.[160] The CJEU had already held that this provision confers discretion on the Member States in this respect.[161]

83. That discretion covers not only the power to define the qualifications required to carry out the paramedical professions but also the power to define the specific medical care activities which are covered by such professions. In fact, since the various qualifications acquired by the service providers do not necessarily prepare them to provide all types of care, a Member State is entitled to take the view, in the exercise of its discretion, that the definition of paramedical professions would

157. *Supra* n. 152, para. 24.
158. *Supra* n. 149, para. 19.
159. *Supra* n. 152, para. 26.
160. *Ibid.*, para. 29.
161. *Supra* n. 53, para. 81.

be incomplete if it were limited to imposing general requirements as to the qualifications of providers, without specifying the care in respect of which they are qualified in the context of those professions. Thus, it must be accepted according to the CJEU that the Member States' discretion in defining the paramedical professions authorizes them not to consider as such and, therefore, to exclude from the exemption from VAT a particular profession and grant the exemption only to providers with the professional qualifications specified in the national legislation on the paramedical professions and only in connection with the specific medical care activities in respect of which those qualifications were acquired, as those activities are defined in the said legislation.[162]

84. However, the discretion enjoyed by the Member States in this respect is not unlimited. It follows from the CJEU's case law that the requirement of a correct and straightforward application of the exemptions does not allow the Member States to prejudice the objectives of the Sixth Directive or the principles of Community law, in particular, the principle of equal treatment. Consequently, where a taxable person requests that his medical care activities be recognized as coming within the ambit of the exercise of paramedical professions, it is for the national courts to examine whether the competent authorities have observed the limits of the discretion provision, having regard to the objective pursued by the latter and the principle of equal treatment.[163]

85. In this respect, concerning, first, the objective pursued by Article 13A, 1c of the Sixth Directive, it should be noted that the condition laid down by that provision that medical care must be provided in the exercise of the paramedical professions as defined by the Member State concerned is to ensure that the exemption applies only to medical care provided by practitioners with the required professional qualifications. Consequently, not all medical care falls within the scope of such an exemption, the latter concerning only that of sufficient quality, having regard to the professional training of the providers. It follows that the exclusion of a particular profession or a specific medical care activity from the definition of the paramedical professions adopted by the national legislation must be capable of justification on objective grounds based on the professional qualifications of the care providers and, therefore, by considerations relating to the quality of the services provided.[164]

86. As regards the second principle of equal treatment, in order to determine whether medical care is similar, it is appropriate to take into account the professional qualifications of the care providers. In fact, where it is not identical, medical care can be regarded as similar only to the extent that it is of equivalent quality from the point of view of recipients. It follows that the exclusion of a profession or specific medical care activity from the definition of the paramedical professions adopted by the national legislation is contrary to the principle of equal treatment

162. *Supra* n. 152, paras 30 and 33–34.
163. *Ibid.*, paras 31 and 34–35.
164. *Ibid.*, paras 37–38.

only if it can be shown that the persons exercising that profession or carrying out that activity have, for the provision of such medical care, professional qualifications which are such as to ensure an equivalent level of quality of care.[165]

87. It was, therefore, for the referring court to determine whether, having regard to all of these factors, the exclusion of activities in the area of disturbance field diagnostics carried out by a physiotherapist from the field of the exercise of the paramedical professions exceeded the limits of the discretion granted to the Member States. In order to establish whether the Netherlands exceeded its discretion, it was appropriate to examine whether treatments using disturbance field diagnostics are exempted from VAT, where they are carried out by doctors or dentists. When it was questioned on this point at the hearing, the Netherlands Government, without wishing to adopt a firm position in this respect, nevertheless indicated, in respect of doctors, that it was not a priori excluded that, taking into account their expertise and more comprehensive medical training, they could benefit from the exemption from VAT if they carried out the said treatments. Under these circumstances, it was for the referring court to determine whether, by not excluding from VAT the treatments using disturbance field diagnostics given by the applicant in the main proceedings, the Netherlands had exceeded its discretion, having regard to the VAT regime applied to doctors and dentists in respect of the same treatments and to the quality of the care provided in this context by each of them. In this respect, the referring court could take into account, in particular, the fact that, in his capacity as a physiotherapist, the applicant in the main proceedings exercised a paramedical profession within the meaning of the national legislation of the Netherlands, that he undertook specific additional training to be able to carry out the said treatments and that treatment often began following referral of his patients by doctors or dentists.[166]

88. In a judgment of 27 March 2015, the Netherlands Supreme Court judged that *Solleveld* should be exempted from VAT for the so-called disturbance field diagnostics services he delivered.[167]

C. Physiotherapy and Osteopathy (Non-conventional Therapy)

89. In *Gabarel,*[168] a request for a preliminary ruling from the Administrative and Fiscal Tribunal of Leira (Portugal) concerning the interpretation of Article 132.1c of the VAT Directive was judged by the CJEU. Gabarel obtained his diploma as a physiotherapist in Rennes (France) with a specialization in osteopathy which gave

165. *Ibid.*, paras 40–41.
166. *Ibid.*, paras 44–50.
167. ECLI:NL:HR:2015:744; this judgment has been severely criticized by C. Reckens & B. Scholten, 'Rechters, ga te rade bij een goede dokter', *Nederlands Juristenblad* 998 (2016) (translation: 'Judges, Take the Advice of a Good Doctor').
168. CJEU, *Gabarel*, Case C-555/15, ECLI:EU:C:2016:272. This is a so-called Reasoned Order of the CJEU (*see* Art. 99 Rules of Procedure CJEU); the text of the judgment is only available in French and Portuguese.

him the right to pursue osteopathy in France. From 1986 onwards, Gabarel practised physiotherapy in Portugal. The Portuguese VAT law exempts from VAT, services in the exercise of the profession of physician, dentist, midwife, nurse and other paramedical professions. Physiotherapy is recognized as a paramedical profession in Portugal. Osteopathy is recognized as a so-called non-conventional therapy under Law No. 45/2003 of 22 August 2003. According to the Portuguese fiscal services, Gabarel could not be exempted from VAT for his services, as osteopathy is not a paramedical profession according to Portuguese law. He appealed this decision before the Administrative and Fiscal Tribunal of Leira which asked two questions to the CJEU: (a) For the purposes of the interpretation of Article 132.1c of the VAT Directive, should non-conventional therapies, in particular osteopathy, be regarded as paramedical activities? (b) Must a taxable person who is authorized under national law to practice a paramedical activity, namely physiotherapy, but who, in the context of his professional health activity, uses either indistinctively or complementarily both therapies characteristic of physiotherapy and therapies characteristic of osteopathy be regarded, for the purposes of Article 132.1c of the VAT Directive as a professional who, overall, carries out a paramedical activity which is, accordingly, exempt from VAT?

90. Referring to *Solleveld* and *van den Hout-van Eijnsbergen* (*see* paragraphs 78 et seq.), the CJEU repeated that according to a literal interpretation of Article 132.1c of the Sixth Directive, the practitioner must satisfy two conditions to benefit from the exemption laid down in that provision, which are, first, that he must provide 'medical care' and, second, that this must be carried out 'in the exercise of the medical and paramedical professions as defined by the Member State concerned'. While the first condition was not under discussion, the referring court wondered whether the second condition was satisfied by activities that, according to the national law, belonged partially to a paramedical activity and partially not. It is for each Member State to define, in its own domestic law, the paramedical professions in the context of which medical care is exempt from VAT. The Member States have discretion in this respect.

91. However, the exclusion of a particular profession or a specific medical care activity from the definition of the paramedical professions adopted by the national legislation for the purpose of the exemption laid down by Article 132.1c must be capable of justification on objective grounds based on the professional qualifications of the care providers and, therefore, by considerations relating to the quality of the services provided. In the given case, the quality of the osteopathic services was not under discussion, but it was up to the referring court to evaluate this.

92. According to the CJEU, Article 132.1 of the VAT Directive has to be interpreted in the sense that a physiotherapist who, in the context of his professional health activity, uses indistinctively or complementarily therapies[169] characteristic of

169. *See* on complementary therapies in the EU, Directorate-General for Internal Policies, *Complementary and Alternative Therapies for Patients Today and Tomorrow, Study for the ENVI Committee,* Brussels, 16 Oct. 2017.

physiotherapy and therapies characteristic of osteopathy should be exempted from VAT for the first kind of therapies and the second kind of therapies if the exclusion of the second category from paramedical activities exceeds the discretion granted to the Member States by that provision. In a later case, the CJEU has given more guidance on the limits of this discretion. In a request for a preliminary ruling, the Belgian Constitutional Court asked the CJEU whether the exemption laid down by Article 132.1c is only applicable to services provided by healthcare professionals who are regulated by law in the Member State concerned and whether providers of healthcare who are not regulated by law but who are a member of a (private) professional organization of chiropractors or osteopaths and who respect the conditions imposed by this organization are excluded.[170] The CJEU first remarked that this article does not oblige the Member States to preserve the exemption exclusively to healthcare professionals regulated by law. The CJEU referred to the discretion of the Member States in this respect.[171] But they have to guarantee that the exemption is only granted for medical care of a sufficient level of quality. This requirement, however, does not necessarily imply the provision of healthcare by a regulated professional because other efficient means to supervise the professional qualifications are possible with regard to the organization of the medical and paramedical professions in a given Member State. The importance of the latter addition may not be underestimated. In Member States, such as Belgium and France, where the medical and paramedical professions have, in general, a legal monopoly, it is almost impossible to grant the exemption to not regulated healthcare providers because their activities are illegal, be it often without being prosecuted and even being tolerated, while this is not the case in other Member States, such as Denmark and the Netherlands that have fairly liberal regulations, with limited reserved activities and protection of titles instead of protection of professions.[172] The CJEU continued that it cannot be excluded in a general and absolute way that healthcare providers who do not belong to a regulated profession nevertheless dispose of the required qualifications to provide healthcare of a sufficient level of quality comparable with that provided by regulated professionals, in particular, if they have been trained in an educational institution licensed by the Member State concerned.[173] A national court may not make use of a national provision empowering it to maintain certain effects of a provision of national law which it has found to be incompatible with Council Directive 2006/112/EC of 28 November 2006 on the common system of VAT, on the basis of an alleged impossibility of refunding the VAT wrongly levied to the customers of the services provided by a taxable person, in particular by reason of the large number of persons concerned or where those persons do not have an accounting system enabling them to identify those services and their value.[174]

---

170. CJEU, *Belgian Syndicate of Chiropraxy*, C-597/17, ECLI:EU:C:2019:544, para. 16.
171. *Supra* n. 58, paras 40–41.
172. *See* for France, E. Cloatre, 'Regulating Alternative Healing in France, and the Problem of "Non-medicine"', 27 *Medical Law Review* 189–214 (2019); E. Cloatre & F. Salvini Ramas, 'The Regulation of Acupuncture in France and the United Kingdom: Shifts and Fragmentation in Contrasting Healthcare Systems', 19 *Medical Law International* 235–257 (2019).
173. *Supra* n. 168, paras 22–31.
174. CJEU, *BV Osteopathie Van Hauwermeier,* Case C-355/22, ECLI:EU;C:2023:737, para. 41.

D. Psychotherapy

93. Psychotherapeutic treatment, given in an outpatient facility by a foundation employing qualified psychologists who are not registered as doctors, qualifies as 'medical care'.[175] The term 'medical care' in Article 13A, 1b of the Sixth Directive must be interpreted as covering all provision of medical care envisaged in letter (c) of the same provision, including services provided by persons who are not doctors but who provide paramedical services, such as psychotherapeutic treatment given by qualified psychologists.[176]

94. In *Solleveld* and *van den Hout-van Eijnsbergen,*[177] a reference for a preliminary ruling concerning the interpretation of Article 13A, 1c of the Sixth Directive from the Netherlands Supreme Court was judged by the CJEU. By its question, the referring court asked in substance whether the exemption from VAT applied to treatments carried out by a psychotherapist outside the context of the exercise of the medical and paramedical professions as defined by the Dutch legislation.

95. Ms *van den Hout-van Eijnsbergen* worked as a self-employed psychotherapist and had a teaching diploma in this field. The Principal Mental Health Inspector found that she satisfied the legal conditions, and she was entered into the Register as a psychotherapist in 1988. As Ms *van den Hout-van Eijnsbergen* did not pay VAT on the services relating to her activities, notices of additional assessment were sent to her. The objection which she made to these notices was rejected by the Inspector. By judgment of 20 March 2003, the Hague Regional Court of Appeal dismissed the action brought by Ms *van den Hout-van Eijnsbergen* against the decision to reject her objection on the ground, in essence, that 'services provided by doctors and psychologists' as referred to in Article 11.1g of the 1968 Law on turnover tax, in the version in force during the tax years at issue in the main proceedings, must be construed solely as services provided by persons authorized to use the title of doctor or psychologist. Ms *van den Hout-van Eijnsbergen* brought an appeal against the said judgment before the Netherlands Supreme Court. In its order for reference, that court, after having observed that it is beyond reasonable doubt that the purpose of treatments provided by self-employed psychotherapists is therapeutic, noted that psychotherapists did not appear on the list of professions referred to in Article 11.1g of the 1968 Law on turnover tax in the version applicable to the dispute, even if they satisfied the statutory requirements for registration and were actually entered in the Register of Psychotherapists. Moreover, the referring court indicated that that provision, in the version in force since 1 December 1997, states that medical care provided by psychotherapists is exempt from VAT. The said court was accordingly uncertain as to whether the exhaustive list of the medical professions in the 1968

175. Opinion AG Stix-Hackl, in *Dornier,* C-45/01, ECLI:EU:C:2002:737, para. 56; answer given by Mr Moscovici on behalf of the Commission (10 Jan. 2019) on a Parliamentary question of L. Boylan, Vat rate to counselling and psychotherapy services, E-005658/2008: 'The Commission is aware that Ireland applies a 13.5% VAT rate to counselling and psychotherapy services, treating them as non-exempt medical services.'.

176. *Supra* n. 53, para. 50.

177. *Supra* n. 155.

Law on turnover tax, in the version in force prior to 1 December 1997, could be sufficient to exclude the medical care at issue from the exemption laid down by Article 13A, 1c of the Sixth Directive. Under these circumstances, the Netherlands Supreme Court decided to refer a question to the ECJ for a preliminary ruling.[178]

96. According to a literal interpretation of Article 13A, 1c, the practitioner must satisfy two conditions to benefit from the exemption laid down in that provision, which are, first, that he must provide 'medical care' and, second, that this must be carried out 'in the exercise of the medical and paramedical professions as defined by the Member State concerned'. With regard to the first condition, the CJEU considered that 'it is common ground that the treatments given by the applicant in the main proceedings constitute medical care within the meaning of that provision, since those treatments are carried out for the purpose of diagnosing, treating and, in so far as possible, curing diseases or health disorders, thus pursuing a therapeutic aim'.[179] With regard to the second condition, the CJEU considered that it was apparent from the orders for reference that the treatments in question were given by a provider who did not belong, at the time of the facts in the main proceedings, to one of the paramedical professions defined by the national legislation.

97. According to the CJEU, from the previous, it followed that by its question, the referring court asked in substance whether the Member States may exclude certain specific medical care activities from the definition of paramedical professions. In that respect, it was clear, according to the CJEU, from the wording of Article 13A, 1c, that that provision did not itself define the concept of 'paramedical professions' but referred instead to the definition adopted by the national legislation of the Member States. Under these circumstances, it is for each Member State to define, in its own domestic law, the paramedical professions.[180]

98. That discretion covers not only the power to define the qualifications required to carry out the paramedical professions but also the power to define the specific medical care activities which are covered by such professions. In fact, since the various qualifications acquired by the service providers do not necessarily prepare them to provide all types of care, a Member State is entitled to take the view, in the exercise of its discretion, that the definition of paramedical professions would be incomplete if it were limited to imposing general requirements as to the qualifications of providers, without specifying the care in respect of which they are qualified in the context of those professions. Thus, it must be accepted according to the CJEU that the Member States' discretion in defining the paramedical professions authorizes them not to consider as such and, therefore, to exclude from the exemption from VAT a particular profession such as that of psychotherapist even if certain aspects of that profession are governed by specific rules under national law. It was, therefore, for the referring court to determine whether, having regard to all these

178. *Ibid.*, paras 16–20.
179. *Ibid.*, paras 23–26.
180. *Ibid.*, paras 27–29.

factors, the exclusion of the profession of psychotherapist from the field of the exercise of the paramedical professions exceeded the limits of the discretion granted to the Member States. In that respect, the CJEU, at the outset, pointed out that, contrary to the line of argument put forward by the Netherlands Government, the fact that all psychotherapists have been treated in the same way in respect of VAT, whatever their legal status, was not relevant. The referring court had to examine whether, as Ms *van den Hout-van Eijnsbergen* submitted, the Netherlands made the activities of psychotherapists with a teaching diploma subject to a VAT regime which was different from those applied to psychiatrists and psychologists carrying out the same activities. If that were the case, it was for the referring court to examine whether psychotherapists with a teaching diploma actually had, like psychiatrists and psychologists, the professional qualifications required to carry out the psychotherapy treatments practised by the applicant and, if so, whether they benefited, in respect of such activities, from the exemption from VAT. If so, the Dutch legislation at issue in the main proceedings would exceed the discretion enjoyed by the Member States only if the quality of the treatments carried out by psychotherapists could be regarded, having regard to their professional qualifications, as equivalent to that of similar treatments carried out by psychiatrists, psychologists or any other medical or paramedical profession, a matter which it is for the referring court to determine in the light of all the relevant circumstances of the case before it. In that respect, the referring court could take into account, in particular, the fact that the applicant had a teaching diploma and that the psychotherapy treatments which she carried out took place within a statutory framework, under the control of the Public Health Inspectorate and in accordance with conditions set out in specific legislation, respect of which was attested to by entry in a register provided for that purpose, these circumstances being such as to ensure that she had, for the exercise of her activities, the required professional qualifications.[181]

181. *Ibid.*, paras 30 and 36–42.

Part II. Access and Pursuit of the Healthcare Professions

Chapter 1. The Mutual Recognition of Professional Qualifications

99. The mutual recognition of the professional qualifications of the health professions in the EU is regulated in Directive 2005/36/EC of the European Parliament and the Council of 7 September 2005 on the recognition of professional qualifications (the Professional Qualifications Directive).[182] This Directive has been revised several times, lastly by Directive (EU) 2024/505 as regards the recognition of professional qualifications of nurses responsible for general care in Romania.[183] The Professional Qualifications Directive is, in particular, based on Article 46 (free movement of workers), Article 53.1. (right of establishment) and Article 62 (freedom to provide services) TFEU. Member States are free to regulate the professions and define the scope of their practice in compliance with Union law. However, when it comes to cross-border recognition of the qualifications giving access to those professions in other EU Member States, the rules of the Professional Qualifications Directive apply.[184]

§1. Purpose

100. The Professional Qualifications Directive establishes rules according to which a Member State which makes access to or pursuit of a regulated profession in its territory contingent upon possession of specific professional qualifications (referred to hereinafter as the host Member State) recognizes professional qualifications obtained in one or more other Member States (referred to hereinafter as the home Member State) and which allow the holder of the said qualifications to pursue the same profession there, for access to and pursuit of that profession. The Directive also establishes rules concerning so-called partial access to a regulated profession and recognition of professional traineeships pursued in another Member State (Article 1).

182. *OJ* 2005, L 255/22; L. Kortese, 'Exploring Professional Recognition in the EU: A Legal Perspective', 4 *Journal of International Mobility* 43–58 (2016).
183. *OJ* L 2024/505, 1.
184. Answer given by Mr Breton on behalf of the European Commission to a written Parliamentary question of T. Zdechovsky, Oral and maxillo-facial surgery, 17 Aug. 2021, E-003123/2021.

§2. Effects of Recognition

101. The recognition of professional qualifications by the host Member State allows beneficiaries to gain access in that Member State to the same profession as that for which they are qualified in the home Member State and to pursue it in the host Member State under the same conditions as its nationals (Article 4.1). Also, any restriction of the right to free movement by their home Member State could only be accepted if justified in line with EU law and, in particular, with the case law of the Court.[185]

§3. The European Professional Card

I. Limited Implementation of European Professional Card for the Healthcare Professions

102. A European Professional Card (EPC) is an electronic certificate proving either that the professional has met all the necessary conditions to provide services in a host Member State on a temporary and occasional basis or the recognition of professional qualifications for establishment in a host Member State (Article 3k Directive). Member States issue holders of a professional qualification with an EPC upon their request and on condition that the Commission has adopted the relevant implementing acts provided for in Article 7 (Article 4a, 1). The introduction of an EPC for a particular profession by means of the adoption of relevant implementing acts is subjected to all of the following conditions: (a) there is significant mobility or potential for significant mobility in the profession concerned; (b) there is sufficient interest expressed by the relevant stakeholders; (c) the profession or the education and training geared to the pursuit of the profession is regulated in a significant number of Member States. Those implementing acts have to be adopted in accordance with the examination procedure referred to in Article 58.2. (Article 4a, 7). An EPC is an electronic certificate proving either that the professional has met all the necessary conditions to provide services in a host Member State on a temporary and occasional basis or the recognition of professional qualifications for establishment in a host Member State (Article 3k Directive).

103. The Commission Implementing Regulation (EU) 2015/983 of 24 June 2015 on the procedure for issuance of the EPC and the application of the alert mechanism pursuant to Directive 2005/36/EC of the European Parliament and of the Council has introduced the EPC for five professions among which the following healthcare professions: nurses responsible for general care, pharmacists (basic training) and physiotherapists.[186]

---

185. Answer given by Vice-President Schinas on behalf of the European Commission to a written Parliamentary question of L. Vincze, Emigration of physicians from Central European Member States, 27 Sep. 2023, E-002128/2023.

186. *OJ* 2015, L 159/27, *see* Annex I to the Regulation.

104. When an EPC has been introduced for a particular profession by means of relevant implementing acts, the holder of a professional qualification concerned may choose to apply for such a Card or to make use of the procedures provided for in Titles II (Free Provision of Services) and III (Freedom of Establishment) (Article 4a, 2 Directive). The EPC is an instrument that is widely accepted by the professionals covered by it.[187]

105. Any fees which applicants may incur in relation to administrative procedures to issue an EPC have to be reasonable, proportionate and commensurate with the costs incurred by the home and the host Member States and may not act as a disincentive to apply for an EPC (Article 4a, 8).

II. Application for an EPC and Creation of an Internal Market Information System File

106. The home Member State enables a holder of a professional qualification to apply for an EPC through an online tool provided by the Commission that automatically creates an Internal Market Information System (IMI) file for the particular applicant. Where a home Member State also allows for written applications, it puts in place all necessary arrangements for the creation of the IMI file, any information to be sent to the applicant and the issuance of the EPC (Article 4b, 1).

III. Processing and Access to Data Regarding the EPC (Prohibition and Restriction of Activities)

107. Without prejudice to the presumption of innocence, the competent authorities of the home and the host Member States update, in a timely manner, the corresponding IMI file with information regarding disciplinary actions or criminal sanctions which relate to a prohibition or restriction and which have consequences for the pursuit of activities by the holder of an EPC under the Directive. In so doing, they respect personal data protection rules provided for in Directive 95/46/EC of the European Parliament and of the Council of 24 October 1995 on the protection of individuals with regard to the processing of personal data and on the free movement of such data and Directive 2002/58/EC of the European Parliament and of the Council of 12 July 2002 concerning the processing of personal data and the protection of privacy in the electronic communications sector. Such updates include the deletion of information which is no longer required. The holder of the EPC and the competent authorities that have access to the corresponding IMI file have to be informed immediately of any updates. That obligation is without prejudice to the alert obligations for Member States under Article 56a (*see* paragraph 186) (Article 4e, 1).

---

187. Answer given by Mr Breton on behalf of the European Commission to a written question of S. Verheyen et al., European Professional Card, 20 Jul. 2020, E-003091/2020.

108. The content of the information updates referred to in Article 4e, 1 is limited to the following: (a) the identity of the professional; (b) the profession concerned; (c) information about the national authority or court which has adopted the decision on restriction or prohibition; (d) the scope of the restriction or the prohibition; and (e) the period for which the restriction or the prohibition applies (Article 4e, 2).

109. Access to the information in the IMI file is limited to the competent authorities of the home and the host Member States, in accordance with Directive 95/46/EC (now General Data Protection Regulation (GDPR)). The competent authorities inform the holder of the EPC of the content of the IMI file upon that holder's request (Article 4e, 3).

110. The information included in the EPC is limited to the information that is necessary to ascertain its holder's right to exercise the profession for which it has been issued, namely the holder's name, surname, date and place of birth, profession, formal qualifications, and the applicable regime, competent authorities involved, EPC number, security features and reference to a valid proof of identity. Information relating to professional experience acquired by the holder of the EPC has to be included in the IMI file (Article 4e, 4).

111. The personal data included in the IMI file may be processed for as long as it is needed for the purpose of the recognition procedure as such and as evidence of the recognition or of the transmission of the declaration required under Article 7 Member States ensure that the holder of an EPC has the right at any time, and at no cost to that holder, to request the rectification of inaccurate or incomplete data, or the deletion or blocking of the IMI file concerned. The holder is informed of this right at the time the EPC is issued and reminded of it every two years thereafter. The reminder is sent automatically via IMI, where the initial application for the EPC was submitted online (Article 4e, 5).

IV. Verification of the Authenticity and Validity of an EPC by Third Parties

112. Without prejudice to Article 4e, 3 (*see* paragraph 109), host Member States provide that employers, customers, patients, public authorities and other interested parties may verify the authenticity and validity of an EPC presented to them by the EPC holder (Article 4e, 7). The European Commission provides an online verification system which enables interested third parties who do not have access to the IMI to verify online the validity and authenticity of the EPC (Article 22.1. Commission Implementing Regulation (EU) 2015/983).

§4. Partial Access

113. Article 4f of the consolidated version of the Professional Qualifications Directive deals with the so-called partial access. The principle of partial access is the codification of the CJEU's case law.[188] In *Nasiopoulos*, the referring court asked, in essence, whether Article 49 TFEU must be interpreted as precluding national legislation which precludes partial access to the profession of physiotherapist, which is regulated in the host Member State, being granted to a national of that State who has obtained, in another Member State, a qualification, such as that of medical masseur-hydrotherapist, which authorizes him to carry out, in that second Member State, some of the activities coming under the profession of physiotherapist.[189]

114. Since the conditions for access to the profession of physiotherapist have not been harmonized at the EU level, the Member States remain competent in defining such conditions since the Professional Qualifications Directive does not restrict their powers at that point. They must, however, exercise their powers in this area in a manner which respects the basic freedoms guaranteed by the Treaty. Legislation of a host Member State which excludes all partial access to a regulated profession and, accordingly, is liable to hinder or make less attractive the exercise of freedom of establishment may be justified, *inter alia*, by overriding reasons relating to the public interest, provided that it does not go beyond what is necessary in order to attain the objective which it pursues. With regard to the objective of legislation such as that at issue in the main proceedings, the overriding reasons relating to the public interest relied upon by the Governments which submitted observations are, first, consumer protection and, second, health protection.

115. As regards consumer protection, it must be noted that, indeed, partial recognition of professional qualifications could, theoretically, have the effect of fragmenting the professions regulated in a Member State into various activities. That would lead essentially to a risk of confusion in the minds of the recipients of services provided by professionals established in that Member State, which recipients might well be misled as to the scope of the qualifications associated with the profession of physiotherapist. However, exclusion from even partial access to the profession of physiotherapist goes beyond what is necessary to achieve the objective of consumer protection. The legitimate objective of protection of consumers may be achieved through less restrictive means than total exclusion of even partial access to a profession, particularly the obligation to use the professional title of origin or the academic title both in the language in which it was awarded and in its original form, and in the official language of the host Member State.

116. As regards health protection, the Czech Government argues that healthcare professions fall within a particularly sensitive area, and the French Government is of the opinion that those professions are specific and cannot be equated with other regulated professions. That approach is shared, *inter alia*, by the Italian Government, which does not see how professional activities in the healthcare profession can be detachable without the protection of public health, the standard of the services and the confidence of consumers in the corresponding qualification being

188. A.M. Duguet & N. De Grove-Valdeyron, 'Regulation of Health Professions in Europe', *in European Health Law* 652 (A. Den Exter ed., Maklu 2017).
189. *Supra* n. 154, para. 16.

affected. In that regard, it must be held that, indeed, a particular vigilance is required, as stated in Article 52 TFEU, when examining national measures for the protection of public health.

117. As the French Government points out, the mere fact that a Member State has chosen a system of protection different from that adopted by another Member State cannot affect the appraisal of the need for and proportionality of the provisions adopted. Nonetheless, first, it must be pointed out that the profession of physiotherapist and, accordingly, that of any type of masseur does not fall within the sector of medical professions, in the strict sense, but within the paramedical sector. That sector, covering a wide range of different activities, cannot, by definition, avoid the system of mutual recognition of regulated professions as established by EU law. Second, it must be noted that the recipient of the services provided by a medical masseur-hydrotherapist de facto enjoys the particular vigilance required as regards the protection of health. The provision of the services supplied by a medical masseur-hydrotherapist consists merely of the implementation of a therapy prescribed to the patient not by that masseur but by a doctor. It is that doctor whom the patient sees first and that doctor who then indicates to the masseur what is to be done as regards the technical execution of the therapy. Thus, the medical masseur-hydrotherapist is not chosen directly by the patient and does not act on his instructions but is designated by and acts in close liaison with a representative of the medical profession, depending on and cooperating with each other. It follows from the foregoing that exclusion from even partial access to the profession of physiotherapist goes beyond not only what is necessary to achieve the objective of consumer protection but also what is required as regards protection of health.[190]

118. The competent authority of the host Member State grants partial access, on a case-by-case basis, to a professional activity in its territory only when all the following conditions are fulfilled: (a) the professional is fully qualified to exercise in the home Member State the professional activity for which partial access is sought in the host Member State; (b) differences between the professional activity legally exercised in the home Member State and the regulated profession in the host Member State as such is so large that the application of compensation measures would amount to requiring the applicant to complete the full programme of education and training required in the host Member State to have access to the full regulated profession in the host Member State; (c) the professional activity can objectively be separated from other activities falling under the regulated profession in the host Member State. For the purpose of this point, the competent authority of the host Member State takes into account whether the professional activity can be pursued autonomously in the home Member State (Article 4f, 1).

119. Partial access may be rejected if such rejection is justified by overriding reasons of general interest, suitable for securing the attainment of the objective pursued, and does not go beyond what is necessary to attain that objective (Article 4f, 2).

190. *Ibid.*, paras 20–30.

120. Partial access does not apply to professionals benefiting from automatic recognition of their professional qualifications (Article 4f, 6). It follows from the wording of that provision that the professionals benefiting from the automatic recognition of the professional qualifications under Chapters II, III and IIIa of Title III of the directive, and not the professions which are concerned by such recognition, which are excluded from the partial access provided for in Article 4f, 1 to 5 of Directive 2005/36. Hence, Article 4f, 6 must be interpreted as not precluding legislation allowing for the possibility of partial access to one of the professions covered by the mechanism for the automatic recognition of professional qualifications laid down by the provisions of Chapter III of Title III of that directive, as amended.[191]

§5. Proportionality Principle and Proportionality Test

121. Member States are free to decide within the limits of Union law, i.e., the freedom of establishment, the freedom to provide services and the principles of proportionality and necessity, whether and how to regulate a profession. In doing so, Member States need to ensure that regulation governing the taking-up and pursuit of a professional activity is justified by public interest objectives such as those within the meaning of Article 52 TFEU, namely public policy, public security and public health or by overriding reasons of general interest, recognized as such in the case law of the CJEU, to ensure that the regulation is proportionate to achieving the objectives, in particular, because regulation of a profession has an impact on professional mobility between Member States.[192] The competence to reserve access to a profession to holders of certain qualifications belongs to the Member States. European standards of competence, knowledge and skills can guarantee a certain level of expertise but do not necessarily lead to the education being organized at the same level. However, in case the current regulatory situation undermines patient safety, a standard could remediate this.[193]

122. Article 59.3. of the Professional Qualifications Directive obliges the Member States to examine whether requirements under their legal system restrict the access to a profession or its pursuit to the holders of a specific professional qualification, including the use of professional titles and the professional activities allowed under such title, referred to in this article as 'requirements' are compatible

191. CJEU, *Les chirurgiens-dentistes de France,* Case C-940/19, ECLI:EU:C:2021:135, paras 22 and 35; 28 *European Journal of Health Law* 399–403 (2021); J. Pertek, 'Partial Access to the Professions for Which Recognition Is Automatic: Directive 2005/36 Does Not Organise It, but Does Not Prevent It', *Revue des Affaires Européennes* 217–221 (2021).

192. Answer given by Ms Bienkowska on behalf of the Commission (26 Oct. 2017) on a written Parliamentary question of N. Marias, Legal status of podiatrists in Greece, 26 Sep. 2017, P-2017-005975.

193. Answer given by Mr Breton on behalf of the Commission on a written Parliamentary question of M. S. Rodríguez Ramos, Standardisation of the *Dental Hygienist Profession* in the EU, 28 Aug. 2022, E-002678/2022.

with the following principles: (a) requirements must be neither directly nor indirectly discriminatory on the basis of nationality or residence; (b) requirements must be justified by overriding reasons of general interest; (c) requirements must be suitable for securing the attainment of the objective pursued and must not go beyond what is necessary to attain that objective.

123. In January 2017, the European Commission proposed a Directive on a proportionality test before adoption of new regulations of professions.[194] After a relatively short preparatory period, Directive (EU) 2018/958 of the European Parliament and the Council of 28 June 2018 on a proportionality test before the adoption of a new regulation of professions (the Proportionality Test Directive) entered into force on 29 July 2018.[195] Member States had to comply with it by 30 July 2020 (Article 13). The Directive results from the outcome of the mutual evaluation exercise provided for in Article 59 of the Professional Qualifications Directive. The contents of the Directive directly relate to the experience acquired during that exercise, where thorough assessments were sometimes lacking, or the scrutiny of regulation of professions was uneven across the Member States. A common approach at the Union level, preventing disproportionate measures from being adopted by Member States, was proposed by the Commission in its Communication of 28 October 2015 on 'Upgrading the Single market: More opportunities for people and business' (Recitals 5 and 6 in the Preamble). The material scope of the proposed Directive was the same as for the Professional Qualifications Directive, namely all regulated professions, including the healthcare professions. The inclusion of the healthcare professions without any exception raised a lot of criticism. The Committee on the Environment, Public Health and Food Safety called on the Committee on the Internal Market and Consumer Protection (IMCO) as the committee responsible for taking into account amendments. In the Preamble, Recital 7a was proposed reading as follows: 'There is a need to ensure that the Member States fulfil to the letter their responsibilities, set out in Article 168 TFEU, regarding the details of their health policies and how they organise the provision of healthcare services and medical care by dedicated, regulated professions. *In order to achieve that result, such regulated professions should be excluded from the scope of this Directive.*'[196] It also proposed an amendment that the Directive should not apply to any requirements restricting access to, or to the pursuit of, regulated health professions in relation to the provision of healthcare services, including pharmaceutical services.[197] The IMCO did not go that far and proposed a specific status for healthcare services. Finally, a compromise was reached. With regard to the proportionality tests itself, required by Article 7 of the Directive, section 5 of this article contains the

194. *See* for a critical assessment R. Baeten, *Was the Exclusion of Health Care from the Services Directive a Pyrrhic Victory? A Proportionality Test on Regulation of Health Professions,* Brussels, OSE Opinion Paper No. 18 Apr. 2017, 25; R. Baeten, 'Healthcare Regulation: An Obstacle to Cross-Border Trade in Services? On the Muffled Application of the EU Single Market Strategy', in B. Vanhercke, S. Sabato & D. Bouqet (eds), *Social Policy in the EU: State of Play* 133–154 (European Trade Union Institute and European Social Observatory 2017).
195. *OJ* 2018, L 173/25-34.
196. E.P. 2014–2019, 2016/0404(COD), 13 Oct. 2017, Rapporteur: F. Grossetête, 3–4, italics added.
197. *Ibid.*, 10–11.

following provision: 'Where provisions referred to in this article concern the regulation of healthcare professions and have patient safety implications, Member States shall take account of the objective of ensuring a high level of human health protection.' Recital 30 in the Preamble contains the following guidance in this regard: 'As confirmed by settled case-law, the health and life of humans ranks foremost among the interests protected by the TFEU. Consequently, Member States should duly take account of the objective of ensuring a high level of human health protection when assessing requirements for healthcare professions, such as reserved activities, protected professional title, continuous professional development or rules relating to the organisation of the profession, professional ethics and supervision, while respecting the minimum training conditions, laid down in Directive 2005/36/EC. Member States should in particular ensure that the regulation of healthcare professions, having public health and patient safety implications, is proportionate and contributes to the guaranteeing of access to healthcare, recognised as a fundamental right in the Charter, as well as to safe, high quality and efficient healthcare for citizens on their territory. In establishing policies for healthcare services, account should be taken of the need to ensure accessibility, a high quality of service, and an adequate and safe supply of medicinal products, in accordance with the public health needs in the territory of the Member State concerned, as well as of the need to ensure the professional independence of healthcare professionals. With regard to the justification for the regulation of healthcare professions, Member States should take into account the objective of ensuring a high level of human health protection, including accessibility and high quality of healthcare for citizens, and adequate and safe supply of medicinal products, taking into consideration the margin of discretion referred to in Article 1 of this Directive.'[198]

198. H. Nys, 'Editorial: The Directive on a Proportionality Test and Healthcare Professions', 26 *European Journal of Health Law* 1–3 (2019).

Chapter 2. Free Provision of Services

124. Title II of the Professional Qualifications Directive regulates the free provision of services on a temporary and occasional basis. The temporary and occasional nature of the provision of services has to be assessed case by case, in particular in relation to its duration, its frequency, its regularity and its continuity (Article 5.2).

§1. Principle of Free Provision of Services

I. No Restriction of Free Provision of Services

125. Without prejudice to specific provisions of Community law, as well as to Articles 6 and 7 of the Directive, Member States may not restrict, for any reason relating to professional qualifications, the free provision of services in another Member State: (a) if the service provider is legally established in a Member State for the purpose of pursuing the same profession there (hereinafter referred to as 'the Member State of establishment') and (b) where the service provider moves, if he has pursued that profession in the Member State of establishment for at least two years during the ten years preceding the provision of services when the profession is not regulated in that Member State. The condition requiring two years' pursuit does not apply when either the profession or the education and training leading to the profession is regulated (Article 5.1).

II. Subject to Professional Rules Directly Linked to Professional Qualifications

126. Where a service provider moves, he is subjected to professional rules of a professional, statutory or administrative nature which are directly linked to professional qualifications, such as the definition of the profession, the use of titles and serious professional malpractice which is directly and specifically linked to consumer protection and safety, as well as disciplinary provisions which are applicable in the host Member State to professionals who pursue the same profession in that Member State (Article 5.3).

127. According to Advocate General Cruz Vallanon, Article 5.3 of the Professional Qualifications Directive is 'on a first reading a source of some perplexity'.[199] At first sight, it appears to be a provision divided into two sections, one governing rules of professional conduct linked to professional qualifications and the other governing the disciplinary rules applicable to the professionals concerned. However, the provision only appears to be divided, since it refers to the same legislative framework in which both substantive and disciplinary provisions are laid down. That is

199. Opinion AG Cruz Vallanon in Case C-475/11, *Kostas Konstantinides*, ECLI:EU:C:2013:51, para. 27.

confirmed by Recital 8 in the Preamble to the Directive, which states that 'the service provider should be subject to the application of disciplinary rules of the host Member State having a direct and specific link with the professional qualifications'. Some argue that cross-border agreements on such rules may help foster the rights of free-moving professionals within the EU while at the same time granting a high level of protection for patients' needs.[200]

128. According to the Advocate General, there is further cause for perplexity in that the article provides that all professionals are also subject to rules which are linked to 'serious professional malpractice which is directly and specifically linked to consumer protection and safety'. The provision is surprising because the Professional Qualifications Directive has a material scope which is strictly confined to the harmonization of the conditions for access to a regulated profession in another Member State and not to the conditions for the pursuit of that profession. In fact, the harmonization of professional activities is one of the functions assigned to the Services Directive which does not apply to medical services.[201]

129. The Advocate General, therefore, considered that the Professional Qualifications Directive, in particular Article 5.3 thereof, must be interpreted uniformly, meaning that it contains a single requirement directed to the Member States, pursuant to which service providers may be subject to all provisions (governing professional conduct and disciplinary matters) which are closely linked to professional qualifications. To give meaning to the provision under which rules relating to 'serious professional malpractice' apply, he believed that these words must be understood as a reference to situations in which disciplinary rules aimed at certain types of professional conduct entail disciplinary penalties affecting the holding or the use of a title. Thus, where serious professional malpractice resulting from the pursuit of medical activities leads to the revocation or temporary suspension of a title, this will be a disciplinary measure which combines access to the profession and pursuit of the activity. Article 5.3 supports Member States whose legal systems provide for measures of this kind, but in view of their onerous nature, it restricts such measures to 'serious' cases.[202]

130. In the light of the interpretation he proposed of Article 5.3, the Advocate General considered that the disciplinary provisions relating to the rules on fees and to the advertising of a regulated professional activity, as is the case of medical services, do not fall within the material scope of Professional Qualifications Directive. The conduct alleged against Dr Konstantinides is related to the business strategy used to win clients and charge for his services. None of that has any connection with a disciplinary measure linked to professional qualifications or serious professional malpractice, the disciplinary consequences of which would affect his title.[203]

---

200. S. Patuzzo & E. Pulice, 'Towards a European Code of Medical Ethics. Ethical and Legal Issues', 43 *Journal of Medical Ethics* 41 (2017).
201. *Supra* n 199, para. 28.
202. *Ibid.*, para. 29.
203. *Ibid.*, para. 30.

131. The CJEU agreed with the opinion of the Advocate General. According to the Court, it appears from the object and purpose and from the general scheme of the Professional Qualifications Directive that professional rules are covered by Article 5.3 of the Directive only if they are directly linked to the actual practice of medicine and failure to observe them harms the protection of patients. It follows that neither the rules for calculating fees nor the rule prohibiting unprofessional advertising by doctors, as applied in the dispute in the main proceedings, are professional rules which are directly and specifically linked to professional qualifications relating to access to the regulated profession concerned within the meaning of Article 5.3.[204]

III. Exemption from Authorization by, Registration with or Membership of a Professional Organization

132. Pursuant to Article 5.1, the host Member State exempts service providers established in another Member State from the requirements which it places on professionals established in its territory relating to authorization by, registration with, or membership of a professional organization or body. In order to facilitate the application of disciplinary provisions in force on their territory, Member States may provide either for automatic temporary registration with or for pro forma membership of such a professional organization or body, provided that such registration or membership does not delay or complicate in any way the provision of services and does not entail any additional costs for the service provider. A copy of the declaration and, where applicable, of the renewal referred to in Article 7.1 accompanied for professions which have implications for public health and safety referred to in Article 7.4 or which benefit from automatic recognition under Title III, Chapter III, by a copy of the documents referred to in Article 7.2 is sent by the competent authority to the relevant professional organization or body, and this constitutes automatic temporary registration or pro forma membership for this purpose.

133. The host Member State is also exempted from the requirement of registration with a public social security body for the purpose of settling accounts with an insurer relating to activities pursued for the benefit of insured persons. The service provider has, however, to inform in advance or, in an urgent case, afterwards, this body of the services which he has provided (Article 6).

§2. Declaration to Be Made in Advance

134. Member States may require that, where the service provider first moves from one Member State to another in order to provide services, he has to inform the competent authority in the host Member State in a written declaration to be made in advance, including the details of any insurance cover or other means of personal or collective protection with regard to professional liability. Such declaration has to be

204. CJEU, *Kostas Konstantinides,* Case C-475/11, ECLI:EU:C:2013:542, paras 39–40.

renewed once a year if the service provider intends to provide temporary or occasional services in that Member State during that year. The service provider may supply the declaration by any means (Article 7.1).

135. Moreover, for the first provision of services or if there is a material change in the situation substantiated by the documents, Member States may require that the declaration be accompanied by the following documents: (a) proof of the nationality of the service provider; (b) an attestation certifying that the holder is legally established in a Member State for the purpose of pursuing the activities concerned and that he is not prohibited from practising, even temporarily, at the moment of delivering the attestation; (c) evidence of professional qualifications; (d) for cases referred to in point (b) of Article 5.1, any means of proof that the service provider has pursued the activity concerned for at least one year during the previous ten years; (e) for professions in, among others, the health sector, where the Member State so requires for its own nationals, an attestation confirming the absence of temporary or final suspensions from exercising the profession or of criminal convictions; (f) for professions that have patient safety implications, a declaration about the applicant's knowledge of the language necessary for practising the profession in the host Member State (Article 7.2).[205]

136. Submission of a required declaration by the service provider in accordance with Article 7.1 entitles that service provider to have access to the service activity or to exercise that activity in the entire territory of the Member State concerned. A Member State may require additional information listed in Article 7.2 concerning the professional qualifications of the service provider if: (a) the profession is regulated in parts of that Member State's territory in a different manner; (b) such regulation is applicable also to all nationals of that Member State; (c) the differences in such regulation are justified by overriding reasons of general interest[206] relating to public health or safety of service recipients; and (d) the Member State has no other means of obtaining such information (Article 7.2a).

§3. Use of the Professional Title of the Member State of Establishment

137. The service has to be provided under the professional title of the Member State of establishment, in so far as such a title exists in that Member State for the professional activity in question. That title has to be indicated in the official language or one of the official languages of the Member State of establishment in such a way as to avoid any confusion with the professional title of the host Member State. Where no such professional title exists in the Member State of establishment, the service provider has to indicate his formal qualification in the official language or

205. E. Daniel, 'La liberté de circulation des professionels face aux exigences linguistiques', *Revue des Affaires Europeénnes* 371–379 (2016).
206. Overriding reasons of general interest are reasons recognized as such in the case law of the CJEU (Art. 3m).

one of the official languages of that Member State. By way of exception, the service has to be provided under the professional title of the host Member State for cases referred to in Title III, Chapter III (Article 7.3).

§4. Prior Check of Professional Qualifications

138. For the first provision of services, in the case of regulated professions that have public health or safety implications which do not benefit from automatic recognition under Chapters II, III or IIIa of Title III, the competent authority of the host Member State may check the professional qualifications of the service provider prior to the first provision of services. Such a prior check is possible only where the purpose of the check is to avoid serious damage to the health or safety of the service recipient due to a lack of professional qualification of the service provider and where the check does not go beyond what is necessary for that purpose. No later than one month after receipt of the declaration and accompanying documents (*see* paragraph 134), the competent authority informs the service provider of its decision: (a) not to check his professional qualifications; (b) having checked his professional qualifications: (i) to require the service provider to take an aptitude test;[207] or (ii) to allow the provision of services. Where there is a difficulty which would result in a delay in taking a decision, the competent authority notifies the service provider of the reason for the delay within the same deadline. The difficulty has to be solved within one month of that notification, and the decision must be finalized within two months of resolution of the difficulty.

139. Where there is a substantial difference between the professional qualifications of the service provider and the training required in the host Member State, to the extent that that difference is such as to be harmful to public health or safety and that it cannot be compensated by the service provider's professional experience or by knowledge, skills and competences acquired through lifelong learning[208] formally validated to that end by a relevant body, the host Member State gives that service provider the opportunity to show, by means of an aptitude test, that they have acquired the knowledge, skills or competence that were lacking. The host Member State takes a decision on that basis on whether to allow the provision of services. In any case, it must be possible to provide the service within one month of the decision taken in accordance with the second subparagraph. In the absence of a reaction from the competent authority within the deadlines set out in the second and third subparagraphs, the service may be provided. In cases where professional qualifications have been verified under this paragraph, the service has to be provided under the professional title of the host Member State (Article 7.4).

207. An aptitude test is a test of the professional knowledge, skills and competences of the applicant, carried out or recognized by the competent authorities of the host Member State with the aim of assessing the ability of the applicant to pursue a regulated profession in that Member State (Art. 3h).

208. Lifelong learning is all general education, vocational education and training, non-formal education and informal learning undertaken throughout life, resulting in an improvement in knowledge, skills and competences, which may include professional ethics (Art. 3l).

§5. Administrative Cooperation in the Event of Justified Doubts or Complaints

140. The competent authorities of the host Member State may ask the competent authorities of the Member State of establishment, in the event of justified doubts, to provide any information relevant to the legality of the service provider's establishment and good conduct, as well as the absence of any disciplinary or criminal sanctions of a professional nature. In the event that the competent authorities of the host Member State decide to check the service provider's professional qualifications, they may ask the competent authorities of the Member State of establishment for information about the service provider's training courses to the extent necessary to assess substantial differences likely to be harmful to public health or safety. The competent authorities of the Member State of establishment provide that information in accordance with Article 56. In the case of non-regulated professions in the home Member State, the assistance centres referred to in Article 57b may also provide such information (Article 8.1). Each Member State designates an assistance centre whose remit is to provide citizens, as well as assistance centres of the other Member States, with assistance concerning the recognition of professional qualifications provided for in the directive, including information on the national legislation governing the professions and the pursuit of those professions, social legislation, and, where appropriate, the rules of ethics (Article 57b.1).

141. The competent authorities ensure the exchange of all information necessary for complaints by a recipient of a service against a service provider to be correctly pursued. Recipients have to be informed of the outcome of the complaint (Article 8.2).

§6. Information to Be Given to the Recipients of the Service

142. In cases where the service is provided under the professional title of the Member State of establishment or under the formal qualification of the service provider, in addition to the other requirements relating to information contained in Community law, the competent authorities of the host Member State may require the service provider to furnish the recipient of the service with any or all of the following information: (a) if the service provider is registered in a commercial register or similar public register, the register in which he is registered, his registration number, or equivalent means of identification contained in that register; (b) if the activity is subject to authorization in the Member State of establishment, the name and address of the competent supervisory authority; (c) any professional association or similar body with which the service provider is registered; (d) the professional title or, where no such title exists, the formal qualification of the service provider and the Member State in which it was awarded; (e) if the service provider performs an activity which is subject to VAT, the VAT identification number referred to in the VAT Directive; (f) details of any insurance cover or other means of personal or collective protection with regard to professional liability (Article 9).

Chapter 3. Freedom of Establishment Through Recognition on the Basis of Coordination of Minimum Training Conditions

§1. Doctors of Medicine

I. Principle of Automatic Recognition

143. Each Member State recognizes evidence of formal qualifications as a doctor in medicine, giving access to the professional activities of doctors with basic training and specialized doctor, which satisfy the minimum training conditions referred to in Articles 24 (*see* paragraph 145) and 25 (*see* paragraph 146) and gives, for the purposes of access to and pursuit of these professional activities, this evidence the same effect on its territory as the evidence of formal qualifications which it itself issues.[209] Such evidence of formal qualifications must be issued by the competent bodies in the Member States and accompanied, where appropriate, by the certificates listed in Annex V (Article 21.1.). Recognition of evidence of formal qualifications, including a degree in medicine with basic training and a degree in dentistry, is automatic and unconditional in that it obliges Member States to accept the equivalence of evidence of formal qualifications covered by Directive 2005/36 and cannot require the persons concerned to comply with requirements other than those laid down by that Directive. That recognition is based on the Member States' mutual trust in the adequacy of the evidence of formal qualifications issued by the other Member States, such trust being based on a training system, the standards of which were determined by mutual agreement. Articles 21 and 22a must be interpreted as precluding the host Member State from verifying compliance with the condition that the overall duration, level and quality of part-time training are not lower than those of continuous full-time training.[210]

144. Directive 2005/36/EC must be interpreted as meaning that the competent authorities of a Member State must recognize, under the system of automatic recognition defined in Article 21 of that directive, evidence of a formal qualification as a specialized doctor issued in another Member State and referred to in point 5.1.2

209. In her answer on a Parliamentary question regarding the recognition of physiotherapists (who do not fall under the automatic recognition) by L. Michel on 23 Jun. 2017, Ms Bienkowska on behalf of the Commission answered on 15 Sep. 2017 that 'the Commission is not aware of specific systemic problem affecting the recognition of the professional qualifications of physiotherapists under the general system of recognition, which could justify the need to change the current system' (E-004190/2017). The Commission does not intend to propose the harmonization of the profession of radiation therapist at EU level; *see* answer given by Mr Navracsics on behalf of the European Commission (12 Jun. 2019) on a written question of M. McGuinness, Education of radiation therapists, E-001473/2019. Cross-border recognition of qualifications of clinical embryologist, to the extent the profession is regulated, falls under the general system; *see* answer given by Ms Kyriakides on behalf of the European Commission on a written Parliamentary question of I. Corrao, Paradox of the clinical embryologist profession in Italy and the need to harmonize the postgraduate curriculum at EU level, 19 Jun. 2023, E-000818/2023.

210. CJEU, *Preindl,* Case C-675/17, ECLI:EU:C:2018:990, paras 31 and 41.

of Annex V to that directive, only where the doctor holding that evidence of a formal qualification also has evidence of a formal qualification in basic medical training issued by a Member State and referred to in point 5.1.1 of Annex V to that directive. This interpretation is without prejudice to the possibility, in the absence of such evidence of a formal qualification in basic medical training, of recognizing evidence of a formal qualification as a specialized doctor on the basis of the general system for the recognition of evidence of training defined in Chapter I of Title III of Directive 2005/36 or, where appropriate, on the basis of Article 45 or Article 49 TFEU.[211]

II. (Admission to) Basic Medical Training

145. Admission to basic medical training is contingent upon possession of a diploma or certificate providing access to universities. Basic medical training comprises a total of at least five years of study, which may, in addition, be expressed with the equivalent European Credit Transfer and Accumulation System (ECTS) credits,[212] and consists of at least 5,500 hours of theoretical and practical training provided by, or under the supervision of, a university. Basic medical training provides an assurance that the person in question has acquired the following knowledge and skills: (a) adequate knowledge of the sciences on which medicine is based and a good understanding of the scientific methods including the principles of measuring biological functions, the evaluation of scientifically established facts and the analysis of data; (b) sufficient understanding of the structure, functions and behaviour of healthy and sick persons, as well as relations between the state of health and physical and social surroundings of the human being; (c) adequate knowledge of clinical disciplines and practices, providing him or her with a coherent picture of mental and physical diseases, of medicine from the points of view of prophylaxis, diagnosis and therapy and of human reproduction; (d) suitable clinical experience in hospitals under appropriate supervision (Article 24). These objectives can be reached by the Member States with different structures of training, which nonetheless have to comply with these requirements. While it is for the Commission to oversee the implementation of the Directive's requirements in national law, the national authorities have to supervise the education and training institutions to ensure compliance with these requirements.[213]

III. (Admission to) Specialist Medical Training

146. Admission to specialist medical training is contingent upon completion and validation of a basic medical training programme as referred to in Article 24 in the

211. Opinion AG Pikamäe in Case C-8/23, *FH v. Conseil national de l'ordre des médecins* ECLI:EU:C:2024:198, para. 74.
212. European Credit Transfer and Accumulation System (*see* Art. 3n Directive).
213. Answer given by Ms Bienkowska on behalf of the European Commission to a written Parliamentary question of D. Bilde, Medical studies in Romania, 20 Feb. 2019, E-005916/2018.

course of which the trainee has acquired the relevant knowledge of basic medicine. Specialist medical training comprises theoretical and practical training at a university or medical teaching hospital or, where appropriate, a medical care establishment approved for that purpose by the competent authorities or bodies. The Member States ensure that the minimum duration of specialist medical training courses referred to in Annex V, point 5.1.3, is not less than the duration provided for in that point.[214] Member States may provide, in national legislation, for partial exemptions from parts of the specialist medical training courses listed in this Annex, to be applied on a case-by-case basis provided that that part of the training has been followed already during another specialist training course listed in this Annex, for which the professional has already obtained the professional qualification in a Member State. Member States ensure that the granted exemption equates to not more than half of the minimum duration of the specialist medical training course in question. Each Member State notifies the Commission and the other Member States of the national legislation concerned for any such partial exemptions. Training is given under the supervision of the competent authorities or bodies. It includes personal participation of the trainee specialized doctor in the activity and responsibilities entailed by the services in question (Article 25.1–3a). The Commission is empowered to adopt delegated acts in accordance with Article 57c concerning the adaptation of the minimum periods of training referred to in point 5.1.3 of Annex V to scientific and technical progress (Article 25.5.).

147. Training is given on a full-time basis at specific establishments which are recognized by the competent authorities. It entails participation in the full range of medical activities of the department where the training is given, including duty on call, in such a way that the trainee specialist devotes all his professional activity to his practical and theoretical training throughout the entire working week and throughout the year, in accordance with the procedures laid down by the competent authorities. Accordingly, these posts are the subject of appropriate remuneration (Article 25.3.).

148. The Member States make the issuance of evidence of specialist medical training contingent upon possession of evidence of basic medical training referred to in Annex V, point 5.1.1 of the Directive (Article 25.4.).

214. Minimum period of training of three years: anaesthetics; ophthalmology; otorhinolaryngology; general haematology; endocrinology; physiotherapy; dermato-venerology; stomatology. Minimum period of training of four years: obstetrics and gynaecology; paediatrics; respiratory medicine; pathological anatomy; neurology; radiology; clinical biology; radiotherapy; diagnostic radiology; psychiatry; cardiology; gastroenterology; child psychiatry; renal diseases; geriatrics; rheumatology; biological chemistry; microbiology-bacteriology; communicable diseases; community medicine; pharmacology; occupational medicine; biological haematology; nuclear medicine; dermatology; venerology; tropical medicine; clinical neurophysiology; dental, oral or maxillo-facial surgery. Minimum period of training of five years: general surgery; neurological surgery; general (internal) medicine; urology; orthopaedics; plastic surgery; maxilla-facial surgery; paediatrics surgery; vascular surgery; neuropsychiatry; gastroenterological surgery; accident and emergency medicine.

IV. Types of Specialist Medical Training

149. Evidence of formal qualifications as a specialized doctor referred to in Article 21 is such evidence awarded by the competent authorities or bodies referred to in Annex V, point 5.1.2 as corresponds, for the specialized training in question, to the titles in use in the various Member States and referred to in Annex V, point 5.1.3. In order to take due account of changes in national legislation and with a view to updating this Directive, the Commission is empowered to adopt delegated acts in accordance with Article 57c concerning the inclusion in point 5.1.3 of Annex V of new medical specialities common to at least two-fifths of the Member States (Article 26).

V. Specific Training in General Medical Practice

150. Admission to specific training in general medical practice is contingent upon completion and validation of a basic medical training programme, as referred to in Article 24.2. in the course of which the trainee has acquired the relevant knowledge of basic medicine (Article 28.1.). The specific training in general medical practice leading to the award of evidence of formal qualifications issued before 1 January 2006 is of a duration of at least two years on a full-time basis. In the case of evidence of formal qualifications issued after that date, the training is of a duration of at least three years on a full-time basis (Article 28.2.).

151. The specific training in general medical practice is carried out on a full-time basis under the supervision of competent authorities or bodies. It is more practical than theoretical.

The practical training is given, on the one hand, for at least six months in an approved hospital possessing appropriate equipment and services and, on the other hand, for at least six months as part of an approved general medical practice or an approved centre at which doctors provide primary healthcare. The practical training takes place in conjunction with other health establishments or structures concerned with general medicine. Without prejudice to the minimum periods, however, the practical training may be given during a period of not more than six months in other approved establishments or health structures concerned with general medicine. The training requires the personal participation of the persons with whom he is working. Member States make the issuance of evidence of formal qualifications in general medical practice subject to possession of evidence of formal qualifications in basic medical training referred to in Annex V, point 5.1.1 (Article 28.3. and 28.4.).

VI. Pursuit of the Professional Activities of General Practitioners

152. Each Member State makes, subject to the provisions relating to acquired rights, the pursuit of the activities of a general practitioner in the framework of its national social security system contingent upon possession of evidence of formal qualifications referred to in Annex V, point 5.1.4 (Article 29).

§2. NURSES RESPONSIBLE FOR GENERAL CARE

I. Principle of Automatic Recognition

153. Each Member State recognizes evidence of formal qualifications as a nurse responsible for general care which satisfy the minimum training conditions referred to in Article 31 and gives, for the purposes of access to and pursuit of professional activities, this evidence the same effect on its territory as the evidence of formal qualifications which it itself issues. Such evidence of formal qualifications must be issued by the competent bodies in the Member States and accompanied, where appropriate, by the certificates listed in Annex V (Article 21.1.). The Directive allows for two training paths: university (or equivalent) and/or vocational level. Each Member State decides how many training paths it offers and ensures that these comply with the minimum conditions.[215] A host Member State may not refuse access to a regulated profession of a specialized nurse only because the applicant's qualifications, obtained in another EU country, are of post-secondary non-university level. If the applicant is qualified to exercise the same profession and activities in his or her Member State, the host country must assess the application under the general system recognition regime. Any decision of the host Member State authority shall be duly justified and subjected to appeal.[216]

II. Training of Nurses Responsible for General Care

154. Admission to training for nurses responsible for general care is contingent upon either: (a) completion of general education of twelve years, as attested by a diploma, certificate or other evidence issued by the competent authorities or bodies in a Member State or a certificate attesting success in an examination of an equivalent level and giving access to universities or to higher education institutions of a level recognized as equivalent; or (b) completion of general education of at least ten years, as attested by a diploma, certificate or other evidence issued by the competent authorities or bodies in a Member State or a certificate attesting success in an examination of an equivalent level and giving access to a vocational school or vocational training programme for nursing (Article 31.1.).

155. Training of nurses responsible for general care is given on a full-time basis and includes at least the programme described in Annex V, point 5.2.1 of the Directive. The Commission is empowered to adopt delegated acts in accordance with Article 57c concerning amendments to the list set out in point 5.2.1 of Annex V with a view to adapting it to scientific and technical progress. These amendments may not entail an amendment of existing essential legislative principles in the Member States regarding the structure of professions as regards training and conditions of

215. Answer given by Ms Bienkowska on behalf of the European Commission to a written question of P. Arimont, Training for nursing staff, 18 Oct. 2019, E-002580/2019.

216. Answer given by Mr Breton on behalf of the European Commission to a written question of P. Arimont, Training as a nurse, 4 Feb. 2020, E-003427/2019.

access by natural persons. Such amendments also respect the responsibility of the Member States for the organization of education systems, as set out in Article 165.1 TFEU (Article 31.2.).

156. The training of nurses responsible for general care comprises a total of at least three years of study, which may, in addition, be expressed with the equivalent ECTS credits, and consists of at least 4,600 hours of theoretical and clinical training, the duration of the theoretical training representing at least one-third and the duration of the clinical training at least one half of the minimum duration of the training. Member States may grant partial exemptions to professionals who have received part of their training in courses which are of at least an equivalent level. The Member States ensure that institutions providing nursing training are responsible for the coordination of theoretical and clinical training throughout the entire study programme (Article 31.3.).

157. Theoretical education is that part of nurse training from which trainee nurses acquire the professional knowledge, skills and competences required under Article 31.6. and 31.7. The training is given by teachers of nursing care and by other competent persons at universities and higher education institutions of a level recognized as equivalent or at vocational schools or through vocational training programmes for nursing (Article 31.4.).

158. Clinical training is that part of nurse training in which trainee nurses learn, as part of a team and in direct contact with a healthy or sick individual and/or community, to organize, dispense and evaluate the required comprehensive nursing care on the basis of the knowledge, skills and competences which they have acquired. The trainee nurse learns not only how to work in a team but also how to lead a team and organize overall nursing care, including health education for individuals and small groups within health institutes or in the community. This training takes place in hospitals and other health institutions and in the community, under the responsibility of nursing teachers, in cooperation with and assisted by other qualified nurses. Other qualified personnel may also take part in the teaching process. Trainee nurses participate in the activities of the department in question insofar as those activities are appropriate to their training, enabling them to learn to assume the responsibilities involved in nursing care (Article 31.5.).

159. Training for nurses responsible for general care provides an assurance that the professional in question has acquired the following knowledge and skills: (a) comprehensive knowledge of the sciences on which general nursing is based, including sufficient understanding of the structure, physiological functions and behaviour of healthy and sick persons, and of the relationship between the state of health and the physical and social environment of the human being; (b) knowledge of the nature and ethics of the profession and of the general principles of health and nursing; (c) adequate clinical experience; such experience, which should be selected for its training value, should be gained under the supervision of qualified nursing staff and in places where the number of qualified staff and equipment are appropriate for the nursing care of the patient; (d) the ability to participate in the practical training of health personnel and experience of working with such personnel; (e) experience of working together with members of other professions in the health sector (Article 31.6.).

160. Formal qualifications as a nurse responsible for general care provide evidence that the professional in question is able to apply at least the following competences regardless of whether the training took place at universities, higher education institutions of a level recognized as equivalent or at vocational schools or through vocational training programmes for nursing: (a) competence to independently diagnose the nursing care required using current theoretical and clinical knowledge and to plan, organize and implement nursing care when treating patients on the basis of the knowledge and skills acquired in accordance with points (a), (b) and (c) of Article 31.6. in order to improve professional practice; (b) competence to work together effectively with other actors in the health sector, including participation in the practical training of health personnel on the basis of the knowledge and skills acquired in accordance with points (d) and (e) of Article 31.6.; (c) competence to empower individuals, families and groups towards healthy lifestyles and self-care on the basis of the knowledge and skills acquired in accordance with points (a) and (b) of Article 31.6.; (d) competence to independently initiate life-preserving immediate measures and to carry out measures in crises and disaster situations; (e) competence to independently give advice to, instruct and support persons needing care and their attachment figures; (f) competence to independently assure the quality of, and to evaluate, nursing care; (g) competence to comprehensively communicate professionally and to cooperate with members of other professions in the health sector; (h) competence to analyse the care quality to improve his own professional practice as a nurse responsible for general care (Article 31.7.).

§3. Dental Practitioners

I. Principle of Automatic Recognition

161. Each Member State recognizes evidence of formal qualifications as a dental practitioner which satisfy the minimum training conditions referred to in Article 34 (*see* paragraph 162) and gives, for the purposes of access to and pursuit of professional activities, this evidence the same effect on its territory as the evidence of formal qualifications which it itself issues. Such evidence of formal qualifications must be issued by the competent bodies in the Member States and accompanied, where appropriate, by the certificates listed in Annex V (Article 21.1.).

II. Basic Dental Training

162. Admission to basic dental training presupposes possession of a diploma or certificate giving access to the studies in question to universities or higher institutes of a level recognized as equivalent in a Member State (Article 34.1.).

163. Basic dental training comprises a total of at least five years of study, which may, in addition, be expressed with the equivalent ECTS credits, and consists of at least 5,000 hours of full-time theoretical and practical training that comprises at least the programme described in point 5.3.1 of Annex V and that is provided in a university, in a higher institute providing training recognized as being of an equivalent level or under the supervision of a university. The Commission is empowered to adopt delegated acts in accordance with Article 57c concerning the amendment of the list set out in point 5.3.1 of Annex V with a view to adapting it to scientific and technical progress. These amendments may not entail an amendment of existing essential legislative principles in the Member States regarding the structure of professions as regards training and conditions of access by natural persons. Such amendments also respect the responsibility of the Member States for the organization of education systems, as set out in Article 165.1 TFEU (Article 34.2.).

164. Basic dental training provides an assurance that the person in question has acquired the following knowledge and skills: (a) adequate knowledge of the sciences on which dentistry is based and a good understanding of scientific methods, including the principles of measuring biological functions, the evaluation of scientifically established facts and the analysis of data; (b) adequate knowledge of the constitution, physiology and behaviour of healthy and sick persons as well as the influence of the natural and social environment on the state of health of the human being, in so far as these factors affect dentistry; (c) adequate knowledge of the structure and function of the teeth, mouth, jaws and associated tissues, both healthy and diseased, and their relationship to the general state of health and to the physical and social well-being of the patient; (d) adequate knowledge of clinical disciplines and methods, providing the dentist with a coherent picture of anomalies, lesions and diseases of the teeth, mouth, jaws and associated tissues and of preventive, diagnostic and therapeutic dentistry; (e) suitable clinical experience under appropriate supervision. This training provides him or her with the skills necessary for carrying out all activities involving the prevention, diagnosis and treatment of anomalies and diseases of the teeth, mouth, jaws and associated tissues (Article 34.3.). Article 34 sets out harmonized minimum training requirements for basic dental training, which allow for the automatic recognition of these qualifications. These requirements can be met by the Member States with different structures of training, which nonetheless have to comply with Article 34. Nevertheless, the CJEU has pointed out that Article 50.2. of the Directive allows a host Member State, where there is justified doubt, to require, in individual cases, confirmation from the competent authorities of a Member State of the authenticity of the evidence of formal qualifications awarded in that other Member State, as well as, where applicable, confirmation of the fact that the beneficiary fulfils the minimum training conditions for the respective profession.[217]

217. *Supra* n. 210, para. 38.

III. Specialist Dental Training

165. Admission to specialist dental training is contingent upon completion and validation of basic dental training referred to in Article 34 or possession of the documents referred to in Articles 23 (acquired rights in general) and 37 (acquired rights specific to dental practitioners) (Article 35.1.).

166. Specialist dental training comprises theoretical and practical instruction in a university centre, in a treatment teaching and research centre or, where appropriate, in a health establishment approved for that purpose by the competent authorities or bodies. Full-time specialist dental courses have a minimum of three years' duration and are supervised by competent authorities or bodies. They involve the personal participation of the dental practitioner training to be a specialist in the activity and in the responsibilities of the establishment concerned (Article 35.2.).

167. The Member States make the issuance of evidence of specialist dental training contingent upon possession of evidence of basic dental training referred to in Annex V, point 5.3.2 (Article 35.3.).

168. The Commission is empowered to adopt delegated acts in accordance with Article 57c concerning the adaptation of the minimum period of training referred to in Article 35.2. to scientific and technical progress. In order to take due account of changes in national legislation, and with a view to updating this Directive, the Commission is empowered to adopt delegated acts in accordance with Article 57c concerning the inclusion in point 5.3.3 of Annex V of new dental specialities common to at least two-fifths of the Member States (Article 35.4. and 35.5.).

IV. Pursuit of the Professional Activities of Dental Practitioners

169. The Member States ensure that dental practitioners are generally able to gain access to and pursue the activities of prevention, diagnosis and treatment of anomalies and diseases affecting the teeth, mouth, jaws and adjoining tissue, having due regard to the regulatory provisions and rules of professional ethics on the reference dates referred to in Annex V, point 5.3.2 (Article 36.1. and 36.3.).

The profession of dental practitioner is based on dental training referred to in Article 34 and constitutes a specific profession which is distinct from other general or specialized medical professions. Pursuit of the activities of a dental practitioner requires the possession of evidence of formal qualifications referred to in Annex V, point 5.3.2 (Article 36.2.).

§4. MIDWIVES

I. The Training of Midwives

170. The training of midwives comprises a total of at least: (a) specific full-time training as a midwife comprising at least three years of theoretical and practical study (route I) comprising at least the programme described in Annex V, point 5.5.1; or (b) specific full-time training as a midwife of eighteen months' duration (route II), comprising at least the study programme described in Annex V, point 5.5.1, which was not the subject of equivalent training of nurses responsible for general care.

The Member States ensure that institutions providing midwife training are responsible for coordinating theory and practice throughout the programme of study. The Commission is empowered to adopt delegated acts in accordance with Article 57c concerning the amendment of the list set out in point 5.5.1 of Annex V with a view to adapting it to scientific and technical progress.

These amendments may not entail an amendment of existing essential legislative principles in the Member States regarding the structure of professions as regards training and conditions of access by natural persons (Article 40.1.).

171. Admission to training as a midwife is contingent upon one of the following conditions: (a) completion of at least twelve years of general school education or possession of a certificate attesting success in an examination of an equivalent level for admission to a midwifery school for route I; (b) possession of evidence of formal qualifications as a nurse responsible for general care referred to in point 5.2.2 of Annex V for route II (Article 40.2.).

172. Training as a midwife provides an assurance that the professional in question has acquired the following knowledge and skills: (a) detailed knowledge of the sciences on which the activities of midwives are based, particularly midwifery, obstetrics and gynaecology; (b) adequate knowledge of the ethics of the profession and the legislation relevant for the practice of the profession; (c) adequate knowledge of general medical knowledge (biological functions, anatomy and physiology) and of pharmacology in the field of obstetrics and of the newly born, and also knowledge of the relationship between the state of health and the physical and social environment of the human being, and of his behaviour; (d) adequate clinical experience gained in approved institutions allowing the midwife to be able, independently and under his or her own responsibility, to the extent necessary and excluding pathological situations, to manage the antenatal care, conduct the delivery and its consequences in approved institutions, and supervise labour and birth, postnatal care and neonatal resuscitation while awaiting a medical practitioner; and (e) adequate understanding of the training of health personnel and experience of working with such personnel (Article 40.3.).

II. Procedures for the Automatic Recognition of Evidence of Formal Qualifications as a Midwife

173. The evidence of formal qualifications as a midwife referred to in point 5.5.2 of Annex V is subject to automatic recognition pursuant to Article 21 in so far as they satisfy one of the following criteria: (a) full-time training of at least three years as a midwife, which may in addition be expressed with the equivalent ECTS credits, consisting of at least 4,600 hours of theoretical and practical training, with at least one-third of the minimum duration representing clinical training; (b) full-time training as a midwife of at least two years, which may in addition be expressed with the equivalent ECTS credits, consisting of at least 3,600 hours, contingent upon possession of evidence of formal qualifications as a nurse responsible for general care referred to in point 5.2.2 of Annex V; (c) full-time training as a midwife of at least eighteen months, which may in addition be expressed with the equivalent ECTS credits, consisting of at least 3,000 hours, contingent upon possession of evidence of formal qualifications as a nurse responsible for general care referred to in point 5.2.2 of Annex V, and followed by one-year professional practice for which a certificate has been issued by the competent authorities in the home Member State. It certifies that the holder, after obtaining evidence of formal qualifications as a midwife, has satisfactorily pursued all the activities of a midwife for a corresponding period in a hospital or a healthcare establishment approved for that purpose (Article 41). The Directive does not require the midwifery training to be an academic discipline.[218]

III. Pursuit of the Professional Activities of a Midwife

174. The Member States ensure that midwives are able to gain access to and pursue at least the following activities: (a) provision of sound family planning information and advice; (b) diagnosis of pregnancies and monitoring normal pregnancies; carrying out the examinations necessary for the monitoring of the development of normal pregnancies; (c) prescribing or advising on the examinations necessary for the earliest possible diagnosis of pregnancies at risk; (d) provision of programmes of parenthood preparation and complete preparation for childbirth including advice on hygiene and nutrition; (e) caring for and assisting the mother during labour and monitoring the condition of the foetus *in utero* by the appropriate clinical and technical means; (f) conducting spontaneous deliveries including where required episiotomies and in urgent cases breech deliveries; (g) recognizing the warning signs of abnormality in the mother or infant which necessitate referral to a doctor and assisting the latter where appropriate; taking the necessary emergency measures in the doctor's absence, in particular the manual removal of the placenta, possibly followed by manual examination of the uterus; (h) examining and caring for the newborn infant; taking all initiatives which are necessary in case

218. Answer given by Ms Bienkowska on behalf of the European Commission to a written Parliamentary question of A. Geriche, State of transposition of Directive 2005/36/EC, particularly regarding training for midwives, 5 Jul. 2018, E-002230-18.

of need and carrying out where necessary immediate resuscitation; (i) caring for and monitoring the progress of the mother in the postnatal period and giving all necessary advice to the mother on infant care to enable her to ensure the optimum progress of the newborn infant; (j) carrying out treatment prescribed by doctors; (k) drawing up the necessary written reports (Article 42).

§5. PHARMACISTS

I. Principle of Automatic Recognition

175. Each Member State recognizes evidence of formal qualifications as pharmacist which satisfy the minimum training conditions referred to in Article 44 and gives, for the purposes of access to and pursuit of professional activities, this evidence the same effect on its territory as the evidence of formal qualifications which it itself issues. Such evidence of formal qualifications must be issued by the competent bodies in the Member States and accompanied, where appropriate, by the certificates listed in Annex V (Article 21.1.).

II. Training as a Pharmacist

176. Admission to a course of training as a pharmacist is contingent upon possession of a diploma or certificate giving access, in a Member State, to the studies in question at universities or higher institutes of a level recognized as equivalent. Evidence of formal qualifications as a pharmacist will attest to training of at least five years' duration, which may, in addition, be expressed with the equivalent ECTS credits, comprising at least: (a) four years of full-time theoretical and practical training at a university or at a higher institute of a level recognized as equivalent, or under the supervision of a university; (b) during or at the end of the theoretical and practical training, six-month traineeship in a pharmacy which is open to the public or in a hospital under the supervision of that hospital's pharmaceutical department. This training cycle includes at least the programme described in point 5.6.1 of Annex V.

177. The Commission is empowered to adopt delegated acts in accordance with Article 57c concerning the amendment of the list set out in point 5.6.1 of Annex V with a view to adapting it to scientific and technical progress, including the evolution of pharmacological practice. These amendments may not entail an amendment of existing essential legislative principles in the Member States regarding the structure of professions as regards training and conditions of access by natural persons. Such amendments have to respect the responsibility of the Member States for the organization of education systems, as set out in Article 165.1 TFEU (Article 44.1. and 44.2.).

178. Training for pharmacists provides an assurance that the person concerned has acquired the following knowledge and skills: (a) adequate knowledge of medicines and the substances used in the manufacture of medicines; (b) adequate knowledge of pharmaceutical technology and the physical, chemical, biological and microbiological testing of medicinal products; (c) adequate knowledge of the metabolism and the effects of medicinal products and of the action of toxic substances, and of the use of medicinal products; (d) adequate knowledge to evaluate scientific data concerning medicines in order to be able to supply appropriate information on the basis of this knowledge; (e) adequate knowledge of the legal and other requirements associated with the pursuit of pharmacy (Article 44.3.).

III. Pursuit of the Professional Activities of a Pharmacist

179. For the purposes of this Directive, the activities of a pharmacist are those, access to which and pursuit of which are contingent, in one or more Member States, upon professional qualifications and which are open to holders of evidence of formal qualifications of the types listed in Annex V, point 5.6.2. The Member States ensure that the holders of evidence of formal qualifications in pharmacy at university level or a level recognized as equivalent, which satisfies the requirements of Article 44, are able to gain access to and pursue at least the following activities, subject to the requirement, where appropriate, of supplementary professional experience: (a) preparation of the pharmaceutical form of medicinal products; (b) manufacture and testing of medicinal products; (c) testing of medicinal products in a laboratory for the testing of medicinal products; (d) storage, preservation and distribution of medicinal products at the wholesale stage; (e) supply, preparation, testing, storage, distribution and dispensing of safe and efficacious medicinal products of the required quality in pharmacies open to the public; (f) preparation, testing, storage and dispensing of safe and efficacious medicinal products of the required quality in hospitals; (g) provision of information and advice on medicinal products as such, including on their appropriate use; (h) reporting of adverse reactions of pharmaceutical products to the competent authorities; (i) personalized support for patients who administer their medication; (j) contribution to local or national public health campaigns (Article 45). Article 25.1. of Delegated Regulation (EU) 2016/161, laying down detailed rules for the safety features appearing on the packaging of medicinal products for human use, obliges persons authorized or entitled to supply medicinal products to the public to verify the safety features and decommission the unique identifier of any medicinal product bearing the safety features they supply to the public at the time of supplying it to the public.[219]

219. *OJ* 2016, L 32. Between 2013 and 2017, the Commission received 400 notifications of falsified medicines which showed that the problem persisted; *see* answer given by Ms Kyriakides on behalf of the European Commission to a written Parliamentary question of E. Jurzycan, Effectiveness of medicine authentication, 29 May 2020, E-001188/2020.

Chapter 4. Freedom of Establishment Through the General System for the Recognition of Evidence of Training

180. Healthcare professions other than those healthcare professions for which automatic recognition is applicable are covered by the so-called general system for the recognition of evidence of qualifications. For those healthcare professions, Member States retain the right to lay down the minimum level of qualification required to ensure the quality of the services provided on their territory. This general system for the recognition of qualifications is governed by the provisions laid down in Chapter I of Title III of the Directive. Member States are required to consider, on a case-by-case basis, whether a qualification from another Member State is equivalent to its own qualification. Host Member States must take into account professional qualifications and experience of practice in another Member State and compare the knowledge and abilities certified by the professional qualification and experience with those required by national rules. If the qualification is not equivalent, then the Member State must decide what 'compensating measures' should be taken by the healthcare professional concerned (Article 14).[220] Speech therapists fall under this general system.[221]

220. *Supra* n. 3, 137.
221. Answer given by Mr Breton on behalf of the European Commission to a written Parliamentary question of P. Arimont, Directive 2005/36/EC and the automatic recognition of professional qualifications in speech therapy, 3 Nov. 2022, E-002792/2022.

Chapter 5. Common Provision on Establishment: Use of Professional Titles

181. If, in a host Member State, the use of a professional title relating to one of the activities of the profession in question is regulated, nationals of the other Member States who are authorized to practise a regulated profession on the basis of establishment have to use the professional title of the host Member State, which corresponds to that profession in that Member State, and make use of any associated initials (Article 52.1.).

Chapter 6. Detailed Rules for Pursuing the Profession

§1. Knowledge of Languages

182. Article 20.3. of Council Directive 75/362/EEC of 16 June 1975 concerning the mutual recognition of diplomas, certificates and other evidence of formal qualifications in medicine (the Physicians Directive)[222] already provided that Member States had to see to it that, where appropriate, the persons concerned acquired, in their interest and in that of their patients, the linguistic knowledge necessary to the exercise of their profession in the host country. In the proposed directive, such a provision was not yet provided for, but the Economic and Social Committee advised this kind of provision. A comparable obligation appeared in Article 15.2. General Nurses Directive, Article 18.3. Dentists Directive, Article 16.3. Midwives Directive and Article 15.3. Pharmacists Directive. The Preamble to those Directives contained no explanation of this provision. The scope of the provision was limited to acquiring the necessary linguistic knowledge and did not encompass having already acquired this knowledge. A linguistic test or another means of controlling was not provided for. Taken literally, this provision did not require the knowledge of the language or one of the languages of the host Member State. This vision has been confirmed by the CJEU: 'However, it is important that language requirements to ensure that the dental practitioner will be able to communicate effectively with his patients … do not go beyond what is necessary to attain that objective. In this respect, it is in the interest of patients whose mother tongue is not the national language that there exist a certain number of dental practitioners who are capable of communicating with such persons in their own language.'[223] The CJEU joined the opinion of the Advocate General that the reliability of a dental practitioner's communication with patients constitutes an overriding reason of general interest, such as justifying making the appointment as a dental practitioner subject to language requirements. Dialogue with patients and compliance with rules of conduct and law specific to dentistry in the Member State of establishment requires appropriate knowledge of the language of that Member State.[224] According to Advocate General Mischo, the obligation in Article 18.3. Dentists Directive imposed on Member States is an obligation to achieve the result since it required them to 'see to it' that those entitled to freedom of movement 'acquire the linguistic knowledge necessary for the exercise of their profession'. According to the Advocate General, 'no-one would attempt to deny that in order for a doctor or a dentist to provide effective treatment to a patient it is essential both that the practitioner is able fully to understand the problem which the patient has described to him in order for it to be treated, and that the explanations provided as to the nature of the problem and the advice accompanying the recommended treatment should be fully understood by the patient so that he can assist

222. *OJ* 1975, L 167.
223. CJEU, *Haim II*, Case C-424/97, ECLI:EU:C:2000:55, para. 60.
224. *Ibid.*, para. 59; M. Peeters, 'Free Movement of Medical Doctors: The New Directive 2005/36 on the Recognition of Professional Qualifications', 12 *European Journal of Health Law* 381–382 (2005).

his own recovery'.[225] Also, the Advocate General was of the opinion that this provision did not specify at what point the necessary knowledge must be acquired. It is reasonable to suppose that the persons concerned do not need this knowledge when they take up their activity in the host Member State, since otherwise the Council would have used the words 'Member States shall check whether the persons concerned have the linguistic knowledge necessary.' However, this provision would have no practical effect if a Member State were not able to test for the existence of the 'necessary' linguistic knowledge at any time. As regards how the knowledge should to be checked, he shared the Commission's view that 'written or oral language test would, for example, constitute an appropriate means'.[226] The so-called sectoral directives have been replaced by the Professional Qualifications Directive that is not limited to the healthcare professions. Article 53 of the original version of this Directive provided as follows regarding the knowledge of languages: 'Persons benefiting from the recognition of professional qualifications shall have a knowledge necessary for practising the profession in the host Member State.' It applied to free establishment and free provision of services as well. Its content was similar to the knowledge provision in the sector directives, and it neither required explicit knowledge of the language or one of the languages of the host Member State. On the occasion of the profound revision of the Professional Qualifications Directive in 2013, the language knowledge requirements have been sharpened, especially with regard to the healthcare professions. First, in the case of provision of services, Member States may require that the declaration be made in advance and also to include for professions that have patient safety implications a declaration of the applicant's language knowledge. The Preamble does not give an explanation, particularly regarding whether this regards the language of the host Member State. Second, Article 53 has been revised. Article 53.1. recapitulates the former Article 53: 'Professionals benefiting from the recognition of professional qualifications must have a knowledge of languages necessary for practising the profession in the host Member State.' Article 53.2. is also applicable to all professions and provides that a Member State ensures that any control carried out by, or under the supervision of, the competent authority for controlling compliance with this obligation is limited to the knowledge of one official language of the host Member State, or one administrative language of the host Member State provided that it is also an official language of the Union. According to Article 53.3. such controls may be imposed if the profession to be practised has patient safety implications. Controls may be imposed in respect of other professions in cases where there is a serious and concrete doubt about the sufficiency of the professional's language knowledge in respect of the professional activities that that professional intends to pursue. Controls may be carried out only after the issuance of an EPC or after the recognition of a professional qualification, as the case may be. Any language controls have to be proportionate to the activity to be pursued. The professional concerned should be allowed to appeal such controls under national law. Recital 26 in the Preamble to the Professional Qualifications Directive deals extensively with the obligation for professionals to have the necessary language skills. It also states that: 'It is important for professions that

225. Opinion AG Mischo in *Haim II*, Case C-424/97, ECLI:EU:C:199, paras 90 and 105.
226. *Ibid.*, paras 93, 95 and 97.

have patient safety implications in particular that language controls under Directive 2005/36/EC be applied before the professional accesses the profession in the host Member State.' This may give the impression that Member States are obliged to impose a language test for such professionals. However, this is not what the Directive provides: 'the legislative text imposes no obligations, although it does give Member States discretion to adopt such controls'.[227] Moreover, it has to be emphasized that the word 'control' in Article 53 does not mean 'testing' the language knowledge. Essentially, the host Member State may check whether a professional can prove his language knowledge based on a certificate or other means of proof. A language test shall only be the last resort, e.g., when the professional cannot provide other proof, to make sure that the professional has acquired an appropriate level of language knowledge. It is also important to stress that the controls should be proportionate to the activity. Thus, a doctor may be required to have a better level than a nurse.[228]

§2. USE OF ACADEMIC TITLES

183. Without prejudice to Articles 7 (*see* paragraphs 133 et seq.) and 52 (*see* paragraph 181), the host Member State ensures that the right is conferred on the persons concerned to use academic titles conferred on them in the home Member State and possibly an abbreviated form thereof, in the language of the home Member State. The host Member State may require that the title be followed by the name and address of the establishment or examining board which awarded it. Where an academic title of the home Member State is liable to be confused in the host Member State with a title which, in the latter Member State, requires supplementary training not acquired by the beneficiary, the host Member State may require the beneficiary to use the academic title of the home Member State in an appropriate form, to be laid down by the host Member State (Article 54).

§3. APPROVAL BY HEALTH INSURANCE FUNDS FOR DOCTORS AND DENTAL PRACTITIONERS

184. Without prejudice to Articles 5.1 and 6.1b, Member States, which require persons who acquired their professional qualifications in their territory to complete

227. *Supra* n. 3, 151. Article 53 does not establish rules as regards language examinations prior to obtaining full professional qualification; *see* answer given by Ms Bienkowska on behalf of the European Commission to a written question by G. La Vie, Language controls and the recognition of professional qualifications, 13 Nov. 2018, P-004340/2018. With regard to third-country qualifications, it is up to the Member States to set up their specific requirements; *see* answer given by Ms Thyssen on behalf of the European Commission to a priority written question of B. Winter, Possible sources of support for specialist training in Thuringia and Lviv, 21 May 2019, P-001447/2019.

228. EP 2014–2019, *Committee on Petitions*, Petition N° by A. Rijkenberg (Austria) on introducing uniform EU-wide language exams from specialist professions, 29 Jun. 2018, Commission reply.

a preparatory period of in-service training and/or a period of professional experience in order to be approved by a health insurance fund, have to waive this obligation for the holders of evidence of professional qualifications of doctor and dental practitioner acquired in other Member States.

Chapter 7. Exchange of Information Regarding Disciplinary Action and Criminal Sanctions and Alert Mechanism

§1. Exchange of Information Regarding Disciplinary Action and Criminal Sanctions

185. The competent authorities of the home and the host Member States exchange information regarding disciplinary action or criminal sanctions that have been taken or any other serious, specific circumstances which are likely to have consequences for the pursuit of activities under this Directive. In so doing, they respect personal data protection rules. The home Member State examines the veracity of the circumstances, and its authorities decide on the nature and scope of the investigations which need to be carried out and informs the host Member State of the conclusions which it draws from the information available to it (Article 56.2.). For this purpose, competent authorities use IMI (Article 56.2a). The suspension of healthcare workers in France because they had refused to be vaccinated against COVID had according to the European Commission no effect with regard to their right of free movement of workers, as enshrined in Article 45 TFEU. Therefore, those healthcare workers could still undertake employed or self-employed activities in other Member States that are in line with national law. If a professional is no longer entitled to practise, even temporarily, his/her professional activities in a Member State, an alert is sent to all other EU/EEA countries. The Member States receiving the alert can request further information and remain free to take a decision under national law based on the information available.[229]

§2. Alert Mechanism

186. The competent authorities of a Member State inform the competent authorities of all other Member States about a professional whose pursuit on the territory of that Member State of the following professional activities in their entirety or parts thereof have been restricted or prohibited, even temporarily, by national authorities or courts: (a) doctor of medicine and of general practice; (b) specialist doctor of medicine; (c) nurse responsible for general care; (d) dental practitioner; (e) specialist dentists; (g) midwife; (h) pharmacist; (k) other professionals exercising activities that have patient safety implications, where the professional is pursuing a profession regulated in that Member State (Article 56a, 1). According to Hervey and McHale, 'the extent of the concept of a professional exercising activities that have patient safety implications is unclear … given the integrated nature of patient safety'.[230]

229. Answer given by Ms Kyriakides on behalf of the European Commission on a written Parliamentary question of V. Joron, 115.000 healthcare workers suspended in France, how many across Europe? 25 Jul. 2022, E-001992/2022.

230. *Supra* n. 3, 149.

187. Competent authorities send the information referred to in the previous paragraph by way of alert via IMI at the latest within three days from the date of adoption of the decision restricting or prohibiting pursuit of the professional activity in its entirety or in part by the professional concerned. That information is limited to the following: (a) the identity of the professional; (b) the profession concerned; (c) information about the national authority or court adopting the decision on restriction or prohibition; (d) the scope of the restriction or the prohibition; and (e) the period during which the restriction or the prohibition applies (Article 56a, 2).

188. The competent authorities of a Member State concerned inform, at the latest within three days from the date of adoption of the court decision, the competent authorities of all other Member States, by way of alert via IMI, about the identity of professionals who have applied for the recognition of a qualification under this Directive and who have subsequently been found by courts to have used falsified evidence of professional qualifications in this context (Article 56a, 3).

189. The competent authorities of all Member States have to be informed without delay when a prohibition or a restriction referred to in Article 56a, 1 has expired. For that purpose, the competent authority of the Member State which provides this information is also required to provide the date of expiry as well as any subsequent change to that date (Article 56a, 5).

190. Member States provide that professionals, in respect of whom alerts are sent to other Member States, are informed in writing of decisions on alerts at the same time as the alert itself, may appeal under national law against the decision or apply for rectification of such decisions and have access to remedies in respect of any damage caused by false alerts sent to other Member States, and in such cases, the decision on the alert has to be qualified to indicate that it is subject to proceedings by the professional (Article 56a, 6).

191. Data regarding alerts may be processed within IMI for as long as they are valid. Alerts have to be deleted within three days from the date of adoption of the revoking decision or from the expiry of the prohibition or the restriction referred to in Article 56a, 1 (Article 56a, 7).

192. Member States appoint competent authorities to handle outgoing and incoming alerts. In order to ensure that incoming alerts are only handled by the relevant competent authorities, each Member State assigns the task of coordinating incoming alerts to one or more competent authorities. These competent authorities ensure that alerts are assigned to the appropriate competent authorities without undue delay. Member States may assign the task of coordinating outgoing alerts to one or more competent authorities (Article 23 IMI Regulation). Alerts contain the information set out in Article 56a, 2 or 3 of the Professional Qualifications Directive. Only competent authorities appointed to handle an alert have access to this information. Competent authorities assigned with the task of coordinating incoming alerts only have access to the data referred to in points (b) and (d) of Article 56a, 2 of this Directive unless the alert was subsequently also assigned to them as an authority handling incoming alerts. In case a competent authority handling incoming alerts needs information other than that set out in Article 56a, 2 or 3 of the Directive, it uses the IMI information request functionality (Article 24 IMI Regulation).

193. Where the holder of an EPC is subject to an alert, the competent authorities that dealt with the EPC application under Article 2.1 of the IMI Regulation ensure the update of the corresponding IMI file with information contained in the alert, including any consequences for the pursuit of professional activities. To ensure that updates of the IMI files are carried out in a timely manner, Member States grant access to the incoming alerts to the competent authorities responsible for handling EPC applications (Article 25 IMI Regulation).

194. The IMI provides for a possibility for the competent authorities handling incoming or outgoing alerts to consult any alert they sent or received in IMI and for which the closure procedure referred to in Article 28 has not been launched (Article 26 IMI Regulation). IMI provides the following functionalities to be undertaken by the competent authorities appointed to handle incoming and outgoing alerts: (a) sending alerts as provided for in Article 56a, 1, 2 and 3 of the Directive; (b) withdrawing alerts which have been sent on the basis of a decision which has been subsequently revoked or annulled; (c) correcting information contained in alerts and modifying alerts; (d) closing and deleting alerts as provided for in Article 56a, 5 and 7 of the Directive 2005/36/EC (Article 26 IMI Regulation).

195. Data regarding alerts may be processed within IMI for as long as they are valid including the completion of the closure procedure referred to in Article 56a, 7 of the Directive. When the alert is no longer valid due to the expiry of the sanction, the competent authority which sent the alert modifies its content or closes the alert within three days from the adoption of the relevant decision or receiving the relevant information where adoption of such decision is not required under national law. The competent authorities that handled the incoming alert and the professionals concerned have to be immediately informed about any modifications concerning the alert. The IMI sends regular reminders to the competent authorities which handle the outgoing alert to verify whether the information contained in the alert is still valid. In case of a revoking decision, the alert is immediately closed by the competent authority which originally sent it, and personal data shall be deleted from the IMI within three days. In the case of a sanction that has expired on the date specified in Article 56a, 5 of the Directive, the alert is automatically closed by the IMI and personal data are deleted from the system within three days as provided for in Article 56a, 7 of the Directive (Article 27 IMI Regulation).

196. In a Parliamentary question, reference was made to a report published in a Dutch newspaper according to which inquiries of journalists have revealed that, two years after its introduction, the so-called European blacklist of medical practitioners, which is intended to alert those concerned to serious health risks arising from certain activities in this field, was not yet in use in ten of the Member States. In her answer, Ms Bienkowska, on behalf of the Commission, remarked that 'in the context of the alert mechanism, it is important to keep in mind that national systems as regards sanctions for professionals for misconduct are not harmonised across the EU. Consequently, the numbers of alerts might vary significantly between Member States depending on their national supervisory rules, and a low number of alerts alone might not per se indicate a violation of EU rules'. She added that the Commission continuously monitors Member States' compliance, offers practical assistance and assesses the need for potential improvements in the usage of the alert system.[231] In another Parliamentary question, it was claimed that 'if a physiotherapist working in Spain is struck off the physiotherapist register for misconduct, they can very move to France and continue working in the profession'.[232] In her answer, Ms Bienkowska on behalf of the Commission referred to the alert mechanism in Article 56a of the Professional Qualifications Directive.[233] Figures obtained by the Danish broadcaster DR showed that nine Member States did not use the alert system at all, so doctors whose authorizations had been withdrawn in the countries concerned could go straight to other EU countries and be authorized there. Taken together, the Directive contains a range of safeguards to allow effective control by Member States, according to the European Commission. Ensuring a coherent application of these rules to the benefit of citizens, including patients and professionals, is of particular concern for the Commission.[234] In a few instances, the Commission found that the alert mechanism was not implemented at all for certain professions (e.g., health professions).[235]

197. The European Commission is not planning to adopt new implementing acts for the Alert Mechanism. Where problems of implementation of the Alert Mechanism in Member States were uncovered, the Commission included the issue in its package of infringement actions. The Commission will continue to monitor on a case-by-case basis the correct practical implementation of the alert mechanism to ensure compliance by national authorities.[236]

231. 'Blacklisted doctors frequently able to practice elsewhere in Europe', *NRC Handelsblad* 12 Jan. 2018; answer to a written question of A. Schreijer-Pierik, 10 Apr. 2018, E-000352/2018.

232. L. Michel, Question for written answer to the Commission, European recognition of physiotherapist training, 19 Jul. 2017, E-004975/2017.

233. *Ibid.*

234. Answer given by Ms Bienkowska on behalf of the European Commission to a written priority Parliamentary question of C. Schaldemose, Using the IMI to report doctors, 8 Apr. 2019, P-001125/2019.

235. European Commission, *Report from the Commission to the European Parliament, the Council, the European Economic and Social Committee and the Committee of the Regions on the Implementation of Certain New Elements Introduced by Directive 2013/55/EU*, Brussels, 11 May 2020, Com (2020) 191 final, 20.

236. Answer given by Mr Breton on behalf of the European Commission to a written Parliamentary question of N. Colin-Oesterlé, Better Implementation of Directive 2005/36/EC on the Recognition of Professional Qualifications, 19 Jan. 2022, E-005046/2021.

Part III. The Practice of the Healthcare Professions

Chapter 1. The (Illegal) Practice of Medical Acts

§1. OSTEOPATHY

198. A French national, M. *Bouchoucha,* was prosecuted in France on the basis of the national provisions which penalize the unlawful practice of medicine on the ground that he had practised osteopathy. He held a French diploma as a *Masseur-kinésithérapeute* and a British diploma in osteopathy. The Court of Appeal of Aix-en Provence referred to the CJEU the question of whether the prohibition on the practice of medicine on the ground that he did not hold the qualification of doctor of medicine was compatible with the freedom of establishment. In his opinion, Advocate General Darmon stated that there were no Community rules on the practice of osteopathy (which is still the case today). In the absence of Community rules governing the practice of osteopathy, each Member State is free to regulate the matter and to decide that it should be restricted to doctors, provided that Community nationals are treated in the same way as nationals of the host State as regards access to that activity. However, he also warned that the possibility cannot be ruled out that a Member State may commit abuse by artificially linking the practice of medicine with an activity alien to it. But in an area such as the protection of human health, a very circumspect approach must be taken in determining what does and does not fall to be classified as a medical activity. In the absence of Community coordination, it is a matter for the Member States alone to say which of the activities that come within the medical sphere in the broad sense are to be regarded as medical activities *stricto sensu* and which may be practised separately from the activity of a doctor. The question of abuse would arise only in the case of the manifestly artificial inclusion within the medical sphere of an activity which is *incontestably* alien to it. The circumstances of this case concern an activity, osteopathy, which cannot be regarded as alien to the field of medicine, and the Court could not even contemplate the possibility of any abuse.[237]

199. The CJEU noted that there were no Community provisions governing the exercise of professions allied to medicine, such as, in particular, osteopathy and that

237. Opinion AG Darmon, in Case C-61/89, *Bouchoucha,* ECLI:EU:C:1990:93, paras 4, 7, 9 and 10.

the then-existing Directive 75/362/EEC of 16 June 1975 concerning the mutual recognition of diplomas in medicine contained no community definition of what activities are to be regarded as those of a doctor (which is still the case actually). So far as there is no Community definition of medical acts, the definition of acts restricted to the medical profession is, in principle, a matter for the Member States. In the absence of community legislation on the professional practice of osteopathy, each Member State is free to regulate the exercise of that activity within its territory without discriminating between its own nationals and those of the other Member States.[238]

§2. Eye Examinations

200. The Belgian Court of Cassation ruled in a judgment that 'while opticians who are not medical doctors are authorised to perform acts designed to correct defects of a purely optical nature, whether or not they use equipment or instruments for that purpose, they are none the less prohibited from examining the state of vision of their clients otherwise than by using a method under which the patient alone determines the sight defects from which he suffers, *inter alia* on the basis of printed scales which may be incorporated in a control instrument and which the patient himself corrects by choosing, as the optician proposes, the lenses which satisfy him. The optician is obliged to advise his client to consult an ophthalmologist if the indications thus obtained leave any doubt as to the nature of the defect which has been established'. The Tribunal of First Degree of Brussels was unsure whether the Belgian legislation, as thus construed, was compatible with the freedoms recognized by Community law concerning establishment, the provision of services and the movement of goods and decided to stay proceedings in order to refer to the CJEU for a preliminary ruling several questions. By its questions, the national court was in substance asking whether by then Articles 5.30., 52 and 59 of the Treaty precluded the competent authorities of a Member State from interpreting the national law governing the practice of medicine in such a way that within the context of the correction of purely optical defects, the objective examination of a client's eyesight, that is to say, an examination which does not use a method under which the client alone determines the optical defects from which he is suffering, is reserved to ophthalmologists, to the exclusion, in particular of opticians who are not qualified medical doctors.[239]

201. Referring to the *Bouchoucha* judgment, Advocate General Mischo proposed that the Court should primarily follow the same line of reasoning, which was that Article 52 did not preclude a Member State from restricting an activity ancillary to medicine to persons holding the qualification of doctor of medicine.[240] Only as a subsidiary argument, in the event that the Court should take the view that national rules such as those here in issue must nevertheless be regarded as an

238. CJEU, *Bouchoucha*, Case C-61/89, ECLI:EU:C:1990:343, paras 8 and 12.
239. CJEU, *McQuen,* Case C-108/96, ECLI:EU:C:2001:67, para. 19.
240. Opinion AG Mischo, in Case C-108/96, *McQuen,* ECLI:EU:C:2000:131, paras 37–38.

obstacle to freedom of establishment, one must go on to examine whether those rules can be justified on the basis of the criteria formulated in the case law of the Court.[241]

202. The CJEU opted for an approach other than the AG and immediately turned to his subsidiary argument. While it is true that, in the absence of harmonization of the activities at issue in the main proceedings, Member States remain, in principle, competent to define the exercise of those activities, they must nonetheless, when exercising their powers in this area, respect the basic freedoms guaranteed by the Treaty. According to the Court's case law, national measures liable to hinder or make less attractive the exercise of fundamental freedoms guaranteed by the Treaty can be justified only if they fulfil four conditions: they must be applied in a non-discriminatory manner; they must be justified by overriding reasons based on the general interest; they must be suitable for securing the attainment of the objective which they pursue; and they must not go beyond what is necessary in order to attain that objective.[242]

203. The CJEU expressed doubts about whether the condition of necessity was fulfilled. In that regard, the Court pointed out that (unlike the prohibition in *Bouchoucha*) the prohibition under challenge was not expressly provided for by any legislative provision of national law but followed rather from the interpretation which the Belgian Cour de Cassation gave to a number of relevant national provisions with a view to attaining a high level of protection of public health. It appeared that that interpretation was based on an assessment of the risks to public health which might result if opticians were authorized to carry out certain eyesight examinations. An assessment of this kind is liable to change with the passage of time, particularly as a result of technical and scientific progress. It is significant in this regard that the Federal Constitutional Court (Germany) concluded, in its decision of 7 August 2000, that the risks which might follow from authorizing opticians to carry out certain examinations of their clients' eyesight, such as tonometry and computerized perimetry, are not such as to preclude them from conducting those examinations. And the CJEU concluded that it is for the national court to assess, in the light of the Treaty requirements relating to freedom of establishment and the demands of legal certainty and the protection of public health, whether the interpretation of domestic law adopted by the competent national authorities in that regard remains a valid basis for the prosecutions brought in the case in the main proceedings.[243]

241. *Ibid.*, para. 45.
242. *Supra* n. 239, paras 24 and 26.
243. *Ibid.*, paras 35–38.

Chapter 2. Professional Rules of Conduct

§1. Single-Practice Rule

204. Under Article L 412 of the French Public Health Code, any doctor or dental surgeon who practices must be enrolled on a register kept by the area council of the Order of Physicians. It also provided that a doctor or dental surgeon 'may be enrolled on only one register' and that 'a doctor enrolled or registered as a doctor in another country might not be enrolled on any register of the order of physicians'. The European Commission brought an action before the CJEU to declare that by requiring doctors and dental surgeons established in another Member State to cancel their enrolment or registration in that other State in order to be able to practise in France, the French Republic had failed to fulfil its obligations under Treaty (freedom of establishment).

205. In its defence, the French Government submitted that the disputed system was justified on grounds of public health, the importance of which is recognized in the Treaty. The protection of patients' health requires that the doctor or dental surgeon should be in their vicinity and that medical care should be continuous, particularly in the case of illnesses in which complications may arise. The frequency and continuity of medical treatment could not be ensured if doctors or dental surgeons were not easily accessible to their patients.[244] It also argued that differences in treatment between the Member States continue to exist in areas which have not yet been harmonized, such as medical ethics.[245]

206. Advocate General Slynn initially had some doubts as to whether the exceptions on the ground of public health really covered this kind of situation. They seemed primarily directed at persons who may be excluded from the freedom of establishment because they suffer from a communicable disease or may carry on activities or set up businesses which may endanger public health, such as by allowing the emission of noxious substances. But at the end of the day, he did not consider that the words public health need to be read in that limited way. A doctor who carries on practice in a way which puts his patient at risk may be restricted, as may a person who seeks to carry on an activity which endangers public security or public order. Therefore, it was relevant to consider whether the French rules were justified in the interests of protecting patients. In that regard, he admitted that a patient may need his doctor more quickly and more continuously than the client needs his lawyer and that telephonic communication may, in many cases, clearly be insufficient. However, it equally had to be recognized that, increasingly, doctors belong to group practices and that a patient may not always see the same general practitioner. It may thus be perfectly compatible with the care of group practice patients for a doctor to take a period as a *locum tenens* employed elsewhere in the EU. Moreover, he added, doctors are not all in the same position. A list of patients or sessions in

244. CJEU, *Commission v. France,* Case C-96/85, ECLI: EU:C:1986:189, para. 6.
245. *Ibid.*, para. 7.

hospitals in different cities of one country may be compatible with the specialist surgeon's duty of care. If such a surgeon could, in fact, operate in a hospital in Paris and Bordeaux, there was no reason why he should not do so in Paris and Brussels or Bonn. Other specializations may even less require the continued nearness of the doctor to a one-time patient. A striking example is that of the radiologist. There are others, such as that of the dermatologist, where continuing geographic proximity may be unnecessary. Accordingly, although ethical rules to ensure that the general practitioner and the specialist practice their profession in a way which provides adequate medical care to their patients can be accepted as necessary, it seemed to the Advocate General that the blanket prohibition on all doctors and dental surgeons from being registered in another Member State and maintaining a practice there, while having a practice in France, was unduly restrictive and had not been shown to be required in the interests of the patients.[246]

207. The Court, at first, pointed out that nationals of a Member State who pursue their occupation in another Member State are obliged to comply with the rules which govern the pursuit of the occupation in question in that Member State. As the French Government rightly observed, in the case of the medical profession, those rules reflect in particular a concern to ensure that individuals enjoy the most effective and complete health protection possible. However, in so far as those rules have the effect of restricting freedom of movement, the right of establishment and the freedom to provide services within the Community, they are compatible with the Treaty only if the restrictions which they entail are actually justified in view of the general obligations inherent in the proper practice of the professions in question and apply to nationals and foreigners alike.[247]

208. The Court then stated first of all that the principle that a practitioner may have only one practice, put forward by the French Government as indispensable to the continuity of medical care, is applied more strictly with regard to practitioners from other Member States than practitioners established in France. Second, the Court observed that the general rule prohibiting doctors and dental surgeons established in another Member State from practising in France is unduly restrictive. First of all, in the case of certain medical specialities, it is not necessary that the specialist should be close to the patient on a continuous basis after the treatment has been given. That is so where the specialist carries out a single procedure, as is often the case of a radiologist, for example, or where subsequent care is provided by other medical personnel, as is often the case of a surgeon. Furthermore, as the French Government indeed recognized, recent developments in the medical profession show that even in the area of general medicine, the increasing trend is for practitioners to belong to group practices so that a patient cannot always consult the same general practitioner.[248]

246. Opinion AG Slynn, in Case C-96/85, *Commission v. France* ECLI: EU:C:1986:189.
247. *Supra* n. 244, paras 10–11.
248. *Ibid.*, paras 12–13.

209. Those considerations showed that the prohibition on the enrolment in a register of the Order of Physicians in France of any doctor or dental surgeon who is still enrolled or registered in another Member State was too absolute and general in nature to be justified by the need to ensure continuity of medical treatment or of applying French rules of medical ethics in France. The Commission was, therefore, correct to argue that the French legislation prohibiting any doctor or dental surgeon established in another Member State from practising in France as a locum, as a principal in practice or as an employee is contrary to the provisions of the Treaty on freedom of movement for persons.[249]

210. Article 16 of the Luxembourg Law of 29 April 1983 concerning the exercise of the professions of medicine, dentistry and veterinary medicine provided that a doctor or dentist may not have more than one surgery. The European Commission lodged an application before the CJEU because Luxembourg had failed to fulfil its obligations under the Treaty.

211. The Luxembourg Government considered that the one-surgery rule was justified in view of both reasons of public health and general interest considerations. It was a matter of the restrictions set out in the Treaty. The practice of medicine requires the physical presence of the practitioner, who should be present within an hour of being called or even sooner. The Luxembourg Government also contended that the medical contract is a contract *intuitu personae.* In entering into the contract, the patient would be moved by considerations regarding the identity of the doctor. The relationship of confidence would break down if, on the very day of surgery or of providing care, the doctor was no longer physically present in the event of a relapse or post-operative complications.[250]

212. In its reply, the Commission stated that the above-mentioned judgment in Case 96/85 was wholly applicable to this case. The Luxembourg legislation which, unlike the French, contained no discriminatory elements, nevertheless prevented any doctor or dentist established in another Member State or employed there who wished to establish himself in Luxembourg from keeping his practice or continuing to be employed in that other Member State.[251]

213. The CJEU observed first of all that the single-practice rule, which, according to the Luxembourg Government, was essential to continuity of care, applied more strictly to doctors and dentists practising in other Member States than to those practising in Luxembourg: the Law permitted derogation from the single-practice rule only for persons practising in Luxembourg. It observed next that a general rule prohibiting practitioners established in another Member State or employed there from carrying on their practice from an establishment in Luxembourg is unduly restrictive. The Court could not accept the argument that the single-practice rule was

249. *Ibid.*, para. 14.15.
250. CJEU, *Commission v. Luxembourg*, Case C-351/90, Report for the Hearing by P.J.G. Kapteyn, judge-rapporteur, paras 16–18.
251. *Ibid.*, para. 21.

objectively justified on the grounds of public health and public policy, and also on the grounds of the general interest and that because a medical contract was a contract *intuitu personae*, the continuous presence of the practitioner at his surgery or place of employment was required in order to ensure that care is permanently available.

214. First, it is not essential for a practitioner, whether a general practitioner, a dentist or even a medical specialist, to be close to the patient at all times. Moreover, the practitioner's permanent availability is not necessarily guaranteed by the single-practice rule when, for example, the practitioner is travelling, practises part-time or belongs to a group practice. Second, the permanent availability of care may be achieved in less restrictive ways, such as by requiring minimum attendance or having arrangements for providing replacements. From these considerations, it was apparent that the prohibition in question was too absolute and general in nature for it to be justified by the need to have care permanently available.[252]

§2. Advertising for Medical Services

I. Legal Prohibition of Advertising

215. Article 1 of the Belgian Law on advertising in dental care matters of 15 April 1958 provided that no person may, whether directly or indirectly, engage in advertising of any kind with a view to treating or providing treatment, whether or not by a qualified person, in Belgium or abroad, for dental or oral ailments, injuries or abnormalities, by means, *inter alia*, of displays or signs, inscriptions or plaques liable to be misleading as to the lawful nature of the activity advertised, leaflets, circulars, hand-outs and brochures, via the medium of the press, broadcasting or cinema. Article 8d of the Royal Decree laying down rules for the practice of dentistry of 1 June 1934 provides that for the purpose of informing the public, it is permissible to affix only an inscription or a plaque of modest dimensions and appearance to the building in which a competent person practises dentistry, stating the name of the practitioner and possibly his legal designation, his sessions days and times, the name of the undertaking or healthcare organization within which the practitioner carries out his professional activity; it may also state the branch of dentistry in which the practitioner specializes, such as surgical dentistry, oral prosthesis, orthodontics, dental surgery.[253]

216. Vanderborght, a Belgian dentist practising dentistry in Belgium, was prosecuted for contravening these rules prohibiting all advertising for the provision of

252. CJEU, *Commission v. Luxembourg,* Case C-351/90, ECLI:EU:C:1992:266, paras 19–23.

253. CJEU, *Vanderborght,* Case C-339/15, ECLI:EU:C:2017:335, paras 11–12; A. Garcia Vidal, 'Restrictions on Advertising Relating to the Provision of Oral and Dental Care Services and EU Law', *Pharmaceutical Analysis* 1–5 (May 2017); A. den Exter, 'Case Note. Medical Professionals as Digital Marketeers and the Advertising Ban', 5 *Journal of Medical Law and Ethics* 115–122 (2017).

oral and dental care services. The Tribunal of First Instance in Brussels questioned the compatibility of those provisions with, among others, Articles 49 and 56 TFEU.

217. Advocate General Bot considered the prohibition of all advertising of dental care to the public as a restriction on the freedom to provide services. He considered this restriction to be justified on the ground of the protection of public health, where the national legislation at issue does not have the effect of prohibiting a dental care provider from giving basic details, free from enticement or incentive, making known his existence as a professional in a telephone directory or other source of information accessible by the public.[254] The prohibition referred to in Article 1 of the Law of 1958 was not in his view contrary to Article 56 TFEU. With regard to the particular nature of the services at issue in the main proceedings, to what is at stake for the patient when he decides whether or not to have recourse to dental care services and to the relationship of trust that must be protected between the dental care provider and the patient, that prohibition seems to him 'to be perfectly logical'.[255]

218. According to the CJEU national legislation, which imposes a general and absolute prohibition of any advertising for a certain activity, is liable to restrict the possibility, for the persons carrying on that activity, of making themselves known to their potential *clientèle* and of promoting the services which they offer to their *clientèle*. Consequently, national legislation must be regarded as a restriction on the freedom to provide services.[256] The Court noted that the protection of health is one of the objectives which may be regarded as overriding reasons in the public interest that are capable of justifying a restriction on the freedom to provide services.[257] The Court added that with regard to the importance of the relationship of trust which must prevail between a dentist and his patient, the protection of the dignity of the profession of the dentist may also be regarded as being capable of constituting such an overriding reason in the public interest.[258] The extensive use of advertising or the selection of aggressive promotional messages, even such as to mislead patients as to the care being offered, by damaging the image of the profession of a dentist, distorting the relationship between dentists and their patients, and promoting the provision of inappropriate and unnecessary care, may undermine the protection of health and compromise the dignity of the profession of dentist.[259] In that context, a general and absolute prohibition of any advertising is appropriate for attaining the objectives pursued by avoiding any use by dentists of advertising and promotional messages.[260]

254. Opinion AG Bot, in *Vanderborght*, Case C-339/15, ECLI:EU:C:2016:660, para. 14.
255. *Ibid.*, para. 112.
256. *Supra* n. 253, paras 63–64.
257. *Ibid.*, para. 67.
258. *Ibid.*, para. 68.
259. *Ibid.*, para. 69.
260. *Ibid.*, para. 70.

219. However, the Court continued, not all the advertising messages prohibited by the legislation at issue are, in themselves, likely to produce effects that are contrary to the objectives referred to in paragraph 69 of its judgment. And it pointed out further in that regard that, although it had already held in *Konstantinides*[261] that national legislation prohibiting advertising for medical services the content of which is contrary to professional ethics is compatible with Article 56 TFEU, it must be observed that the legislation at issue in *Vanderborght* had a much broader scope. In those circumstances, it must be held that the objectives pursued by the legislation at issue could be attained through the use of less restrictive measures supervising, closely if necessary, the form and manner in which the communication tools used by dentists may legitimately have, without imposing on them a general and absolute prohibition of any form of advertising. In light of all of the foregoing considerations, the answer to the question was that Article 56 TFEU must be interpreted as precluding national legislation, such as that at issue in the main proceedings, which imposes a general and absolute prohibition of any advertising relating to the provision of oral and dental care services.[262]

220. According to the European Commission, promotional advertising for healthcare services that misleads patients by promoting unsuitable and/or unnecessary medical care may undermine the protection of health and compromise the dignity of healthcare professionals, which are objectives in the public interest.[263] A provision that does not impose a general and absolute ban on advertising but rather aims at ensuring that any advertising is compatible with the appropriate independence, dignity and integrity of health professions is not prohibited by EU law.[264]

221. In *Corporacion Dermoestética*, the CJEU held that rules regulating television advertising for medical and surgical treatments provided by private healthcare establishments can be justified in the light of the objective of protection of public health. However, to the extent to which it is possible for a set of rules, such as those laid down in the legislation at issue in the main proceedings, to guarantee that the objective of protection of public health is attained by introducing a measure resulting in a prohibition on advertising medical and surgical treatments on national television networks while at the same time making it possible to broadcast such advertisements on local television networks, such rules exhibit an inconsistency which the Italian Government had not attempted to justify and cannot therefore properly attain the public health objective which they seek to pursue. Consequently, national legislation, such as that at issue in the main proceedings, cannot be

---

261. *Supra* n. 204, para. 57.
262. *Supra* n. 253, paras 73–76.
263. Answer given by Mr Breton on behalf of the European Commission to a written Parliamentary question of K. Konečná, Compliance of a ban on promotional advertising for healthcare services with EU law, 18 Aug. 2022, E-002245/2022.
264. Answer given by Mr Breton on behalf of the European Commission to a written Parliamentary question of D. Oscar Lancini, Misleading advertising in the healthcare sector, 9 Feb. 2024, E-003659.2023.

regarded as being appropriate for the purpose of securing the attainment of the objective of public health and constitutes an unjustified restriction of the freedom to provide services.[265]

222. Article 8 of the Directive on Electronic Commerce must be interpreted as precluding national legislation which imposes a general and absolute prohibition of any advertising by members of the dental profession, in that profession prohibits any recourse to online advertising methods that promote specific dentists or their company.[266]

223. Article 87(3) of Directive 2001/83/EC of the European Parliament and of the Council of 6 November 2001 on the Community code relating to medicinal products for human use must be interpreted as not applying to national legislation which prohibits a pharmacy which sells medicinal products by mail order from organizing an advertising campaign in the form of a prize competition allowing participants to win everyday items other than medicinal products, participation in that competition being subject to the submission of an order for a medicinal product for human use to a medical prescription, together with that prescription.[267] Article 87(3) provides that the advertising of a medicinal product shall encourage the rational use of the medicinal product by presenting it objectively and without exaggerating its properties and shall not be misleading.

II. Prohibition by National Disciplinary Rules

224. In *Konstantinides*,[268] the CJEU had to decide on a reference for a preliminary ruling by the Appeal Court for health professions Giesen (Germany). One of the questions at stake was whether paragraph 27(3) of the Code of Professional Conduct for doctors in the Land of Hesse, which prohibits and penalizes advertising by doctors which is contrary to the image of the profession or contrary to professional ethics, is compatible with Article 56 TFEU.

225. In his opinion, Advocate General Cruz Vallanon first noted that the fact that the national legislative framework is the result of corporate self-regulation adopted by a professional body in no way precludes the application of the provisions of the Treaty relating to fundamental freedoms. As the Court has repeatedly observed, the freedoms of movement must also be respected 'in the case of rules which are not public in nature but which are designed to regulate, collectively, self-employment and the provision of services'.[269] According to the Advocate General, the national framework in the terms proposed by the professional association constituted a

265. CJEU, *Corporacion Dermoestética,* Case C-500/06, ECLI:EU:C:2008:421, paras 38–40.
266. CJEU, *Conseil départemental de l'ordre des chirurgiens-dentistes de la Haute-Garonne,* Case C-296/18, ECLI:EU:C:2018:857.
267. CJEU, *DocMorris,* Case C-190/20, ECLI:EU:C:2021: 609, para. 45; 28 European Journal of Health Law 551–558 (2021).
268. *Supra* n. 204.
269. *Supra* n. 199, para. 37.

restriction of the freedom to provide services.[270] Such restrictions are aimed at protecting consumers and guaranteeing the quality of medical services, which are essential to ensuring public health. Accordingly, regulation of the advertising of professional medical activities may be justified in relation to the objective of protecting consumers and public health.[271]

226. Also, in regard to whether the rules are appropriate for attaining the objective of protecting public health, he noted, albeit on a very general level, that the laying down of specific conditions concerning the content of advertising, which are linked to disciplinary rules, is not in itself inconsistent with the aim of ensuring the protection of consumers and public health. However, a set of rules which lays down, in general and ambiguous terms, the requirement that advertising by professionals must be effected in accordance with ethical standards can be proportionate only if the infringement is clearly defined in the rules or where sufficient clarity is lacking if the rules are applied to a situation which is unquestionably contrary to professional ethics. In the case before the Court, the infringement which *Konstantinides* was alleged to have committed came within the second category, since it involved an infringement which is not defined clearly enough to enable the identification of specific unlawful conduct. The referring court and the professional association submitted, without *Konstantinides* having argued otherwise, that the advertisement on the internet, where the medical services appear under the heading of a so-called European Institute or German Institute, did not reflect the infrastructure available to him in Germany. On the contrary, their provision of services took place in a private clinic in collaboration with other medical professionals established in the Land of Hesse, but without the existence of any research or institutional activities matching those referred to on his website. Should those points be confirmed, it would be a case of advertising which is misleading to potential patients who might believe that they will receive the service in conditions which do not subsequently reflect the true position. Given the clear relationship between medical activities and the safeguarding of public health, which is closely linked to the protection of consumers as patients[272] of medical services, conduct such as that of *Konstantinides* was unlikely to meet the ethical advertising standards expected of a medical professional. This assessment had to be made by the referring court.[273]

227. According to the CJEU, paragraph 27(3) of the Code of Professional Conduct for doctors in Hesse does not prohibit the advertising of medical services as such but requires that the content of such advertising should not be unprofessional. Nevertheless, it suffers from a certain ambiguity, making it liable to constitute an obstacle to the freedom to provide medical services. Such measure may be justified by overriding considerations in the public interest relating to public health and consumer protection, provided that – this being for the referring court to ascertain – the

270. *Ibid.*, para. 61.
271. *Ibid.*, para. 63.
272. Also in the original Spanish version, while one would expect 'patients as consumers of medical services'.
273. *Supra* n. 199, paras 64–68.

application of any penalties to a professional making use of the freedom to provide services is proportionate to the conduct of which he is accused.[274]

§3. Medical Fees

228. Also, in the *Konstantinides* case, the referring court asked whether a professional rule like paragraph 12(1) of the Code of Professional Conduct for doctors in the Land of Hesse pursuant to which medical fees are required to be reasonable on pain of a disciplinary penalty were compatible with EU law and more specifically with Article 56 TFEU. Paragraph 12 provides that doctors who are members of the professional association in the Land of Hesse must calculate their fees in accordance with the 'official list of fees' for medical procedures adopted by the professional association. Where a service is not one of the ones included in the list, paragraph 12 requires the conclusion of an 'agreement on fees' or the adoption of 'reasonable' fees, and the financial situation of the recipient of service must always be taken into account. The referring court pointed out that the service provided by *Konstantinides* was not among the services included in the list of fees for medical procedures. Precisely because there was some latitude for determining it, the fee was challenged by one of his patients. The professional association agreed with the patient and also considered that the fees charged were excessive and justified the imposition of a disciplinary penalty. However, as *Konstantinides* pointed out and the professional association acknowledged, the criterion he applied took account of the fee code for equivalent medical services.[275]

229. According to the Advocate General, the fact that an independent professional risks the imposition of a disciplinary penalty because he charged a fee within the scope of the discretion allowed by the professional association rules clearly creates for that professional a situation of legal uncertainty which is likely to limit or render less attractive his activity. Considered from the point of view of a service provider established in another Member State, the threat of a severe disciplinary penalty liable to amount to EUR 50,000, and even a declaration of his unfitness to pursue the profession, merely because he charged a fee equivalent to that applicable to one of the services included in the list of fees for medical procedures constituted, without any doubt, a restriction of the freedom to provide services.[276] It was for the referring court to assess whether this restriction was justified on the grounds of protection of health and consumers having regard, among others, of the necessity of the measure. On this point, it was important that the referring court analyse the need for the measure from the point of view of a cross-border service provider and not from that of a provider established in the host Member State. Where there is some discretion when it comes to determining the price of the service, and where the service concerned is highly specialized and is provided by a professional from another Member State, it is necessary to ensure that such a professional, within the scope of

274. *Supra* n. 204, paras 54–57.
275. *Supra* n. 199, paras 32, 34 and 35.
276. *Ibid.*, para. 43.

the discretion conferred on him by the professional association rules, is not exposed to onerous procedures which restrict his rights and ultimately discourage him from moving to the host Member State.[277]

230. According to the CJEU, the existence of a restriction within the meaning of the Treaty cannot be deduced from the mere fact that doctors established in Member States other than the Federal Republic of Germany have to submit, for calculating their fees for services provided in the territory of the Land of Hesse, to the rules applicable in that Land. In the absence of any flexibility of the system at issue in the main proceedings, the application of such a system, which would be liable to have a deterrent effect on doctors from other Member States, would constitute a restriction within the meaning of the Treaty. It was then for the referring court to examine whether, on the assumption that their application in the circumstances such as those described in order for reference constituted a restriction of the freedom to provide services, the rules at issue in the main proceedings were based on an objective in the public interest.[278]

277. *Ibid.*, para. 48.
278. *Supra* n. 204, paras 48–51.

Part IV. Patients' Rights in EU Law

Chapter 1. Who Is a Patient in EU Law?

231. According to Article 3h of the Cross-Border Healthcare Directive, 'patient' means 'any natural person who seeks to receive or receives healthcare in a Member State'.[279]

232. There is a striking similarity between the definition of patient in the Cross-Border Healthcare Directive and the definition of 'recipient' in Article 4.3 of the Services Directive which is (*inter alia*) 'any natural person who uses or wishes to use, a service'. The similarity is that both the user of services under the Services Directive and the patient are considered a 'recipient' of services. This is important in order to fully comprehend the exact nature of the rights that the Cross-Border Healthcare Directive confers to patients: these rights are not rights of a patient in the classic sense of an ill person, but rights of a patient in his quality as the recipient and even the potential recipient of healthcare services. There is nothing wrong with the fact that these rights are also considered patient rights as long as one is aware that they are different from the classic patient rights such as informed consent, protection of dignity, integrity and confidentiality.

233. It is, however, puzzling that the Cross-Border Healthcare Directive itself is ambivalent in this respect. Many have already remarked that the words 'patient rights' appear in the title of this Directive, but with a few exceptions and in a different context, these words do not appear in the corpus itself.[280] Again, a comparison with the Services Directive is revealing: Chapter 5 of this Directive deals with 'quality of services' and the first article in this Chapter, Article 22, is entitled 'Information on Providers and Their Services'; Article 23 is entitled 'Professional Liability and Guarantees' and Article 26, 'Policy on Quality and Services'. All these rights of recipients of services also appear in Article 4 of the Cross-Border Healthcare

279. *See also* A. Dubuis, *Les droits du patient en droit de l'Union européenne* 29–36 (Bruylant 2017); L. Klesta, 'Le patient est-il un consommmateur?', *European Journal of Consumer Law-Revue Européenne de Droit de la Consommation* 225–234 (2010).

280. H. Nys, 'The Transposition of the Directive on Patients' Rights in Cross-Border Care in National Law by the Member States: Still a Lot of Efforts to Be Made and Questions to Be Answered', 14 *European Journal of Health Law* 1–14 (2014); *see also supra* n. 3, 159: 'the Patients' Right Directive, a document somewhat confusingly labelled, given that, in contrast to the domestic legislation of certain EU Member States, it does not provide a "patients' rights manifesto", still less a Patients' Rights Act'.

Directive but in a covert way and disguised as responsibilities of the Member States of Treatment, not as rights per se. All of them have rights to transparency and information in order to make informed choices with regard to providers and the services they deliver. In other words, it is the right of a (potential) receiver of healthcare services. Already in 1994, Leenen wrote: 'Patients are the clients of health care … . In industry and business the consumer is king and this rule should also count for health care.'[281] In the implementation of the Directive, there is convergence in moving from a focus on 'the patient as a receiver of health services as a national citizen' towards the 'patient as a consumer in a common European market'.[282]

234. The specific or 'modern' meaning of the patient as a receiver of healthcare services does not mean that the more classic notion of the patient is absent in EU Law, on the contrary. For instance, in *Doulamis,* Advocate General Bot expressed his opinion that the relationship between a patient and a treatment provider is stronger than the relationship with a product, which results merely from consumer habits. In the healthcare sector, that relationship is based on the patient's trust in the service provider as an individual or in a healthcare establishment, and the need for quality with respect to such services is clearly of the highest priority. That trust is based initially on the reputation of the professional or the healthcare establishment and, in general, the more treatment the patient receives, the more that trust is strengthened.[283] And, he added, healthcare services differ from other services. They affect the physical integrity and psychological balance of the recipient. Moreover, a patient who avails himself of those services is responding to a genuine need related to the restoration of his health and, in some cases, the protection of his life. Bearing in mind the importance of what is thus at stake when having to decide whether or not to avail himself of treatment, the patient does not have the same freedom of choice as he does with other services. When he avails himself of treatment, the patient is not satisfying a desire but responding to a need. The dental care sector, as with all activities in the healthcare sector, is one in which, in the Advocate General's opinion, the degree of 'asymmetry of information' between the provider and the recipient of the service to adopt the expression used by the European Commission in its Report on Competition in Professional Services is at its highest. This means that, in his area of activity, the service provider has a level of competence which is very much higher than that of the recipient, so that the latter is not in a position to make a genuine assessment of the quality of the service he is purchasing.[284] It has been acknowledged by the CJEU that Member States may seek to redress imbalances between the consumer and the producer, which might result from asymmetry of information.[285]

---

281. H. Leenen, 'The Rights of Patients in Europe', 1 *European Journal of Health Law* 13 (1994).
282. Z. Nordeng & F. Veggeland, 'The Implementation of European Union (EU) Rules on Cross-Border Care: Moving Towards Convergence', 15 *Health Economics, Policy and Law* 156 (2020).
283. Opinion AG Bot, in *Doulamis*, Case C-446/05, ECLI:EU:C:2007:701, para. 94.
284. *Ibid.*, paras 114–115.
285. Opinion AG Bobek, in C-621/15, *Sanofi Pasteur,* ECLI:EU:C:2017:176, para. 23; *see* E. Büyüksagis, 'L'arrêt Sanofi. La responsabilité du fait des produits défectueux appliquée aux vaccins, une responsabilité objective basée sur des presomptions', *Journal de droit européen* 395 (2017); L.R. Smillie et al., '*C-621/15-W v. Sanofi Pasteur:* An Example of Judicial Distortion and Indifference

235. The different angles from which the patient can be approached are clearly summarized by Advocate General Bot: 'A patient who has been prescribed treatment by his doctor and who then goes to his pharmacist is in a position to understand and put into practice the advice the pharmacist gives him. On the other hand, in a hospital, medicinal products are administered by the nursing staff and the patient is most often in a completely passive situation.'[286] In the former situation, we may speak of a 'participative patient', while in the latter, one may refer to a 'passive patient'.

236. According to Advocate General Cruz Vallanon in *Konstantinides,* the Services Directive and Directive 2000/31 on information society services are not applicable to medical service because medical and surgical services, since they require the provider and the recipient of the service to be physically present, cannot be considered to come under 'information society services' within the meaning of Article 2a of that Directive.[287] The CJEU did not take a position on this in its judgment. However, in the light of Recital 18 in the Preamble of Directive 2000/31, the statement of the Advocate General seems too broad and too general. According to this Recital, 'activities which by their very nature cannot be carried out at a distance and by electronic means, such as statutory auditing of company accounts or medical advice requiring the physical examination of a patient are not information society services'(*see* paragraph 49). In *Vanderborght,* the CJEU expressly recognized that 'advertising relating to the provision of oral and dental care services by means of a website created by a member of a regulated constitutes a commercial communication which is part of an information society service or which constitutes such a service'.[288] Although this statement only relates to advertising and not to the provision of medical services, it is difficult to make a difference when the website used for advertising is also used to inform and advise a patient online. Finally, also in light of the Cross-Border Healthcare Directive, one may seriously question whether the point of view of the Advocate General is correct. Article 3d of this Directive defines the 'Member State of treatment' as the Member State on whose territory healthcare is actually provided to the patient. In the case of telemedicine, healthcare is considered to be provided in the Member State where the healthcare provider is established. This implies that healthcare providers and patients are not physically present.[289]

---

to Science', 26 *Medical Law Review* 134–145 (2018); R. Knol Radoja, 'Vaccine Injury: Burden of Proof of the Defect and the Causal Link in the Light of the Judgment in the Case C-621/15', *EU and Comparative Law Issues and Challenges Series* 255–274 (2019).

286. Opinion AG Bot, in *Commission v. Germany,* Case C-141/07, ECLI:EU:C:2008:218, para. 108.

287. *Supra* n. 204, para. 59.

288. *Supra* n. 253, para. 9; *see* J. Stuyck, 'Arrêt Vanderborght: l'interdiction belge de publicité en matière de soins dentaires à l'épreuve du droit de l'Union europeénne', *Journal de droit européen* 324 (2017).

289. *See* International Association of Mutual Benefits Societies (AIM), *AIM Feedback on 'Cross-Border Healthcare-Evaluation of Patients' Rights,* 2021.

Chapter 2. Patients' Rights in EU Law in General

§1. Introduction

237. In this chapter, the patients' rights in EU Law are discussed in a general way, which means here outside a cross-border healthcare context. The patients' rights in a cross-border care context are specifically regulated in the Cross-Border Healthcare Directive and are discussed in Chapter 3 of this Part. However, it should already be pointed out here that at least some of these rights are also relevant for domestic patients and not only for mobile patients (*see* Chapter 3). Also, the reverse is true: some of the general patients' rights are relevant in a cross-border context.

238. Patients' rights in Europe are regulated predominantly at the national level. However, a supranational framework for patients' rights has developed at the EU level, based on EU secondary legislation,[290] fundamental rights instruments and ethical and legal traditions in Member States.[291] The most important legal source of patients' rights in EU Law is the Charter of Fundamental Rights of the EU.[292] European accession to the European Convention on Human Rights (ECHR) is a legal obligation under Article 6 of the Treaty on European Union (TEU). While a provisional agreement had been negotiated in 2013 between the Council of Europe and the European Commission, the CJEU held in 2014 that parts of it were incompatible with EU law. On 7 October 2019, the Council of the EU adopted supplementary negotiating directives. These directives aim at a certain number of specific amendments to the draft Accession Agreement of 2013. The amendments to be demanded by the Union are limited to what is strictly necessary to address, with the required degree of legal certainty, the objections raised by the CJEU in its opinion of 18 December 2014 against the draft Accession Agreement. When adopting the supplementary negotiating directives, the Council of the EU also unanimously expressed its commitment to the swift resumption of the negotiation on the Accession Agreement. Formal negotiations on amending the draft of the Accession Agreement started in the first half of 2020.[293] With regard to the European Convention for the protection of human rights and dignity of human being with regard to the application of biology and medicine (the European Bioethics Convention), which is also open for signature by the EU, the Commission answered the question: 'Has the Commission carried out studies on whether it would be advisable for the EU to

290. *See* H. Nys, 'Comparative Health Law and the Harmonization of Patients' Rights in Europe', 8 *European Journal of Health Law* 323 (2001).
291. H. Van Kolfschooten, 'EU Regulation of Artificial Intelligence: Challenges for Patients' Rights', 59 *Common Market Law Review* 85 (2022).
292. *OJ* 2012, C 326/391.
293. Answer given by Vice-President Jourová on behalf of the European Commission to a written Parliamentary question of S. Guillaume et al., Accession of the European Union to the ECHR, 12 May 2020, E-003589/2019.

accede to the European Bioethics Convention?' that 'concerning the European Bioethics Convention, the Commission has not carried out such studies'.[294] The EU is not a party to the 1997 Convention on Human Rights and Biomedicine, and neither are some of the Member States.[295]

§2. PATIENTS' RIGHTS IN THE CHARTER OF FUNDAMENTAL RIGHTS OF THE EU

I. Introduction

239. The Charter of Fundamental Rights of the EU aims to strengthen the protection of fundamental rights in the light of changes in society, social progress and scientific and technological developments by making those rights more visible in a Charter. Although the word 'patient' does not even appear in the Charter of Fundamental Rights of the EU, it is obvious that these fundamental rights are also applicable in healthcare. Article 1 of Commission Decision (EU) 2021/156 of 9 February 2021, renewing the mandate of the European Group on Ethics in Science and New Technologies (EGE), has set up the EGE.[296] The task of the EGE is to provide the Commission with independent advice on questions where ethical, societal and fundamental rights dimensions intersect with the development of science and new technologies, either at the request of the Commission or on its own initiative, expressed through its chairperson and agreed with the responsible Commission department. In particular, the EGE shall: (a) identify, define and examine ethical questions raised by developments in science and technologies and (b) provide guidance critical for the development, implementation and monitoring of Union policies or legislation in the form of analyses and recommendations, presented in opinions and statements, that shall be oriented towards the promotion of ethical Union policymaking, in accordance with the Charter of Fundamental Rights of the European Union (Article 2).[297]

240. The provisions of the Charter are addressed to the institutions, bodies, offices and agencies of the Union with due regard to the principle of subsidiarity and to the Member States only when they are implementing Union law. They shall, therefore, respect the rights, observe the principles, and promote the application

294. Answer given by Ms Kyriakides on behalf of the European Commission to a written Parliamentary question of S. Spurek, IVF reimbursement guarantee, 20 Feb. 2020, E-004374/201; *see* S. Heselhaus, *Human Dignity in Europe*, in *Handbook of Human Dignity in Europe* 943–968 (P. Becchi and K. Mathis eds, Springer Nature Switzerland 2019).
295. Answer given by Mr Reynders on behalf of the European Commission to a written Parliamentary question of L. Duris Nicholsonova, Previously expressed wishes (living will), 11 May 2022, E-000358/2022/Rev.1; T. Vidalis, *The Emergence of Biolaw. The European Experience and the Evolutionary Approach* 5–6 (Springer Textbooks in Law, 2022).
296. *OJ* 2021, L 46/34.
297. *See* M. Fartunova-Michel & B. Nabli, *Droit de l'Union Européenne de la Bioéthique* 173–192 (Bruylant 2021); H. Busby, T. Hervey & A. Mohr, 'Ethical EU Law? The Influence of the European Group on Ethics in Science and New Technologies', 33 *European Law Review* 803–842 (2008).

thereof in accordance with their respective powers, as well as respect the limits of the powers of the Union as conferred on it in the Treaties (Article 51.1.).[298]

241. Initially, the application and interpretation of the Charter in the light of patients' rights have mainly been discussed in the context of cross-border movement of patients.[299]

II. Free and Informed Consent (Article 3.1 and 3.2a Charter)

242. 'Everyone has the right to respect for his or her physical and mental integrity' (Article 3.1). 'In the fields of medicine and biology, the following must be respected in particular: the free and informed consent of the person concerned, according to the procedures laid down by law' (Article 3.2a).

243. On 11 April 2024, the European Parliament adopted a resolution on including the right to abortion in the EU Fundamental Rights Charter. The resolution urges the European Council to launch a Convention for the revision of the Treaties, as requested in its resolutions of 9 June 2022 and 22 November 2023, and to adopt its proposal included in its resolution of 22 November 2023 to add sexual and reproductive healthcare and the right to safe and legal abortion to the Charter and amend it as follows: 'Article 3: Right to the integrity of the person and to bodily autonomy: 2a. Everyone has the right to bodily autonomy, to free, informed, full and universal access to sexual and reproductive health and rights, and to all related healthcare services without discrimination, including access to safe and legal abortion.'[300]

244. Article 3 of the Charter consists of two parts. The first part explicitly recognizes a right to respect for physical and mental integrity in general. The second part of Article 3 is specific to the fields of medicine and biology. This second part makes, in its turn, four distinctions, of which only the first one (under a) is of relevance here.

245. According to Dubuis, free and informed consent is not framed in terms of a right to informed consent but as an obligation for the addressees of the Charter of Fundamental Rights of the EU.[301] However, one should bear in mind that the second part of Article 3 is a specification of the right to respect for physical and mental integrity which encompasses, among others, the free and informed consent of the person concerned. This correlation between the right to integrity and free and informed consent had already been made previously by the CJEU (*see* paragraph

298. B. Spinelli, 'First Working Document on the Implementation of the Charter of Fundamental Rights of the European Union in the EU institutional framework', *Committee on Constitutional Affairs*, 22 Jan. 2018, 8p.
299. *See* C.M. Rieder, 'The Application and Interpretation of the EU Charter in the Context of Cross-Border Movement of Patients', 22 *Columbia Journal of European Law* 475–476 (2016).
300. P9_TA(2024)0286.
301. *Supra* n. 270, 344.

643). In its judgment in *Netherlands v. European Parliament and Council* of 9 October 2001,[302] the CJEU confirmed that a fundamental right to human integrity is part of Union Law and encompasses, in the context of medicine and biology, the free and informed consent of the donor and recipient.[303] While one could doubt that the donor is a patient, the recipient of human material certainly is a patient. It seems arguable that Article 3.2a of the Charter contains the patients' right to free and informed consent. The details of this right have to be elaborated by law.

246. While the right to physical and mental integrity as protected under Article 3.1 is attributed to everyone, from competent adults to incompetent adults and children, it is less obvious to establish who can invoke the protection offered by Article 3.2a. Free and informed consent in the context of medicine clearly protects competent adults.[304] With regard to children, Article 24.1. of the Charter provides that children shall have the right to such protection and care as is necessary for their well-being. They may express their views freely. Such views shall be taken into consideration on matters which concern them in accordance with their age and maturity. In the Preamble of its Resolution of 1 June 2017 with recommendations to the Commission on the protection of vulnerable adults, the European Parliament refers to the Charter of Fundamental Rights of the EU and, more particularly, Article 3 thereof which guarantees everyone the right to physical and mental integrity. In the Annex to its Resolution, the European Parliament calls on the Commission to submit to Parliament and the Council before 31 March 2018, pursuant to Article 81.2. of the TFEU, a proposal for a regulation designed to improve cooperation among the Member States, and the automatic recognition and enforcement of decisions of vulnerable adults and mandates in anticipation of incapacity. In its answer to this resolution, the European Commission stated that the potential legislative initiative would be complementary to the Hague framework and that it would bring the desired results only if a sufficient number of Member States acceded to the Hague Convention 2000. It stated that it would encourage Member States to accede to the Hague Convention.[305] The Commission has also taken several measures in order to facilitate Member States' ratification of this Convention, for instance, translation in all EU official languages of the Explanatory Report to the Hague Convention; financial support to protection of adults' related projects; organization of a Joint Conference on Private International Law on the Cross-border Protection of Vulnerable Adults from 5 to 8 December 2018. So far, nine Member States have ratified it.[306]

302. CJEU, *Netherlands v. European Parliament and Council,* Case C-377/98, ECLI:EU:C:2001:523.
303. Explanatory Note on Art. 3 Charter of Fundamental Rights of the EU.
304. S. Michalowski, 'Right to the Integrity of the Person', in S. Peers, T. Hervey & A. Ward (eds), *The EU Charter of Fundamental Rights: A Commentary* 45 (Hart Publishing 2014).
305. P8_TA(2017)0235. Protection of vulnerable adults. European Parliament Resolution of 1 Jun. 2017 with recommendations to the Commission on the protection of vulnerable adults (2015/2085(INL)); European Commission, Answer – Protection of vulnerable adults, E-003844/2017, 30 Aug. 2017. *See* M. Drventic, 'The Protection of Adults in the EU', *EU and Comparative Law Issues and Challenges* 804–829 (2019).
306. Answer given by Mr Reynders on behalf of the European Commission to a written Parliamentary question of A. Schwaab, Cross-border recognition of lasting powers of attorney, 5–8 Mar. 2020, E-000060/2020.

247. By referring to 'procedures laid down by law', this provision on informed consent leaves a considerable degree of discretion to the Member States and thus implicitly recognizes the prospect for a wide range of different approaches as to what informed consent means and who can give consent.[307] It is the competence of Member States to determine and implement the measures necessary for the protection of the health and life of their citizens in accordance with applicable national and EU law. Concerning measures amounting to the mandating of vaccination against COVID-19, the necessity and proportionality must be determined in light of available scientific evidence, the severity of the pandemic and the overall public health situation.[308] The European Commission will not take any action in relation to Member States' actions in this regard.[309]

III. Right to Privacy and Right to Data Protection

248. 'Everyone has the right to respect for his or her private and family life, home and communications' (Article 7). The CJEU has held that the right to respect private life, embodied in Article 8 of the ECHR and deriving from the common constitutional traditions of the Member States, is one of the fundamental rights protected by the legal order of the EU. It includes, in particular, a person's right to keep his state of health secret.[310]

249. 'Everyone has the right to the protection of personal data concerning him or her' (Article 8.1). 'Such data must be processed fairly for specified purposes and on the basis of the consent of the person concerned or some other legitimate basis laid down by law. Everyone has the right of access to data which has been collected concerning him or her, and the right to have it rectified' (Article 8.2). 'Compliance with these rules shall be subject to control by an independent authority' (Article 8.3).

307. J. McHale, 'Fundamental Rights and Healthcare', in E. Mossialos et al. (eds), *Health Systems Governance in Europe: The Role of EU Law and Policy* 300 (Cambridge University Press 2010); *supra* n. 5, 173.
308. Answer given by Ms Kyriakides on behalf of the European Commission to a written Parliamentary question of I. Lagos, Unconstitutional and illegal measures regarding mandatory vaccination, 11 Feb. 2022, E-005489/2021.
309. Answer given by Ms Kyriakides on behalf of the European Commission to a written Parliamentary question of M. Grapini, Austria's wrongful decision not to comply with Regulation (EU) 953/2021 by making vaccination compulsory, 29 Mar. 2022, E-000513/2022.
310. EU Civil Service Tribunal, *V and EDPS*, Case F-46/09, ECLI:EU:F:2011:101, para. 111.

250. The relationship between the right to privacy and the right to data protection is a complex one. In the explanatory memorandum to the Charter of Fundamental Rights of the EU, it is emphasized that the right to data protection is partially based on the right to privacy.[311] The scope of both rights also seems to overlap to a large extent.[312]

251. Mostert et al. have identified three differences between both rights. First, the scope and the substance of the individual rights protected by both human rights differ. On the one hand, all forms of personal data processing fall under the scope of the right to data protection, regardless of whether the right to privacy is interfered with. On the other, whether or not the right to privacy is interfered with depends on both the nature and the context of the specific processing. The individuals' rights based on the right to privacy are more of a context-sensitive nature.[313]

252. The second difference is that the right to data protection contains largely a positive obligation of the EU and its Member States. This is different from the right to privacy that, at least originally, reflects a mere negative obligation of public authorities not to interfere with the private life of citizens.[314]

253. The third difference is that the right to data protection is based on a more comprehensive and systematic approach, one that goes beyond individual rights. It suffices to look at Article 7 and Article 8 of the Charter to become aware of this. Article 8 guarantees a comprehensive system of data protection norms, such as the principles of fair and lawful processing, purpose specification and limitation and the requirement of independent supervision. The right to privacy does not guarantee such a comprehensive system of norms.[315]

IV. Right of Access to Preventive Healthcare and to Benefit from Medical Treatment

254. Everyone has the right to access preventive healthcare and the right to benefit from medical treatment under the conditions established by national laws and practices. A high level of human health protection shall be ensured in the definition

311. Convention Presidium, Explanations relating to the Charter of Fundamental Rights of the European Union, Brussels, 2000, CHARTE 4473/00, CONVENT 49.
312. M. Mostert, et al., 'From Privacy to Data Protection in the EU: Implications for Big Data Health Research', 25 *European Journal of Health Law* 47 (2018).
313. *Ibid.*, 48.
314. *Ibid.*, 49–50.
315. *Ibid.*, 50–51.

and implementation of all the Union's policies and activities (Article 35 of the Charter of Fundamental Rights of the EU). A high level does not mean 'the highest level that is technically possible'.[316]

255. Because there is little jurisprudence, it is difficult to evaluate the scope of application of Article 35.[317] According to Berki, the Charter 'does not create any specific healthcare entitlements for patients'.[318] According to de Ruijter, Article 35, read together with the right to life, can provide the basis for an individual claim, for instance, when access to healthcare is denied on the argument that resources are limited or read in relation to Article 4 on the infliction of inhuman or degrading treatment. In this situation, a patient in pain or a disabled person who is waiting for healthcare in the home state while access to cross-border healthcare is denied could potentially claim the infliction of inhuman or degrading treatment in combination with a right to healthcare.[319]

§3. Patients' Rights in Secondary EU Law

I. Right to Report Suspected Side Effects of Medicinal Products

256. Member States have to take all appropriate measures to encourage patients, doctors, pharmacists and other healthcare professionals to report suspected adverse reactions to the national competent authority; for these tasks, organizations representing consumers, patients and healthcare professionals may be involved as appropriate and to facilitate patient reporting through the provision of alternative reporting formats in addition to web-based formats (Article 102a and b Directive 2001/83/EC on the Community code relating to medicinal products for human use,[320] amended by Directive 2010/84 of 15 December 2010).[321] For the purposes of point a, the Member States may impose specific obligations on doctors, pharmacists and other healthcare professionals (Article 102f). According to Recital 21 in the Preamble to Directive 2010/84, Union rules in relation to pharmacovigilance should continue to rely on the crucial role of healthcare professionals in monitoring the safety of medicinal products and should take account of the fact that patients are also well placed to report suspected adverse reactions to medicinal products. It is, therefore, appropriate to facilitate the reporting of suspected adverse reactions to

316. General Court, *TestBioTech and others*, T-177/13, ECLI:EU:T:2016:736, para. 106; appeal against this judgment has been dismissed, CJEU, C-82/17 P, ECLI:EU:C:2019:719. *See* M. Frischhut, *Standards on Quality and Safety in Cross-Border Healthcare, in Cross-Border Health Care and European Union Law* 65 (A. den Exter ed., Erasmus University Press 2017).
317. *Supra* n. 304, 475.
318. *Supra* n. 62, 29.
319. *Supra* n. 5, 171–172.
320. *OJ* 2001, L 311.
321. *OJ* 2010, L 348.

medicinal products by both healthcare professionals and patients and to make methods for such reporting available to them. The right of individual European patients to report suspected side effects is a very important novelty of European pharmacovigilance legislation.[322]

II. Right to Report Suspected Adverse Reactions of Medicinal Products

257. Marketing authorization holders shall not refuse to consider reports of suspected adverse reactions received electronically or by any other appropriate means from patients and healthcare professionals (Article 107.2 Directive 2001/83/EC on the Community code relating to medicinal products for human use,[323] amended by Directive 2010/84 of 15 December 2010).[324] According to Recital 21 in the Preamble to Directive 2010/84, Union rules in relation to pharmacovigilance should continue to rely on the crucial role of healthcare professionals in monitoring the safety of medicinal products and should take account of the fact that patients are also well placed to report suspected adverse reactions to medicinal products. It is, therefore, appropriate to facilitate the reporting of suspected adverse reactions to medicinal products by both healthcare professionals and patients and to make methods for such reporting available to them.

III. Right to Receive Information Regarding Implantable Medical Devices on an Implant Card

258. Article 18.1. of the Medical Device Regulation obliges the manufacturer of an implantable device to provide together with the device the following: (a) information allowing the identification of the device, including the device name, serial number, lot number, the UDI, the device model, as well as the name, address and the website of the manufacturer; this information has to be provided on an implant card delivered with the device; (b) any warnings, precautions or measures to be taken by the patient or a healthcare professional with regard to reciprocal interference with reasonably foreseeable external influences, medical examinations or environmental conditions; (c) any information about the expected lifetime of the device and any necessary follow-up; (d) any other information to ensure safe use of the device by the patient, including the information in point (u) of section 23.4 of Annex I. The information has to be provided for the purpose of making it available to the particular patient who has been implanted with the device by any means that allow rapid access to that information and has to be stated in the language(s) determined by the concerned Member State. The information has to be written in a way that is readily understood by a layperson and has to be updated where appropriate. Updates of the information have to be made available to the patient via the website of the

322. A. Altavilla, 'Safe, Innovative and Accessible Medicines in Europe: A Renewed Strategy for Patients and the Pharmaceutical Sector', 25 *European Journal of Health Law* 145 (2018).
323. *Supra* n. 320.
324. *Supra* n. 321.

manufacturer. Article 18.2. obliges the Member States to require health institutions to make the information referred to in Article 18.2. available, by any means that allow rapid access to that information, to any patients who have been implanted with the device, together with the implant card, which bears their identity. According to Article 2.36, a 'health institution' means an organization, the primary purpose of which is the care or treatment of patients or the promotion of public health. Recital 39 of the Preamble contains the following clarifications: 'Patients who are implanted with a device should be given clear and easily accessible essential information allowing the implanted device to be identified and other relevant information about the device, including any necessary health risk warnings or precautions to be taken, for example, indications as to whether or not it is compatible with certain diagnostic devices or with scanners used for security controls.' According to McHale, the implant card 'can be seen as something which can effectively be built into the consent process'.[325]

§4. Patients' Rights in EU Soft Law Documents

I. Documents Approved by the European Parliament

A. *European Charter on the Rights of the Patient*

259. On 19 January 1984, the European Parliament approved a Resolution on a European Charter on the Rights of the Patient.[326,327] In this Resolution, the European Parliament invited the Commission 'to submit as soon as possible a proposal for a European Charter on the Rights of Patients'. The European Commission had already expressed a favourable opinion on this matter in an answer to a written question.[328] According to the opinion of the Legal Affairs Committee, Article 235 of the EEC Treaty could be invoked as a legal basis for a Charter on the Rights of the Patient. This article made a general provision for action to attain Community objectives, one of which is the improvement of living conditions.[329]

260. In Recital 1 of the Resolution, the European Parliament considered that a considerable amount of work had already been done with a view to establishing the rights of patients, but the patient's ability to assert his rights was not yet assured.

325. J.V. McHale, 'Health Law, Brexit and Medical Devices: A Question of Legal Regulation and Patient Safety', 18 *Medical Law International* 211 (2018).
326. *Supra* n. 270, 404; *supra* n. 3, 59, 'Softer' types of law; T. Hervey, 'EU Law and National Health Policies: Problem or Opportunity?', *Health Economics, Policy and Law* 6 (2007): 'We may see the development of EU-level norms (probably in first instance, soft law norms, such as an agreed EU Charter of Patients' Rights) in this field'; H.D.C. Roscam Abbing, 'Twenty Years WHO Principles of Patients' Rights in Europe, a Common Framework: Looking Back to the Future', 21 *European Journal of Health Law* 326 (2014): 'To be implemented in the daily healthcare practice … soft law is a useful instrument.'
327. *OJ* 1984, C 46/104; *see* H.J.J. Leenen, 'Patients' Rights in Europe', 8 *Health Policy* 37 (1987).
328. Opinion of the Legal Affairs Committee, Doc. 1-970/83, Ann. III, 19, para. 12.
329. *Ibid*., para. 16.

261. Paragraph 3 of the Resolution stressed that the Charter must incorporate the following fifteen patients' rights: (a) the right to available treatment and care appropriate to the illness; (b) the right to prompt treatment; (c) the right to adequate social security cover to allow the rights set out in (a) to be exercised; (d) the right to free choice of medical practitioner and healthcare establishment; (e) the right of access to hospital service within a reasonable travelling distance; (f) the right to information concerning diagnosis, therapy and prognosis, the patient's right of access to his own medical data, and the patient's right to give his consent to or to refuse the treatment proposed; (g) the right to medical confidentiality, the only possible exceptions to which should be on a limited number of serious and well-defined grounds, having due regard for the integrity of the human person; (h) the patient's right to lift the obligation of confidentiality completely or in part as regards his own medical records; (i) the right to complaint based 'on damage to the interests of the patient'; (j) the right to an appeal procedure before the courts; (k) the rights and duties of medical practitioners; (l) the patient's right to be represented by independent associations and organizations; (m) the definition of the legal status of the patient in a healthcare establishment; (n) the right to respect for private life and for religious and philosophical convictions; and (o) the right to a dignified death.

262. Paragraph 4 of the Resolution considered that it might be necessary, in well-defined circumstances, to limit the rights of patients where they would involve a danger to public health.

263. Finally, paragraph 5 expressed the opinion that the specific problems pertaining to the rights of the mentally ill and of children should not be dealt with in the context of this Charter but in a specific Charter (*see* paragraphs 266 et seq.).

264. With regard to the 'right' mentioned under (k), the Legal Affairs Committee had expressed the opinion that most Member States already had rules establishing the rights and duties of medical practitioners. If these rules need to be supplemented, it should be done in some other way and not by a Charter on the Rights of Patients.[330]

265. Although the European Commission had stated previously to be able to endorse 'the general objectives of a Charter designed to safeguard the rights of hospital patients', the Commission never submitted a proposal for a European Charter on the Rights of Patients, not even one limited to so-called hospital patients. In paragraph 3 of the Resolution of 13 May 1986 on a European Charter for Children in Hospital, the European repeated its call to the Commission to submit 'as soon as possible' a proposal for a European Charter on the rights of patients.

330. *Ibid.*, para. 13.

B. European Charter for Children in Hospital

266. On 13 May 1986, the European Parliament approved a Resolution on a European Charter for Children in Hospital.[331]

267. In paragraph 3, the European Parliament called on the Commission to submit as soon as possible a proposal for a Charter on the Rights of Children in Hospital 'in order to give real meaning to Youth Year'.

268. In paragraph 4, the European Parliament requested that the Charter should incorporate the following twenty-five rights: (a) the right to be admitted to hospital only if the treatment they require cannot be provided at home or on a day basis, and has been so planned as to ensure that they are hospitalized as soon as possible and for the shortest possible time; (b) the right of children to day care without incurring additional costs for the parents; (c) the right to have with them as much as possible during their stay their parents or the person acting in *loco parentis*, not as passive bystanders, but as active participants in hospital life, with no additional costs being incurred thereby; however, the exercise of this right must not prejudice or stand in the way of the best possible administration of the treatment which the child has to receive; (d) the right to be fully informed – as far as their age, degree of mental development and emotional and psychological state allow – about the medical treatment they are undergoing and the positive prospects it offers; (e) the right of the child to individual supervision and care, with, as far as possible, the same nurses and assistants being detailed to look after them; (f) the right to refuse (through their parents or the person acting in *loco parentis*) to serve as research subjects and to refuse any care or examination when the primary purpose is educational or informational rather than therapeutic; (g) the right of the parents or the person acting in *loco parentis* to be given all available information concerning the child's illness and welfare, insofar as this does not conflict with the child's fundamental right to privacy; (h) the right of the parents or the person acting in *loco parentis* to authorize the treatment which the child is to undergo; (i) the right of the parents or the person acting in *loco parentis* to appropriate support and psychosocial counselling by specially trained staff; (j) the right not to be subjected to pharmacological or therapeutic experimentation. Only the parents or the person acting in *loco parentis* having been duly informed of the risks and benefits of such treatment, may give their consent and must retain the right to withdraw this consent; (k) the right of children in hospital, where they are involved in therapeutic experimentation, to protection by the Helsinki Declaration of the World Medical Assembly and its subsequent updates;[332] (l) the right to be protected from unnecessary medical treatment and physical or emotional distress; (m) the right (and the means) to contact their parents

331. *OJ* 1986, C 148, 37. In his answer to a Parliamentary question of J. Zitnanska regarding the presence of parents during hospitalization as a horizontal principle, Commissioner Andriukaities stated 'the Commission cannot take any measures to guarantee children's right to have their parents present during hospitalization, or ensure that the Member States uphold the Charter on the Rights of Children in Hospital' (E-004039/2017).

332. The Helsinki Declaration in many ways is already incorporated in EU law; *see supra* n. 5, 39.

or the person acting in *loco parentis* in times of stress; (n) the right to be treated with tact, civility and understanding and to have their privacy respected; (o) the right to be cared for throughout their hospital stay by appropriately trained staff, fully aware of the physical and emotional needs of each age group; (p) the right to be cared for in hospital with other children, avoiding as far as possible admission to adult wards; (q) the right to an environment furnished and equipped to meet hospital requirements and the educational and recreational needs of children, and in conformity with current safety standards; (r) the right to continue their schooling during their stay in hospital, teachers and teaching materials being supplied by the educational authorities, particularly in the case of prolonged stays in hospital providing that this activity does not have an adverse effect on the child's well-being or hinder its treatment; (s) the right to use books, audio-visual aids and toys appropriate for their age group during their stay in hospital; (t) the right to be taught even when they are admitted to day-hospital or are convalescing in their own homes; (u) the right to be guaranteed the treatment they need – if necessary with the intervention of the legal authorities – in the event of their parents or the person acting in *loco parentis* refusing such treatment on religious grounds, or because of cultural backwardness, prejudice or in the event of their being unable to cope adequately in an emergency; (v) the right to the necessary financial, moral and psychological support when undergoing examinations and/or treatment which have to be carried out abroad; (w) the right of parents or the person acting in *loco parentis* to invoke the Charter where children require hospital treatment or check-ups in non-Community countries.

269. Until today, the European Commission has not made a proposal for a Charter on the Rights of Children in Hospital.

II. The European Charter of Patients' Rights

A. *Introductory Remarks*

270. Contrary to what had been envisaged by the European Parliament, it was not the European Commission that took the initiative for a European Charter of Patients' Rights but the Active Citizen Network that was encouraged by the European Commission to draft such a Charter. A first draft was presented in Brussels on 15 November 2002, while a so-called final version was proclaimed on 18 April 2008.[333] By acting in this way, the EU authorities used an innovative method of producing norms not by taking action themselves but by stimulating a citizen's

333. *Supra* n. 279, 105–106; the draft of 2002 is available on the website of the Active Citizen Network.

organization to draft a Charter. Although this Charter is not legally binding,[334] it has the merit of clarifying what citizens may expect regarding their rights as patients in all the Member States of the EU.[335]

271. In its Resolution of 15 March 2007 on Community Action on the provision of cross-border healthcare, the European Parliament 'considered that there is a need to incorporate a common Charter of patients' rights in a [legislative] framework in order to ensure that such rights are exercised in practice across borders and in the home country'.[336] According to Dubuis, the European Parliament made a reference here to the European Charter of Patients' Rights.[337] However, the text of the Resolution does not explicitly mention the said Charter. According to the same author, also the Resolution 2006/2275 (INI) of the European Parliament of 23 May 2007 on the impact and the consequences of the exclusion of health services from the Directive on services in the internal market[338] would contain a reference to this Charter.[339] However, our research could not confirm this.

272. The European Charter of Patients' Rights is embedded in a so-called Basis Document consisting of four parts preceded by a Preamble.

B. European Charter of Patients' Rights: Part One – Fundamental Rights

273. Part One is devoted to 'Fundamental Rights' and, more particularly, to the Charter of Fundamental Rights of the EU which in 2002 was not yet a binding instrument. Interestingly, the Charter of Fundamental Rights of the EU is called 'the main reference point of the present Charter'. In particular, Article 35 of the Charter of Fundamental Rights of the EU (*see* paragraph 254) is considered to be 'a guiding standard for the national governments. In addition to Article 35, the preceding Preamble to the European Charter of Patients' Rights states that the Charter of Fundamental Rights of the EU 'contains many provisions that refer either directly[340] or indirectly to patients' rights'. In this sense, the European Charter of Patients' Rights can be considered as a 'translation' or 'prolongation' of the confirmation of patients'

334. X. Bioy, 'Le droit fondamental à l'accès aux soins en Europe. Vers un standard de conciliation entre libertés économiques et droits du patient', *Revue des Affaires Européennes* 501 (2011): 'Si la Commission a souhaité la rédaction d'une Charte des droits du patient, ce n'est que sous la forme non contraignante rédigé par une association'.
335. E. Rial-Sebbag, G. Chassang & F. Taboulet, 'Quelle gouvernance pour les droits des patients en Europe?', *Revue des Affaires Européennes* 560 (2011); *see* W. Palm et al., *Patients' Rights: From Recognition to Implementation*, in *Achieving Person-Centred Health Systems. Evidence, Strategies and Challenges* 351 (Cambridge: Cambridge University Press 2020).
336. *OJ* 2007, C 301 E, 202 para. 11.
337. *Supra* n. 279, 107, footnote 462.
338. *OJ* 2008, C 102 E, 279.
339. *Supra* n. 279, 107, footnote 462.
340. *See* however H.D.C. Roscam Abbing: 'The EU Charter contains some pertinent clauses. The addressees of the Charter being the EU institutions and subsidiary organs, the text is indirectly relevant for the patient however', H.D.C. Roscam Abbing, 'Rights of Patients in the European Context, Ten Years and After', 11 *European Journal of Health Law* 4, note 12 (2004).

rights in the Charter of Fundamental Rights of the EU, making these rights more concrete.[341] This is in line with the introductory sentence in Part Two of the European Charter of Patients' Rights that the patients' rights it contains 'together seek to render the fundamental rights concrete, applicable and appropriate to the current transitory situation in the health services … . They must be protected throughout the entire territory of the European Union'. In its opinion on 'Patients Rights' (*see* paragraphs 292 et seq.), the European Economic and Social Committee considers that the rights proposed in the European Charter of Patients' Rights 'are based on the EU Charter' (paragraph 1.1.1. of the opinion).

C. European Charter of Patients' Rights: Part Two – Fourteen Patients' Rights

274. Part Two does not proclaim patients' rights but 'proposes the proclamation of fourteen patients' rights'[342] without making it clear who should take the responsibility to proclaim them. With regard to the fourteen patients' rights, seven 'preliminary statements are called far': (1) The definition of rights implies that both citizens and healthcare stakeholders assume their own responsibilities. Rights are indeed correlated with both duties and responsibilities. (2) The Charter applies to all individuals, recognizing the fact that differences, such as age, gender, religion, socio-economic status, literacy, etc., may influence individual healthcare needs. (3) The Charter does not intend to take sides on ethical issues. (4) The Charter defines rights as they are valid in contemporary European Health Systems. It shall, therefore, be reviewed and modified to allow for their evolution and the development of scientific knowledge and technology. (5) The fourteen rights are an embodiment of fundamental rights, and as such, they must be recognized and respected independently of financial, economic or political constraints, taking the criteria of the appropriateness of care into consideration. (6) Respect for these rights implies the fulfilment of both technical/organizational requirements and behavioural/professional patterns. They, therefore, require a global reform of the ways national health systems operate. (7) Each article of the Charter refers to a right and defines and illustrates it without claiming to foresee all possible situations.

275. The fourteen rights proposed in the Charter all start in the same way: 'Everyone has the right to' or 'the right of', except Article 5 that starts as follows: 'Each individual has the right to'. Each right is followed by a commentary that sometimes also contains another right. This complicates the reading and application of the Charter.

1. Article 1 Right to Preventive Measures

276. Every individual has the right to a proper service in order to prevent illness.

---

341. *Supra* n. 279, 106.
342. And not seventeen as suggested by *supra* n. 279, 393, No. 586.

This right correlates with the duty of 'the health services raising people's awareness, guaranteeing health procedures at regular intervals free of charge and making the results of scientific research and technological innovation available to all'.

2. Article 2 Right of Access

277. Every individual has the right of access to the health services that his or her health needs require. Health services must guarantee equal access to everyone without discriminating on the basis of financial resources, place of residence, kind of illness or time of access to services.

3. Article 3 Right to Information

278. Every individual has the right to access all kinds of information regarding their state of health, health services and how to use them, as well as all that scientific research and technological innovation make available.

According to the comments, this right also includes a right of direct access to his or her clinical file and medical records, to photocopy them, to ask questions about their contents and to obtain the correction of any errors they might contain.

4. Article 4 Right to Consent

279. Every individual has the right of access to all information that might enable him or her to actively participate in the decisions regarding his or her health; this information is a prerequisite for any procedure and treatment, including participation in scientific research.

It is remarkable that only the title, not the article itself, refers to informed consent. Shared decision-making is also very important but does not merely coincide with giving informed consent. In the commentary, informed consent is explicitly mentioned. Also, the right to refuse a treatment or a medical intervention is concealed herein. The comment ends with a reference to the right of a patient to refuse information about his or her health status. This right, however, should have been mentioned under Article 3 and not here.

5. Article 5 Right to Free Choice

280. Each individual has the right to freely choose among different treatment procedures and providers on the basis of adequate information.

This right clearly overlaps with the right to give or refuse informed consent (Article 4). Not only Article 5 itself but also the commentary to this article confirms this: 'The patient has the right to decide which diagnostic exams and therapies to undergo and which primary care doctor, specialist or hospital to use.' It would have been more appropriate to consider the right to free choice of physician and hospital as an autonomous right and not confuse it with the right to informed consent.

This article rightly links the right to free choice of providers with adequate information, which, according to the commentary, also has to relate to 'the results of their activity'.

6. Article 6 Right to Privacy and Confidentiality

281. Every individual has the right to the confidentiality of personal information, including information regarding his or her state of health and potential diagnostic or therapeutic procedures, as well as the protection of his or her privacy during the performance of diagnostic exams, specialist visits, and medical/surgical treatments in general.

Without mentioning it explicitly, the commentary also refers to the right to intimacy: 'treatments must take place in an appropriate environment and in the presence of only those who absolutely need to be there (unless the patient has explicitly given consent or made a request)'.

7. Article 7 Right to Respect of Patients' Time

282. Each individual has the right to receive necessary treatment within a swift and predetermined period of time. This right applies to each phase of the treatment.

This is probably the most innovative patients' right in the Charter and in general. It is to a certain degree contradicted by the following statement in the commentary: 'Doctors must devote adequate time to their patients, including the time dedicated to providing information.' This is very laudable but necessarily implies that it is not always possible that other patients are 'served' within a predetermined period of time.

8. Article 8 Right to the Observance of Quality Standards

283. Each individual has the right of access to high-quality health services on the basis of the specification and observance of precise standards.

The commentary adds that these standards should be fixed by means of a public and consultative procedure and should periodically be reviewed and assessed. In a question for written answer, reference was made to this article of the Charter, but the answer did not.[343]

343. Answer given by Mr Andriukaitis on behalf of the European Commission to a written Parliamentary question by P. Pedicini, Inhuman conditions in S. Giovanni Bosco Hospital in Naples, 7 Feb. 2019, E-006060/2018.

9. Article 9 Right to Safety

284. Each individual has the right to be free from harm caused by the poor functioning of health services, medical malpractice and errors, and the right of access to health services and treatments that meet high safety standards.

The commentary adds an important right for healthcare providers: 'healthcare staff that report existing risks to their superiors and/or peers must be protected from possible adverse consequences'.

10. Article 10 Right to Innovation

285. Each individual has the right of access to innovative procedures, including diagnostic procedures, according to international standards and independently of economic or financial considerations.

This right corresponds, according to the commentary, with an obligation for 'the health services to promote and sustain research in the biomedical field, paying particular attention to rare diseases. Research results must be adequately disseminated'.

11. Article 11 Right to Avoid Unnecessary Suffering and Pain

286. Each individual has the right to avoid as much suffering and pain as possible in each phase of his or her illness.

According to the commentary, 'the health services must commit themselves to taking all measures useful to this end, like providing palliative treatments and simplifying patients' access to them'.

12. Article 12 Right to Personalized Treatment

287. Each individual has the right to diagnostic or therapeutic programmes tailored as much as possible to his or her personal needs.

13. Article 13 Right to Complain

288. Each individual has the right to complain whenever he or she has suffered a harm and the right to receive a response or other feedback.

According to the commentary, this right cannot prejudice the patients' right to take legal action or pursue alternative dispute resolution.

14. Article 14 Right to Compensation

289. Each individual has the right to receive sufficient compensation within a reasonably short time whenever he or she has suffered physical or moral and psychological harm caused by a health service treatment.

According to the commentary, this right exists 'whatever the gravity of the harm and its cause (from an excessive wait to a case of malpractice) even when the ultimate responsibility cannot be absolutely determined'. This comment seems in contradiction with the text of Article 14 itself which requires harm to be caused by a treatment. Harm caused by an excessive waiting period does not fulfil this condition.

D. *European Charter of Patients' Rights: Part Three – Rights of Active Citizenship*

290. Part Three of the European Charter of Patients' Rights consists of the so-called Rights of Active Citizenship. In order to promote and verify the implementation of the above-stated patients' rights, some citizens' rights must be proclaimed.[344] They mainly regard different groups of organized citizens (patients, consumers, advocacy groups, advice-givers, self-help groups, voluntary and grassroots organizations, etc.) that have the unique role of supporting and empowering individuals in the protection of their own rights. These rights are pegged to the rights of civic association, contained in Article 12.1. of the Charter of Fundamental Rights of the EU. These rights consist of the right to perform general interest activities, the right to perform advocacy activities and the right to participate in policymaking in the area of health. Those rights are not rights of an individual patient but of patients.[345]

E. *European Charter of Patients' Rights: Part Four – Guidelines for Implementing the Charter*

291. Finally, Part Four of the European Charter of Patients' Rights contains guidelines for implementing the Charter. From a legal point of view, the most interesting is the last one, regarding 'legislation': 'The Charter rights may be incorporated into national and European laws and regulations in full or in part, to make the goal of protecting patients' rights an ordinary part of public policies, notwithstanding the immediate implementation of such rights in light of the European Union Charter of Fundamental Rights.' It is not clear what is meant by 'immediate implementation'.

344. According to Dubuis the Charter deliberately misuses here the concept of 'citizen', *see supra* n. 279, 107.
345. *Supra* n. 279, 59.

III. Opinion on 'Patients' Rights of the European Economic and Social Committee

A. *Introduction*

292. On 26 September 2007, the European Economic and Social Committee adopted an opinion on Patients' Rights.[346] The European Economic and Social Committee is an EU institution that advises the EU legislature. It decided to draw up this opinion on its own initiative. The European Economic and Social Committee calls on the European Commission to take initiatives 'enabling the implementation of health policy which respects patients rights' (paragraph 1.1.3.). This requires the gathering and analysis of comparative data on the regulatory and ethical obligations in force in each EU country, the devising, in the most appropriate form, of a Community course of action applicable to issues in this field, the planned evaluation of the application of the texts promulgated and policies decided, the dissemination of the results of this work to the relevant national authorities and representatives of the various socio-professional and user groups concerned and finally the establishment of a European Patients' Rights Day.

293. The first European Patients' Rights Day was held on 29 March 2007 in the European Parliament in Brussels, a few months before the European Economic and Social Committee called for the establishment of such a Day. During the first Day, the Active Citizenship Network and the participating organizations committed themselves to pushing forward for the institutionalization of such a Day and the adoption of the Charter. Since 2008, the European Patients' Rights Day has taken place every year on 18 April.[347]

294. According to the European Economic and Social Committee, 'developments in health-related issues reveal a similar pattern in all European countries and *a general and inescapable trend towards the assertion of the rights of people seeking care*' (paragraph 1.1.5., italics added).

295. The opinion contains interesting reflections regarding the shifting position of the patient in the healthcare system and its legal consequences. Advances in medical science and the introduction of social protection systems have led to a general epidemiological transition, which is reflected in fewer short-term care cases and, above all, in the rising incidence of chronic illnesses, a phenomenon accentuated by an ageing population. The provision of care for the chronically sick implies long-term care, as a result of which sick people accumulate knowledge through their experience of accessing the healthcare system and their experience of their illness (paragraph 1.3.). The arrival of new information technologies has reinforced this increase in patients' knowledge and improved their capacity to exchange views and question professionals. In some cases, people sometimes have a thorough knowledge of their illness which must be taken into account (paragraph 1.4.). Generally,

346. *OJ* 2008, C 10/67.
347. Active Citizenship Network, *European Patients' Right Day: Call for Participation,* 2008.

patients' expectations vis-à-vis professionals are not limited solely to technical aspects of care but are also concerned with relational and human aspects (paragraph 1.5.). Finally, living with a long-term illness or disability creates new needs and expectations on the part of the persons concerned. The challenge for treatment has changed: it is no longer a matter of seeking a cure at all costs, but more one of learning to 'live with' an illness in an ongoing effort to combat pain. Such considerations induce people to play an increasingly active role with regard to the treatment they receive, with new needs and expectations (paragraph 1.6.).

296. People's evolving needs and expectations regarding their treatment are part of a more profound change in society which aims to promote a model based on respect for individual autonomy and the assertion of individual rights (paragraph 1.7.). All of these factors lead to the conclusion that the paternalistic model of interaction between doctor and patient has run its course and, consequently, that there is a need to rethink the place of the patient in his interaction with the system, implying the recognition and introduction of new rights and obligations (paragraph 1.8.).

297. The opinion also points to the consequences of these evolutions for professionals. Medical and welfare staff must act as an adviser to their patient without, however, relinquishing their responsibility. Their task is, therefore, to provide care, information and support to the patient. They devise a therapeutic strategy based on hypotheses suggested by the patient's symptoms and the relationship with the patient. Thus, the patient has a legitimate right to request health professionals for a personalized assessment of his condition, which must make it possible to propose a treatment that is the most suitable in technical and psychological terms (paragraph 2.2.2.1.). And also, family members and patient associations have a crucial role to play in this context (paragraph 2.2.3.).

298. The opinion does not contain a call to the Commission to propose a Charter of patients' rights. Taking an original stance, it considers 'the affirmation of patients' rights as a human right on its own. It then refers to 'the European Charter of Patients' Rights, drawn up in 2002 by the Active Citizenship Network [which] proclaims 14 rights'.[348] The European Economic and Social Committee 'welcomes and acknowledges' (in the French version: *que le CESE apprécie et reconnaît*) these rights (paragraph 3.1. of the opinion). Whether this means that the European Economic and Social Committee has 'formally' acknowledged or recognized the Charter as some French authors have pretended is, however, less obvious.[349]

348. This is not correct as the Charter does not itself proclaim rights but proposes to proclaim such rights.

349. *Supra* n. 279, 107: *officiellement reconnu*; *supra* n. 335, 599: *formellement reconnue.*

B. Rights of Patients

299. The opinion is focused on the rights of patients, i.e., people using healthcare systems, whether they are healthy or sick, as defined by the World Health Organization (WHO) (paragraph 1.9.). The opinion considers three patients' rights that are linked horizontally or are preconditions for other rights (paragraph 3.1.). They are all considered to be inalienable rights (Title 3 of the Opinion).

1. Right to Information

300. The information in question primarily concerns the patient undergoing treatment. It must provide details of the person's illness, how it may evolve over time, the courses of treatment possible, including the associated benefits and risks, the health establishments or professionals providing this treatment, and the effects of the illness and the treatment on the person's day-to-day life. The provision of such information is particularly important in the case of chronic illness, dependence, disability or long-term treatment leading to changes in the daily lives of the person and his family and friends (paragraph 3.2.1.). Information is not an end in itself but a means of allowing a person to make free and informed choices. For that reason, the ways in which information is provided are as important as the information itself. They are part of a process which makes use of different information sources, including the Internet and telephone helpline services operated by associations, and where the patient can interact with a wide range of professionals, each of whom has his own role to play. The oral transmission of information is crucial. At regular intervals, the doctor must find out whether the patient understands the facts relating to his case and ascertain his level of satisfaction (paragraph 3.2.2.). In addition, irrespective of the person concerned, the patient's circle of family and friends must also be taken into account in the information process, especially if the patient is a child or a dependent elderly person. Obviously, the level of information provided will depend on the patient's state of health and capacity to decide for himself (paragraph 3.2.3.). It is desirable that the information on a person's state of health, the diagnostic and therapeutic steps taken and the ensuing results be recorded in a 'medical file'. The possibility of the patient accessing this file directly or through a doctor of his choice, according to his wishes, is also part of patient information and autonomy. In any moves to secure further information and transparency, an appropriate legal framework should, however, ensure that when the data is being recorded, it is not used for any purpose for which it is not intended. Efforts should be made to make sure that extreme vigilance is exercised as regards the use of such data, especially where it is electronically stored and sometimes also when it is transmitted across borders (paragraph 3.2.5.).

2. Right to Free and Informed Consent

301. The right of patients to participate in decisions affecting them must be affirmed. This does not mean the transfer of responsibility from doctor to patient but rather the prospect of them interacting in a therapeutic alliance, each maintaining his own position with his own rights and area of responsibility (paragraph 3.3.1.). The patient's consent does not apply automatically to all medical acts, now or in the future. Consent is not given once and for all, but rather, it has to be renewed before each important medical or surgical act. The consent of a patient who has been informed in this way must be explicit and expressed objectively. After having been given the requisite information, the patient may either accept or reject the course of action which has been proposed to him (paragraph 3.3.3.1.).

3. Right to Dignity

302. Under this heading must be included the right to privacy, the right to pain relief, the right to die in dignity, protection of the integrity of the human body, respect for private life and the principle of non-discrimination (paragraph 3.4.1.).

4. Other Individual Rights

303. Right to access to care for all, i.e., not just access to rights and social protection but to the full range of healthcare services and professionals without discrimination on the grounds of a person's social or economic position (paragraph 3.5.1.).

304. Right to high-quality care: every person, taking into account the state of his health, has the right to receive the most appropriate treatment and access to the best therapies and medicines, offering the best cost-effectiveness ratio (promotion of generic drugs). The right to high-quality care also implies the right to screening and therapeutic education, which calls for investment in resources and funding and adequate availability of properly trained professionals (paragraph 3.5.2.).

305. Right to prevention and safety of care: citizens want the health system to be built around and for people. They want to know more about the therapeutic strategies proposed to them, take part in personal and collective prevention efforts, and ensure that social choices, behaviour and consumption do not harm health (paragraph 3.5.3.).

C. Recommendations for Implementing Patients' Rights

306. The affirmation and application of these rights is a source of concern for many professionals, patients, health policymakers and user associations. There is an urgent need to move away from confrontation between the rights of some parties and the obligations of others. Respect for patients' rights also means a new distribution and balance for the obligations and responsibilities of professionals (paragraph 4.1.). In the interests of the common good, it is the collective responsibility to help professionals respond to these expectations by including ethical aspects and respect for the individual and his rights in their training and by rethinking the role of patient, user, consumer, family and citizen associations (paragraph 4.2.).

D. Towards an Affirmation of Collective Rights

307. The opinion closes with a Conclusion towards an affirmation of collective rights (paragraph 5). How effective individual rights turn out to be in practice will depend to a large extent on the collective responses which are made to support this initiative. That is why it is necessary to work for the adoption of health democracy, implying the collective involvement of all users and their representation in different parts of the system (paragraph 5.1.).

IV. Patient's Rights in the Interinstitutional Proclamation on the European Pillar of Social Rights

308. The European Pillar of Social Rights was jointly signed and solemnly proclaimed by the European Parliament, the Council and the Commission on 17 November 2017 at the Social Summit for Fair Jobs and Growth in Gothenburg, Sweden. According to Recital 13 in the Preamble: 'A stronger focus on employment and social performance is particular important to increase resilience and deepen the Economic and Monetary Union. *For this reason, the European Pillar of Social Rights is notably conceived for the euro area* (19 Member States, italics added) but it is addressed to all Member States.' The aim of the European Pillar is to serve *as a guide* (italics added) towards efficient employment and social outcomes when responding to current and future challenges which are directly aimed at fulfilling people's essential needs and towards ensuring better enactment and implementation of social rights (Recital 12). It is a non-binding instrument: 'For them to be legally enforceable, the principles and rights first require dedicated measures or legislation to be adopted at the appropriate level' (Recital 14 in the Preamble).

309. The main challenge remains to bring this reference framework to all citizens across the EU. Due to limited EU competence in the social field, implementation is done by the Member States in cooperation with social partners.[350]

310. Principle 16 of the European Pillar of Social Rights provides that 'Everyone has the right to timely access of affordable, preventive and curative healthcare of good quality.' In organizing the delivery of health services at the national and local level, the EU Member States are guided by the principles established in Article 35 of the Charter of Fundamental Rights of the European Union and Principle 16 of

350. N. Milotay, *At a glance. Implementation of the Social Pillar* (European Parliamentary Research Service, December 2017).

the European Pillar.[351] The European Pillar of Social Rights Action Plan stresses the importance of the European Health Union in building more accessible health systems and commits to improving accessibility metrics. The European Pillar is a joint commitment. The Commission works with the Member States in the framework of the European Semester and the Social Open Method of Coordination. In 2020, all the Member States received Country Specific Recommendations in the health area.[352]

311. According to Principle 18 of the European Pillar, everyone has the right to affordable long-term care services of good quality, in particular home care and community-based services. The European Care Strategy and the Council Recommendation on long-term care call for a person-centred approach in long-term care. The implementation of the Council Recommendation will be monitored by the Commission in the context of the European Semester and the Social Open Method of Coordination on the basis of the framework of indicators to be developed with the Social Protection Committee for this purpose.[353]

---

351. Answer given by Mr Andriukaitis on behalf of the European Commission to a written Parliamentary question by S. Kelly, Cross-border discrimination in public healthcare, 13 Mar. 2019, E-000451/2019.
352. Answer given by Ms Kyriakides on behalf of the European Commission to a written Parliamentary question by E. Tomac, Disparities regarding access to health and healthcare services, 17 Dec. 2021, E-004616/2021.
353. Answer given by Mr Schmit on behalf of the European Commission to a written Parliamentary question by S. Kympouropoulos, Transition from institutional care to home care and community-based services, 14 Feb. 2023, E-003788/2022.

Chapter 3. Patients' Rights and the Cross-Border Healthcare Directive[354]

§1. The Patients' Right to Healthcare

I. The Patients' Right to Healthcare

A. *The Patients' Right to Receive Healthcare in Another Member State*

312. Whether the Cross-Border Healthcare Directive creates a right to receive healthcare in another Member State is discussed. Recital 18 in the Preamble states that the Directive should not give any person an entitlement to enter, stay or reside in a Member State in order to receive healthcare in that State. However, Article 4.3 of the Directive provides that the principle of non-discrimination with regard to nationality has to be applied to patients from other Member States. The European Commission was not aware of circumstances in which a domestic patient is prioritized over a citizen coming from another Member State.[355] According to Davies, 'this discrimination ban should serve as a limited right of access to healthcare in other Member States'.[356] Moreover, Article 7.5 of the Directive provides that Member States may adopt provisions in accordance with the TFEU aimed at ensuring that patients enjoy the same rights when receiving cross-border healthcare as they would have enjoyed if they had received healthcare in a comparable situation in the Member State of affiliation. Thus, a mere possibility, not an obligation.[357] According to the European Commission, the Directive 2011/24/EU provides rules 'for facilitating' the access to safe and high-quality cross-border healthcare and promotes cooperation on healthcare between Member States, with full respect to national competence in organizing and delivering healthcare. Member States must properly implement these rules, and the Commission, as guardian of the Treaties, monitors the implementation and promotes cooperation on healthcare between Member States, with full respect to national competencies in organizing and delivering healthcare.[358] Article 11, however, obliges the Member States to prohibit 'any

354. J. van de Gronden & M. Veenbrink, 'EHDS and Free Movement of Patients: What EU Intervention is Needed?', 31 *European Journal of Health Law* 249–283 (2024), Title 5: The Current EU Legal Framework for the Free Movement of Patients.
355. *Supra* n. 352.
356. G. Davies, *Legislating for Patients' Rights,* in J.W. van de Gronden et al. (eds), *Health Care and EU Law* 197 (The Hague: Asser Press 2011).
357. *See* for critical remarks P. Quinn & P. De Hert, 'The European Patients' Rights Directive: A Clarification and Codification of Individual Rights Relating to Cross-Border Healthcare and Novel Initiatives Aimed at Improving Pan-European Healthcare Cooperation', *Medical Law International* 22–23 (2012).
358. Answer given by Ms Kyriakides on behalf of the European Commission to a written Parliamentary question by C. Daly, Administration of cross-border healthcare schemes in Ireland, 3 Jul. 2023, E-001441/2023.

restrictions on recognition of individual prescriptions' (*see* paragraph 20). According to Sovig, the Directive 'in this respect is establishing a right to access to medicines on a European level'.[359] Ensuring patient access to medical devices and/or medicinal products is also linked to their reimbursement, which is a Member State competence.[360]

313. Also Article 5c and its 'sibling' Article 11.1. 'may be regarded as a genuine right to access to healthcare established by the Directive'.[361] If a patient has received cross-border healthcare and where medical follow-up proves necessary, Member States are obliged to ensure that 'the follow up is available'. Recital 21 in the Preamble nuances the application of the non-discrimination principle: 'Nothing in this Directive should oblige healthcare providers to accept for planned treatment patients from other Member States or to prioritise them to the detriment of other patients, for instance by increasing the waiting time for treatment of other patients. Inflows of patients may create a demand exceeding the capacities existing in a Member State for a given treatment. In such exceptional cases, the Member State should retain the possibility to remedy the situation on the grounds of public health, in accordance with Articles 52 and 62 TFEU.' In line with this, Article 4.2, the second sentence of the Directive, determines the conditions in order that a Member State of treatment may adopt measures regarding access to treatment aimed at fulfilling its fundamental responsibility to ensure sufficient and permanent access to healthcare within its territory. Such measures have to be limited to what is necessary and proportionate, may not constitute a means of arbitrary discrimination and have to be made publicly available in advance. This provision enables Member States to limit the entry of patients coming from other Member States. Only (then) did four Member States (UK, Denmark, Estonia and Romania) report that they had put in place such measures; however, none reported having used them.[362]

314. In line with Article 168 TFEU and the implementation of Directive 2011/24/EC, the Commission encourages Member States to support cooperation in healthcare and complementarity of health systems in border regions, including with its Interreg programmes, as part of the EU's Cohesion Policy. Belgium and Luxembourg signed a bilateral agreement for cooperation in healthcare to improve access

---

359. K.H. Sovig, *Convergence and Divergence in Patients' Rights,* in A. den Exter (ed.), *Cross-Border Health Care and European Union Law* 39 (Rotterdam: Erasmus University Press 2017).
360. Answer given by Ms Kyriakides on behalf of the European Commission to a written Parliamentary question of S. Pietikäinen, Ensuring equal access to breakthrough medical innovations for European patients, 12 Sep. 2023, E-002126/2023.
361. K.H. Sovig, *Convergence and Divergence in Patients' Rights,* in A. den Exter (ed.), *Cross-Border Health Care and European Union Law* 38–39 (Rotterdam: Erasmus University Press 2017).
362. *Supra* n. 352.

to and continuity of care in the border area. This is the outcome of project COSAN funded by the Interreg Greater Region 2014–2020 between Belgium, France, Germany and Luxembourg.[363]

B. The Special Case of Access to Organs for Transplantation

315. According to Article 1.3b, the Directive is not applicable to the allocation of and access to organs for the purpose of organ transplants. According to Recital 15, 'given their specificity, access to and the allocation of organs for the purpose of organ transplants should fall outside the scope of this Directive'. This specificity is not explained, but it undoubtedly has to be traced back to the scarcity of organs for transplantation because of the limited numbers of living and deceased donors. Most Member States have (very long) waiting lists for organs for transplantation. In *Watts,* the CJEU has considered waiting lists to be a legitimate instrument for distributing scarce health resources.[364] However, scarcity and waiting lists also exist for other therapeutic procedures, such as heart surgery. Scarcity, as such, does not legitimise the exclusion of access to organs for transplantation from the Directive. The justification is to be found in the principle of non-discrimination with regard to nationality. Different Member States, among which Belgium, use nationality as a selection criterion to be allowed to be on the waiting list for organ transplantation. Without the explicit exclusion of access to organs for transplantation from the Directive, such selection would have been a violation of EU Law.[365]

§2. Patients' Rights to Information

316. The Directive imposes obligations to inform a patient both upon the Member State of treatment and the Member State of affiliation.[366] For obvious reasons, these obligations differ. The Member State of affiliation has mainly an obligation to

363. Answer given by Ms Kyriakides on behalf of the European Commission on a written Parliamentary question of Parliamentary question of T. Metz and Ch. Goerens, Access to healthcare and emergency services in cross-border territories (case of Alzette-Belval, Luxembourg/France), 14 Jun. 2023, E-001173/2023.
364. CJEU, *Watts*, Case C-372/04, ECLI:EU:C:2006:325.
365. H. Nys, 'Organ Transplantation and the Proposed Directive on Cross Border Care', 17 *European Journal of Health Law* 427–431 (2010); H. Nys, *The Exclusion of Organ Transplantation from the Cross-Border Care Directive: Boundary or Opportunity?,* in M.A. Weimar et al. (eds), *Organ Transplantation: Ethical, Legal and Psychosocial Aspects. Expanding the European Platform* 142–147 (Lengerich: Pabst Science Publishers 2011); H.D.C. Roscam Abbing, 'Editorial. Human Organs for Transplantation: Self-Sufficiency, a European Perspective', 26 *European Journal of Health Law* 96 (2019) who pleas for the introduction of a standardized (non-)donor card in Europe, given that people move around Europe.
366. H. Nys, 'The Information Rights of the Patient in the European Patients' Rights Directive', in J. Loureiro, A.D. Pereira & C. Barbosa (Coord.), *Direito Da Saudo. Estudos em Homenagem ao Prof. Doutor Guilherme de Oliveira,* 3: 67–82 (Coimbra: Almedina 2016); A.-M. Van den Bossche & P. Ploscar, 'Rights of Dental Patients in the EU: A Legal Assessment', 30(1) *Journal of Forensic Odonto-Stomatology* 4–11 (November 2012).

inform a person who intends to travel to another Member State to receive healthcare, concerning reimbursement conditions. This procedural information facilitates the application of the right to receive cross-border healthcare. The Member State of treatment and the healthcare providers offering services in that Member State have substantial information obligations in order to clarify the nature of the healthcare and the circumstances in which it is provided.

I. The Patients' Right to Information with Regard to Reimbursement

317. The Member State of affiliation ensures that there are mechanisms in place to provide patients on their request with information on their rights and entitlements in that Member State relating to receiving cross-border healthcare, in particular as regards the terms and conditions for reimbursement of costs and procedures for accessing and determining those entitlements and for appeal and redress if patients consider that their rights have not been respected, in accordance with Article 9 (Article 5b). According to Article 6.4, this information has to be provided to patients by a National Contact Point for Cross-Border Healthcare (NCP) that each Member State has to designate following Article 6.1 (*see* paragraph 316). This information has to be easily accessible and made available by electronic means and in formats accessible to people with disabilities, as appropriate (Article 6.5). This obligation is an enforceable one.[367]

II. The Patients' Right to Information Regarding the Nature of Healthcare and the Circumstances in Which It Is Provided

A. *Information on Request of the Patient by the NCP of the Member State of Treatment*

318. Article 6.1 obliges each Member State to designate one or more NCPs for cross-border healthcare and communicate their names and contact details to the Commission. The Commission and the Member States make this information publicly available. Member States ensure that the NCP consult with patient organizations, healthcare providers and healthcare insurers. According to Article 6.2, the NCP facilitate the exchange of information and cooperate closely with each other and with the Commission. They provide patients *on request* with contact details of NCPs in other Member States (italics added). On 4 June 2019, the European Court of Auditors (ECA) published a special report on EU actions for cross-border healthcare. In its report, the ECA concluded that despite the cooperation between the Member States has increased thanks to the EU's cross-border healthcare measures, the benefits for patients are still limited. It made recommendations focusing, among others, on the Commission's support for the NCP. The ECA and the Commission

367. V. Michel, 'Entre logique économique et sanitaire: la conception des droits des patients en matière de soins de santé transfrontaliers', *Revue des Affaires Européens* 514–515 (2011).

agreed to an action plan to implement the ECA's recommendations, and this has resulted in the publication of a Toolbox and Manual for Patients to support the work of the NCP.[368]

1. Relevant Information on the Standards and Guidelines on Quality of Safety

319. Article 4.2a, read together with Article 4.1b, obliges the Member State of treatment to ensure that patients receive from the NCP, upon request, relevant information on the standards and guidelines on quality and safety laid down by that Member State, including information on which healthcare providers[369] are subject to these standards and guidelines. The question arises of what 'relevant' information is in this context and who decides on this. A general answer to this question cannot be given (*see* paragraph 325).[370]

320. The Commission initially intended to oblige Member States to define standards for care provided on their territory and to set in place mechanisms aimed at ensuring that providers meet such standards. However, since this would come close to a minimum harmonization, most Member States favoured introducing duties to provide patients with information enabling them to make an informed choice.[371] However, giving this kind of information requires that effective mechanisms for quality of care exist in each Member State.[372] At least Member States might feel pressure to instal such standards and guidelines and/or adjust or evaluate them through mutual comparison.[373]

321. Article 4.1b does not specify what is meant by a standard on quality and safety.[374] According to Roscam Abbing, it is questionable whether the Directive can be considered a legal basis justifying standardization of healthcare services because it is for the Member States to ensure that such services are provided in accordance with the standards and guidelines of quality and security in the Member State of

368. *See* ec.europa.eu/health/sites/health/files/crossborder_care/docs/2019_ncptoolbox_manualpatients_en.pdf; *see also* the answer given by Mr Andriukaitis on behalf of the European Commission to a Parliamentary question of S. in't Veld, EU cross-border healthcare measures, 23 Aug. 2019, E-002425/2019.
369. Healthcare provider means any natural or legal person or any other entity legally providing healthcare on the territory of a Member State (Art. 1g).
370. D. Delnoij & W. Sauter, 'Patient Information under the EU Patients' Rights Directive', 21 *European Journal of Public Health* 272 (2011).
371. A.P. Van Der Meij, 'The New Directive on Patients' Rights in Cross-Border Healthcare', 18 *Maastricht Journal of Comparative and European Law* 389–390 (2011).
372. H. Legido-Quigley et al., 'Cross-Border Healthcare in Europe: Clarifying Patients' Rights', 342 *British Medical Journal* 365 (2011).
373. M. Peeters, 'Free Movement of Patients: Directive 2011/24 on the Application of Patients' Rights in Cross-Border Healthcare', 19 *European Journal of Health Law* 55 (2012).
374. H.D.C. Roscam Abbing, 'Patients' rights to access to quality of healthcare throughout the European Union: the role of EU legislation', in J. Loureiro, A.D. Pereira & C. Barbosa (Coord.), *Direito Da Saudo. Estudos em Homenagem ao Prof. Doutor Guilherme de Oliveira*, 3: 44 (Coimbra: Almedina 2016).

treatment.[375] The adoption and revision of guidelines concerning the treatment of patients affected by a medical condition is not part of the competence of the Commission.[376]

322. The NCPs are not expected to inform patients about the quality of healthcare in other Member States.[377] At least not on their own initiative, one could add. Hendriks expresses his 'surprise' on this and refers to a study that shows that only a few NCPs provide information on the quality and safety of healthcare in other Member States. He finds this 'rather peculiar if not alarming. When one wants or has to undergo treatment in another Member State, easily accessible and comparable information about the quality of the care offered is indispensable to making an informed choice'.[378]

2. Information on Supervision and Assessment of Healthcare Providers

323. The obligatory information based on Article 4.2a also regards provisions for supervision and assessment of healthcare providers.

3. Information on the Accessibility of Hospitals for Persons with Disabilities

324. Article 4.2a also obliges the Member State of treatment to ensure that patients receive from the NCP, upon request, information on the accessibility of hospitals for persons with disabilities.

4. Information on a Specific Provider's Right to Provide Services[379]

325. The question of what 'relevant' information is (*see* paragraph 315) supposed to be has been answered to a certain degree in the Directive itself. In order to enable patients to make use of their rights in relation to cross-border healthcare,[380]

375. *Ibid.*, 45.
376. Answer given by Ms Kyriakides on behalf of the European Commission on a written Parliamentary question of G. Gancia, Evaluation of the administration of triptorelin in paediatrics for the treatment of gender dysphoria, 4 Apr. 2024, E-000242/2024.
377. A. Hendriks, 'Editorial. High-Quality of Care Throughout Europe: But Do We Speak the Same Language?', 23 *European Journal of Health Law* 3 (2016).
378. *Ibid.*
379. L. Bongers, *Moving Towards European Convergence in Classical Individual Patient's Rights. Can the New Individual Patients' Rights to Information under Article 6 (3) of Directive 2011/24/EU Contribute?*, Doctoral thesis, University of Maastricht, 2022, 363 p.
380. Cross-border healthcare means healthcare provided or prescribed in a Member State other than the Member State of affiliation (Art. 1e). It is generally considered to be planned healthcare. *See* however G. Strban (ed.), *Activity Report 2016. Access to Healthcare in Cross-Border Situation,* Brussels, European Commission, DG Employment, Social Affairs and Industry, 2017, 37, referring to 'the lack of distinction between unplanned and planned care in the Directive'; *see also supra* nn. 62, 23, footnote 138.

NCPs in the Member State of treatment have to provide them with information concerning healthcare providers, including, on request, information on a specific provider's right to provide services or any restrictions on its practice (Article 6.3). Healthcare providers include medical specialists. There are no plans to create a register of medical specialists at the EU level, making it easier for patients to consult a specialist.[381]

5. Information on Patients' Rights, Complaints Procedures and Mechanisms for Seeking Remedies

326. Article 6.3 also obliges to provide information on patients' rights, complaints procedures, and mechanisms for seeking remedies according to the legislation of the Member State. The Directive does not clarify what 'patients' rights' in this context mean. It probably refers to the classic patients' rights, such as the right to information and the right to informed consent.

6. Information on the Legal and Administrative Options Available to Settle Disputes, Including in the Event of Harm Arising from Cross-Border Healthcare

327. Finally, Article 6.3 obliges to provide information on the legal and administrative options available to settle disputes, including in the event of harm arising from cross-border healthcare. The obligation to inform mobile patients of mechanisms for their protection and for seeking remedies in the event of harm from healthcare provided on their territory has to be understood against the background of Article 4.2c and 2d. According to those provisions, the Member State of treatment has to ensure that there are transparent complaints procedures and mechanisms in place for patients in order for them to seek remedies in accordance with the legislation of that Member State of treatment if they suffer harm arising from the healthcare they receive as well as systems of professional liability insurance, or a guarantee or similar arrangement that is equivalent or essentially comparable as regards its purpose and which is appropriate to the nature and the extent of the risk. It is difficult to imagine that only mobile patients in a given Member State of treatment could profit from these mechanisms. It is clear that the Directive also has important consequences for domestic patients. This is also illustrated by Recital 23 in the Preamble: 'Systems for addressing harm in the Member State of treatment should be without prejudice to the possibility for Member States to extend the coverage of their domestic systems to patients from their country seeking healthcare abroad, where this is more appropriate for the patient.'[382]

---

381. Answer given by Ms Kyriakides on behalf of the European Commission to a written Parliamentary question of C. Schneider, Cross-border healthcare services, 1 May 2021, E-000799/2021.
382. *Supra* n. 366, 3: 74.

7. Information on NCP in Other Member States

328. NCP provides patients on request with contact details of NCPs in other Member States (Article 6.2 *in fine*).

8. Language in Which Information Is Provided by NCP

329. According to Berki, 'the language gap constitutes a serious obstacle in cross-border healthcare situations: if the patient and the healthcare professional do not speak the same language, the risk of misunderstanding and – as a consequence – of misdiagnosis increases significantly … .'[383] Concerning the language that NCP have to use when providing the aforementioned information, the Directive is ambiguous. On the one hand, Article 4.5 provides that the Directive does not affect laws and regulations in the Member States on the use of languages which means that the information mentioned in, among others, Article 4.2a must only be provided in the official language(s). However, Member States may choose to deliver information in languages other than those which are official languages in the Member State concerned. Dubuis considers this rightly as only a minimal obligation.[384] On the other hand, Article 6.5 provides that the information referred to in *this Article* has to be easily accessible and made available by electronic means and in formats accessible to people with disabilities, as appropriate (italics added). 'This Article' is not limited to Article 6 because Article 6.3 explicitly refers to the information mentioned in Article 4.2a. Information in the patient's own language is not necessarily 'easily accessible' but anyhow more easily accessible than a language one does not know at all or less well. According to de Ruijter, 'it does not need to be ensured that the patient has understood the information, for instance by taking into account cultural differences, expectations and the organization of the healthcare system'.[385]

330. The information to be provided by the NCP is information to patients at their request. For this reason, this information cannot be considered to be only 'collective information'.[386]

383. G. Berki, 'Patient Mobility in the EU: A Playground for All of Us?', *Belgisch Tijdschrift voor Sociale Zekerheid (Belgian Journal on Social Security)* 69 (2019).
384. *Supra* n. 279, 712.
385. *Supra* n. 5, 171.
386. In this sense, S. De La Rosa, 'The Directive on Cross-Border Healthcare or the Art of Codifying Complex Case Law', 49 *Common Market Law Review* 36–37 (2012).

B. Information to Be Provided by Healthcare Providers

331. The Member State of treatment has to ensure that healthcare providers provide relevant information[387] to help individual patients make an informed choice (Article 4.2b). This article does not refer to a request of the patient which means that such information has to be given spontaneously. Nevertheless, Recital 20 in the Preamble states: 'furthermore, healthcare providers should provide patients *on request* with information on specific aspects of the healthcare services they offer and on the treatment options' (italics added). L. Dubouis is also of the opinion that this information only has to be provided on request.[388] This is not in accordance with the clear text of the Directive that takes precedence.

332. Article 4.2b contains a non-comprehensive enumeration of the subjects of this 'relevant' information:[389] (a) the treatment options and the availability, quality and safety of the healthcare they provide in the Member State of treatment; (b) clear invoices and clear information on prices; (c) information on their authorization or registration status, their insurance cover or other means of personal or collective protection with regard to professional liability. Article 20.1. of the Directive requires the Commission to 'draw up a report on the operation of this Directive and submit it to the European Parliament and to the Council' by 25 October 2015[390] and every three years thereafter.[391] In the 2018 report, it is noted that 'the requirement for professional liability insurance came up during the completeness checks as a problematic issue in several Member States. Even if healthcare providers *de facto* have liability insurance, in practice, there was often a lack of legislation requiring such systems to be in place'.[392]

333. Article 4.2b further provides that to the extent that healthcare providers already provide patients resident in the Member State of treatment with relevant information on these subjects, the Directive does not oblige healthcare providers to provide more extensive information to patients from other Member States. 'This apparent restriction instead implies a major expansion: extending the right to information needed to inform choice to all citizens of the different Member States, even when they are not exercising their rights to consume cross-border healthcare. The interaction between the two halves of Article 4.2b is therefore not just that they are corresponding vessels – in that if limited information is available nationally more must be provided for border crossing patients and vice versa, if ample information

387. The draft Directive required *all* relevant information, W. Sauter, *Harmonisation in Healthcare: The EU Patients' Rights Directive,* Research Paper Tilec, 2011, No. 06, 20.
388. L. Dubouis, 'La directive n° 2011/24 relative à l'application des droits des patients en matière des soins de santé', *Revue de Droit Sanitaire et Social* 1068 (2011).
389. The references to information concerning 'outcome of the healthcare provided' have been purged from the draft Directive, *supra* n. 387.
390. Commission Report on the operation of Directive 2011/24/EU, COM(2015) 421 final, 4 Sep. 2015.
391. Report from the Commission on the Operation of Directive 2011/24/EU, COM(2022) 210 final, 12 May 2022, 17: 'While the Directive was successful in enshrining patients' rights, for those rights to be fully enjoyed they need to be known by patients'.
392. Report from the Commission on the operation of Directive 2011/24/EU, COM(2018) 651 final, 21 Sep. 2018, 5.

is provided nationally less is required for patients from abroad – but that a comparable level of comparable information must presumably be provided, as a result, to both kinds of patients. In other words, this Directive may eventually have much more impact on national policies than on cross-border consumption of care. It will trigger national governments to initiate the measurement and publication of quality of care indicators, if they have not done so already. More importantly, these quality indicators have to be relevant for consumer choice.'[393] Also, according to Palm and Baeten, 'the information obligation towards healthcare providers in article 4.2b may indeed help to increase transparency, including for domestic patients'.[394]

334. Especially the 'relevant' information on treatment options and the availability, quality and safety of the care provided raises questions. Should the relevant information concerned facilitate making choices between treatments in different Member States or just between treatment options? At least the latter appears probable, according to Sauter.[395] According to this author, 'as regards relevant information, the main issue would appear to be whether quality (as well as availability and safety) information will have to be made available by the individual healthcare providers in a format that will make it comparable between Member States. To do so would be something like reaching for the holy grail of consumer choice for healthcare in the European Union. If this view is taken, a number of issues are unresolved: presumably, the information would be at a minimum have to be comparable but not actually presented as part of a comparison with other providers in the Member State of treatment or elsewhere. This raises the question what kind of standards would be needed to make information enabling patient choice comparable and who set these standards? Or could there be competing standards allowing some degree of comparison either nationally or between (sets of) Member States. The Directive provides no mechanism for this'.[396] Should the information be presented in a comparative format assessing provider's performance in terms of quality and safety? The Directive does not seem to suggest this in any way.[397] A major challenge for policymakers and for the research community lies in defining what is relevant and what constitutes useful information. Consumers define quality of care differently from how professionals define it. Consumers view quality in terms of access, costs, having a choice of doctors, having doctors who spend enough time with them and doctor qualifications. Professionals present quality information based on performance indicators and on provider's characteristics and services.[398] According to Van Der Meij, the Directive has not much added value in this respect, given the fact that factual information to enable patient choice is often hardly available at the national level.[399]

393. *Supra* n. 370, 271.
394. W. Palm & R. Baeten, 'The Quality and Safety Paradox in the Patients' Rights Directive', 21 *European Journal of Public Health* 273 (2011).
395. *Supra* n. 387.
396. *Supra* n. 370, 271.
397. *Supra* n. 372.
398. *Supra* n. 370, 272.
399. *Supra* n. 371, 390.

335. Some authors understand the obligation to provide information to help patients make an informed choice in a different way. According to Davies, making an informed choice is something that can only be achieved if the patient understands their prognosis, the possible treatments and their risks and side effects. This provision can, therefore, only be sensibly read as requiring Member States to ensure their doctors fully inform patients about all these things. It is hard to object to this idea in abstract terms, according to Davies, but if translated into concrete rules, it may well conflict with well-established medical traditions. The idea that doctors should fully inform patients about risks, side effects or prognoses may well be accepted in some States, but it will not be practised in others. Legislating a patients' right to information is also an intervention in the autonomy and freedom of the doctor. In this sensitive context, an EU demand for national implementing legislation addressing such matters may be expected to provoke some resistance, perhaps intermittently outrage.[400]

336. In my opinion, the obligation to inform patients in order to make an informed choice in Article 4.2b does not coincide with the obligation to inform patients about their health status and the risks and side effects of possible treatments with a view to giving informed consent. There are no indications at all in the Preamble of the Directive that Article 4.2b has to be understood in this sense. The right to receive information to make an informed choice is not the same as the 'classic' right to information about one's health status or the 'classic' right to give an informed consent, although one cannot deny that there is some overlap between them. Also, according to de Ruijter, 'the Directive itself does not safeguard the right to informed consent'.[401] The 'classic' rights to information and consent were already well established in EU law prior to the Directive (*see* above, Article 3.2a Charter of Fundamental Rights of the EU, paragraph 242).

337. It is, therefore, not a surprise that the Directive does not harmonize the right to informed consent. In this respect, the assessment of the Directive by the Active Citizenship Network offers an interesting perspective. It looked at the incorporation of the European Charter of Patients' Rights (*see* paragraphs 270 et seq.) in the Directive, and it came to the following conclusion: 'Of the fourteen rights of the Charter, those most greatly absorbed by the Directive are six in number: the right to access; the right to information; the right to free choice; the right to innovation; the right to complain and to compensation and the right to privacy.'[402] Thus, the Active

---

400. *Supra* n. 356, 206 (discussing Art. 5.1c of the proposed Directive which had the same contents as Art. 4.2b); *see also supra* n. 359, 43 and 54 referring to 'the right to receive information and to provide informed consent' in the context of Art. 4.2; *see also supra* n. 279, 208: 'en effet, le terme de "choix éclairé" semble se rapprocher de la notion de "consentement éclairé"'; however at p. 209 she writes: 'Par ailleurs, on ne trouve aucune mention relative au consentement et le droit au consement libre n'est donc pas non plus reconnu dans cette directive.' *See* more in general H. Nys, 'Editorial. The Right to Informed Choice and the Patients' Rights Directive', 19 *European Journal of Health Law* 327–331 (2012).

401. *Supra* n. 5, 174.

402. Active Citizenship Network, *The EU Charter of Patients' Rights, a Civic Assessment* 77 (2011), available on www.activecitizenship.net.

Citizenship Network concludes that the right to informed consent is not among the rights of the Charter that have been incorporated in the Directive, although the Network 'fought to get the contents of the Charter included in the Directive'.[403]

338. The wording of Article 4.2b indicates that the right to information is more an individual than a collective right.[404] The provision does not state literally that the information has to be *given* to the individual patient. The information has to *help* individual patients make an informed choice, and this leaves room for a more collective form of informing patients. This may be the reason why De Grove is classifying this provision under the heading *droits à l'information collective* (rights to collective information).[405] Because the first addressee of this provision is the individual patient seeking cross-border healthcare who needs the information in order to make an informed choice regarding the healthcare provider who will treat him or her, it is almost evident that he or she has to be informed individually. Looking at it from this perspective, this right to information is closely related to the right to freely choose a healthcare provider. This is also a 'classic' patients' right recognized in a number of patients' rights Charters (*see* above, Article 3d of the European Charter on the Rights of Patients, paragraph 259 and Article 5 of the European Charter of Patients' Rights, paragraph 278). The 'classic' patients' right to free choice is often considered as a 'negative' right or freedom: a patient should not be compelled to be treated by a healthcare provider who is not freely chosen. In a more modern and progressive interpretation, the right to free choice becomes a 'positive' right: the right to select a healthcare provider on the basis of relevant information. The obligation to give information to individual patients in order to make an informed choice fits very well in this new approach.

339. Some authors have rightly expressed doubts about whether healthcare providers are the best placed to provide this kind of information because the information they provide could not be objective and could present a conflict of interests.[406] Moreover, informing patients in an individual way on these aspects is a time-consuming and costly procedure. This pleads for a more collective approach. Interestingly, Recital 20 in the Preamble of the Directive leaves room for such an approach, be it without neglecting an individual one: 'Nothing should prevent the Member State of treatment from also obliging other actors than the healthcare providers, such as insurance providers or public authorities, to provide the information on specific aspects of the healthcare services offered, if that would be more appropriate with regard to the organisation of its healthcare system.'

403. *Ibid.*, 73.
404. J. Legemaate, 'Patients' Rights Relating to Patient Safety', in J. Loureiro, A.D. Pereira & C. Barbosa (Coord.), *Direito Da Saudo. Estudos em Homenagem ao Prof. Doutor Guilherme de Oliveira*, 3: 16 (Coimbra: Almedina 2016).
405. N. De Grove-Valdeyron, 'La Directive sur les droits des patients en matière de soins de santé transfrontaliers. Véritable statut juridique européen du patient ou simple clarification d'un régime de mobilité?', *Revue Trimestrielle de Droit Européen* 318 (2011).
406. *Supra* n. 394.

§3. The Patients' Right to Healthcare That Is Safe and of Good Quality

340. Several provisions in the Directive regard different aspects of the patients' right to healthcare that is safe and of good quality.[407]

I. Healthcare Corresponding with National and Union Quality and Safety Standards

341. According to Article 1, the aim of the Directive is to 'facilitating the access to safe and high-quality cross-border healthcare'. Taking into account the principles of universality, access to good quality care, equity and solidarity, cross-border healthcare has to be provided in accordance with standards and guidelines on quality and safety laid down by the Member State of treatment and Union legislation on safety standards (Article 4.1b and c). The Directive itself does not contribute to the development of a standard of care in Europe.[408] There is no European regulation that determines the standard of care across the EU, and any harmonizing effort in this respect was excluded from the Directive.[409] Also, according to van Leeuwen, 'there has not been any harmonisation of medical standards at the European level'.[410] According to Roscam Abbing, the Directive has had the effect that the legal duties and responsibilities of the EU for safe health products and services have increased.[411] The Commission has gradually broadened its activities in the fields of patient safety and quality of healthcare. The Luxembourg Declaration on Patient Safety of 5 April 2005 considers access to high-quality healthcare as a key human right recognized and valued by the EU, its institutions and the citizens of Europe. Accordingly, patients have a right to expect that every effort is made to ensure their safety as users of all health services. However, Hervey rightly notes that the Directive 'imposes no obligations on Member States *to improve* quality of healthcare'.[412]

342. In the Council Conclusions on 'Common Values and Principles in European Union Health Systems' of June 2006,[413] access to good quality care is considered one of the overarching values. Quality and safety are seen as important operational principles of this value, shared across the EU.[414] According to Axmin,

---

407. *See*, for a discussion of the right to quality healthcare and EU competition law, D. Fornaciari, 'Quality Health Care in the European Union Thanks to Competition Law', *International Journal of Environmental Research and Public Health* 1–8 (2010).
408. *Supra* n. 359, 40.
409. *Supra* n. 5, 170; N. Misic Radanovic & I. Vukusic, 'Causation in Medical Malpractice', *EU Comparative Law Issues and Challenges* 773–775 (2020).
410. B. van Leeuwen, 'The Doctor, the Patient, and EU Law: The Impact of Free Movement on Quality Standards in the Healthcare Sector', 41 *European Law Review* 647 (2016).
411. H. Roscam Abbing, 'Patients' Rights to Quality of Healthcare: How Satisfactory are the European Union's Regulatory Policies?', 19 *European Journal of Health Law* 415–416 (2012).
412. T. Hervey, *Patient Mobility, Solidarity and Equal Access,* in A. Den Exter (ed.), *Cross-Border Health Care and European Union Law* 28 (Rotterdam: Erasmus University Press 2017).
413. *OJ* 2006, C 146/1-3.
414. *Supra* n. 412.

the reference in Recital 5 in the Preamble of the Directive means that the common values and principles shared across the European healthcare systems are binding on the Member States of treatment and are to serve as guiding principles for the provision of cross-border healthcare.[415] In its 2009 Recommendation on Patient Safety, the Council expressed a more general view of patient safety in the EU context. The Recommendation focuses on empowering and informing citizens and patients.[416]

II. Quality and Safety as a Justification for Prior Authorization

343. The right to healthcare that is safe and of good quality is also at stake in Chapter III of the Directive that deals with the reimbursement of cross-border healthcare. According to Article 7.1, the Member State of affiliation ensures that the costs incurred by an insured person who receives cross-border healthcare are reimbursed if the healthcare in question is among the benefits to which the insured person is entitled in the Member State of affiliation. This article contains a clear, precise and unconditional obligation imposed on Member States, intended to confer rights on individuals such that they are able to rely directly on that provision before a national court.[417] The Member State of affiliation cannot make the reimbursement of costs of cross-border healthcare subject to prior authorization except in the situations provided for in Article 8 (Article 7.8). Article 8.2 provides for three cases where a prior authorization may be justified. Two of them are relevant for the quality and the safety of the healthcare, 'the real innovation of the Directive in its codification exercise'.[418] In its third report on the operation of Directive 2011/24/EU3 (2022),[419] the Commission invited Member States to reassess the national measures limiting patients' access to cross-border healthcare.[420] In light of Court of Justice case law, a requirement for prior authorization is a restriction to the free movement of services.[421]

A. The Treatment Presents a Particular Risk for the Patient or the Population

344. A prior authorization is justified when the treatment presents a particular risk for the patient or the population (Article 8.2b). Recital 43 in the Preamble is rather limited in explaining the motifs for this justification: 'It is also important to take into consideration the general principle of ensuring the safety of the patient, in

415. *Supra* n. 64, 195.
416. *Supra* n. 404, 11.
417. CJEU, *Centraal Administratie Kantoor,* Case C-636/19, 29 *European Journal of Health Law* 296–306 (2022).
418. *Supra* n. 386, 41.
419. Com (2022), 210 final, 12 May 2022.
420. Answer given by Ms Kyriakides on behalf of the European Commission to a written Parliamentary question of S. Pietikäinen, Compliance in Finland with Directive 2011/24/EU of the European Parliament and of the Council on the application of patients' rights in cross-border healthcare, 6 Jul. 2022, E-001706/2022.
421. CJEU, *WO,* C-777/18, EU:C;2020:745, para. 58.

a sector well known for information asymmetry, when managing a prior authorisation system.' This ground for justification has not yet been acknowledged in the case law of the ECJ and has been added to the Directive at the request of the Council.[422] According to van de Gronden, one has probably to do with, for instance, an outbreak of a virus where cross-border care could lead to the further spread of the virus.[423] Or one could imagine patients wishing to travel with highly infectious diseases or patients who have highly unstable conditions that might not allow them to safely make long-distance journeys.[424] Whether the European legislator had this kind of situation in mind is, however, not obvious. The Directive envisages treatments that present a particular risk, not patients with such a risk. Moreover, these patients, most of the time, need hospital treatment, in which case a prior authorization is justified under Article 8.2a (healthcare subjected to planning requirements). According to Peeters, this provision may envisage other kinds of risks, such as those related to experimental methods or treatments of low quality.[425]

B. *Serious and Specific Concerns Relating to the Quality or Safety of the Care Provided by a Healthcare Provider*

345. A prior authorization is also justified when healthcare is provided by a healthcare provider that, on a case-by-case basis, could give rise to serious and specific concerns relating to the quality or safety of the care, with the exception of healthcare which is subject to Union legislation ensuring a minimum level of safety and quality throughout the Union (Article 8.2c). Also, this justification for prior authorization raises a lot of questions, including the exception to it. Like in the first situation, there is no case law of the CJEU that provides some clarification. According to van de Gronden, the reverse is true: the CJEU has rejected in the past the pretended low quality of cross-border care and refused reimbursement for such care.[426] In *Stamatelaki,* the Greek authorities had refused to reimburse the costs incurred during an admission to a private hospital in the United Kingdom. The Greek legislation excluded reimbursement for the cost of treatment in private hospitals abroad except in situations of children. The CJEU considered it 'necessary to reject the Greek Government's argument relating to the fact that Greek social security institutions did not check the quality of treatment provided in private hospitals in another Member State'.[427] According to the CJEU, the fact remained that private hospitals located in other Member States are also subject, in those Member States,

422. *Supra* n. 405, 311–312.
423. J.W. van de Gronden, 'Richtlijn Rechten van de patiënt bij grensoverschrijdende gezondheidszorg: veel huiswerk voor de Nederlandse zorgwetgever?', *SEW* 378 (2011).
424. *Supra* n. 356, 56.
425. M. Peeters, 'Richtlijn 2011/24 betreffende de toepassing van de rechten van de patiënt bij grensoverschrijdende zorg: impact op de (Belgische) gezondheidszorg', 17 *Tijdschrift voor Gezondheidsrecht/Revue Droit de la Santé* 99 (2011–2012).
426. *Supra* n. 423, 379.
427. CJEU, *Stamatelaki,* Case C-444/05, ECLI:EU:C:2007:731, para. 36; *see* C.M. Rieder, 'The Application and Interpretation of the EU Charter in the Context of Cross-Border Movement of Patients', 22 *Columbia Journal of European Law* 475–476 (2016).

to quality controls and that doctors established in those States who operate in those establishments provide professional guarantees equivalent to those of doctors established in Greece.[428] According to van de Gronden, one may expect that the CJEU will critically review a requirement for prior authorization justified by concerns regarding the quality of the safety of cross-border care. For this reason, Article 8.2b should not be interpreted too broadly. According to de Ruijter, 'it is doubtful whether healthcare authorities will have enough information available with respect to what goes on in the healthcare facilities cross border, or that this information will be provided to them, to aptly safeguard their patients'.[429]

346. In line with this case law, no prior authorization may be requested when the healthcare provider fulfils the requirements provided for in Directive 2005/36 (*see* paragraphs 98 et seq.). Disputes are to be expected in the event that prior authorization is refused because of concerns regarding the quality of care of a practitioner, even though this care may meet the requirements of this Directive.[430]

347. Peeters raised the question of whether the exception referred to in Article 8.2b refers to Directive 2005/36. She doubts this because this Directive is always applicable to healthcare providers, and the CJEU has considered that this Directive offers sufficient guarantees for the quality and safety of care. She rather considers the exception as referring to future EU Law regarding the minimum level of quality of medical services.[431] Because Article 8.2b makes reference to the quality of healthcare and not to the training and education of healthcare providers, there is reason to believe that she is right.

348. The complex way Article 8.2b has been phrased makes me think that it refers to the phenomenon of the 'problem doctor' or the 'rogue doctor'[432] who have been subjected to a disciplinary or comparable measure resulting in his/her being temporarily or definitely being not competent to practice.[433] This brings me to a provision in the Directive that remained somewhat underexposed in the literature, Article 10.4. that is part of Chapter IV (Cooperation in Healthcare). According to this Article, Member States of treatment shall ensure that information on the right to practice listed in national or local registers established on their territory is, upon request, made available to the authorities of other Member States for the purposes of cross-border healthcare in accordance with Union provisions on the protection of personal data and the principle of presumption of innocence. This requirement of

428. *Ibid.*, para. 37.
429. *Supra* n. 5, 171.
430. *Supra* n. 386, 41, footnote 92.
431. M. Peeters, 'Richtlijn 2011/24 betreffende de toepassing van de rechten van de patiënt bij grensoverschrijdende zorg: impact op de (Belgische) gezondheidszorg', 17 *Tijdschrift voor Gezondheidsrecht/Revue Droit de la Santé* 99 (2011–2012).
432. This expression is used by T. Hervey, *Cooperation Between Healthcare Authorities in the Proposed Directive on Patients' Rights in Cross-Border Healthcare,* in J.W. van de Gronden et al. (eds), *Health Care and EU Law* 169 (The Hague: Asser Press 2011).
433. H.D.C. Roscam Abbing, 'Problem Doctors and Patients' Rights to Good Quality Care in the European Union', 13 *European Journal of Health Law* 301–308 (2006).

transparency accommodates the anxiety that patients are treated by healthcare professionals who lost their right to practice but nevertheless continue treating patients from other Member States.[434]

III. Quality and Safety as a Justification to Refuse a Prior Authorization

349. Where the patient is entitled to healthcare and healthcare cannot be provided within a time limit which is medically justifiable, the Member State of affiliation should, in principle be obliged to grant prior authorization. However, in certain circumstances, cross-border healthcare may expose the patient or the general public to a risk which overrides the interest of the patient in receiving the cross-border healthcare sought (Recital 45 in the Preamble). To accommodate this problem, Article 8.6 provides that the Member State of affiliation may refuse to grant prior authorization in four situations. Three of them have to do with safety and quality concerns and are, so to speak, the reflection of Article 8.2b.

350. The Member State of affiliation has to make publicly available which healthcare is subject to prior authorization for the purposes of this Directive, as well as all relevant information on the system of prior authorization (Article 8.7). Previous studies on the Directive showed that information on the treatments for which patients should request prior authorization is not always sufficient. This may result in patients not knowing which health services are subject to prior authorization and, subsequently, a limited number of individuals requesting such authorization when they seek cross-border healthcare. With regard to administrative procedures in general, the European Commission identified this as one of the priority areas with great potential to act as barriers to patients to seek cross-border healthcare if left unaddressed as well.[435]

A. *The Patient Will Be Exposed to a Safety Risk*

351. The patient will, according to a clinical evaluation, be exposed with reasonable certainty to a patient safety risk that cannot be regarded as acceptable, taking into account the potential benefit for the patient of the sought cross-border healthcare (Article 8.6a).

434. S.A. De Vries, 'De Europese patiëntenrechtenrichtlijn: van privileges naar rechten voor alle patiënten in Europa', *Nederlands Tijdschrift voor Europees Recht* 222 (2011), who refers to a 'Doctor Vodka' who lost his licence because of drinking three bottles vodka each day.

435. *Study on Enhancing Implementation of the Cross-Border Healthcare Directive 20011/24/EU to Ensure Patient Rights in the EU. Final Report,* Brussels, European Commission, DG Health and Food Safety, 2022, 18.

B. The General Public Will Be Exposed to a Substantial Safety Hazard

352. The general public will be exposed with reasonable certainty to a substantial safety hazard as a result of the cross-border healthcare in question (Article 8.6b).

C. Concerns Regarding the Quality and Safety of the Care Provided by a Healthcare Provider

353. Cross-border healthcare is to be provided by a healthcare provider that raises serious and specific concerns relating to the respect of standards and guidelines on quality of care and patient safety, including provisions on supervision, whether these standards and guidelines are laid down by laws and regulations or through accreditation systems established by the Member State of treatment (Article 8.6c).

IV. Healthcare Within a Time Limit Which Is Medically Justifiable and Religious Beliefs

354. According to Article 8.6d, a prior authorization can also be refused by the Member State of affiliation when the healthcare can be provided on its territory within a time limit which is medically justifiable, taking into account the current state of health and the probable course of the illness of each patient concerned. However, and without prejudice to Article 8.6a, b and c, the Member State of affiliation may not refuse to grant prior authorization when the patient is entitled to the healthcare in question in accordance with Article 7 and when this healthcare cannot be provided on its territory within a time limit which is medically justifiable, based on an objective medical assessment of the patient's medical condition, the history and probable course of the patient's illness, the degree of the patient's pain and/or the nature of the patient's disability at the time when the request for authorization was made or renewed (Article 8.5). According to the CJEU Articles 8.5 and 6d, read in the light of Article 21(1) of the Charter of Fundamental Rights of the European Union, must be interpreted as precluding a patient's Member State of affiliation from refusing to grant that patient the authorization provided for in Article 8(1) of the directive, where hospital care, the medical effectiveness of which is not contested, is available in that Member State, although the method of treatment used is contrary to that patient's religious beliefs unless that refusal is objectively justified by a legitimate aim relating to maintaining treatment capacity or medical competence, and is an appropriate and necessary means of achieving that aim, which it is for the referring court to determine.[436] A's son was born with cardiovascular disease, and he had to have open-heart surgery. The operation was available in A's Member State of affiliation (Latvia), but it could not be performed without a blood transfusion. He opposed blood transfusion, however, because he was a Jehova's

436. CJEU, *A/Veselības ministrija,* Case C-243/19, ECLI:EU:C:2020: 872, para. 85.

Witness. He, therefore, requested that the national health service of Latvia issue a prior authorization enabling his son to receive treatment in Poland, where the operation could be done without a blood transfusion.[437]

355. The judgment of the EUCJ in *Veselības ministrija* is a good illustration of what Hervey and De Ruijter have qualified as 'Union law-making in a wide range of aspects of national health systems. These include cross-border access of patients to medical treatments (…) occasionally because of ethical or other differences in the "basket of care" at home, resulting in changes to domestic practices or provision.'[438] Also, Berki refers to examples of treatments which are subject to debate from a bioethical point of view. In this respect, she discusses the example of home birth services. Other examples could be palliative care and end-of-life treatments.[439]

§4. The Patients' Right to Complain

356. According to Article 4.2c, the Member State of treatment ensures that there are transparent complaints procedures and mechanisms in place for patients in order for them to seek remedies in accordance with the legislation of that Member State if they suffer harm arising from the healthcare they receive. Also, this right is of relevance for domestic patients. The application of the Directive's provisions in individual cases is a matter for national courts with the possibility and the obligation if they decide in the last instance to request the CJEU for a preliminary ruling.[440]

§5. The Patients' Right to Receive Compensation for Damages

357. Article 4.2d provides that the Member State of treatment ensures that there are systems of professional liability insurance, or a guarantee or similar arrangement that is equivalent or essentially comparable as regards its purpose and which is appropriate to the nature and the extent of the risk in place for treatment provided on its territory. This obligation does not imply that Member States have to guarantee that healthcare providers have taken a professional liability insurance before

437. M. Axmin, 'Access to Cross-Border Healthcare in the light of Religious Freedom. Commentary on the Case C-243/19', 28 *European Journal of Health Law* 185–196 (2021); R. Tinière, 'L' Europe de la santé à l'épreuve du tourisme médical motivé par les convictions religieuses. The Hypothetical Emergence of a Medical Tourism Founded on Religious Convictions', *Revue des Affaires Européennes* 957–962 (2020); J. Paju, '*Case C-243/19 A v. Veselibas Ministrija*', 28 *Maastricht Journal of European and Comparative Law* 900–907 (2021).

438. T. Hervey & A. De Ruijter, 'The Dynamic Potential of European Union Health Law', 11 *European Journal of Risk Regulation* 730 (2020).

439. *Supra* n. 62, 122–123.

440. Answer given by Ms Kyriakides on behalf of the European Commission to a written Parliamentary question of T. Sokol, Improving the cross-border healthcare system in the EU, 27 Feb. 2020, E-004195/2020.

starting to practice.[441] However, according to Article 4.2b, healthcare providers have to inform their patients about their insurance cover or other means of personal or collective protection with regard to professional liability (*see* paragraph 332). In practice, this results in an obligation to have such insurance or coverage. According to Recital 23 in the Preamble, ensuring clear common obligations in respect of the provision of mechanisms for responding to harm arising from healthcare is essential to prevent lack of confidence in those mechanisms being an obstacle to taking-up cross-border healthcare. Some French authors seem to regret that the concept and operation of these compensation mechanisms are left to the Member States[442] and express the expectation that within a short period of time, these mechanisms will be considered as a matter of common EU interest.[443]

§6. The Patients' Right to Respect of Private Life

358. Ensuring continuity of cross-border healthcare depends on transfer of personal data concerning patients' health. These personal data should be able to flow from one Member State to another (Recital 25 in the Preamble).[444] Article 4.2e obliges the Member State of treatment to ensure that the fundamental right to privacy with respect to the processing of personal data is protected in conformity with national measures implementing Union provisions on the protection of personal data, in particular, Directives 95/46/EC and 2002/58/EC (*see* paragraphs 519 et seq.).[445] The Directive does not oblige the Member States to report the type of condition patients were treated for in another country.[446]

§7. The Patients' Right to a Medical Record and Access to It

359. In order to ensure continuity of care, patients who have received treatment are entitled to a written or electronic medical record[447] of such treatment and access to at least a copy of this record in conformity with and subject to national measures implementing Union provisions on the protection of personal data (Article 4.2f). According to Dubuis, it is misleading to refer to a 'right' to have access to a copy of the medical record because patients are only explicitly entitled to a medical

441. M. Peeters, 'Richtlijn 2011/24 betreffende de toepassing van de rechten van de patiënt bij grensoverschrijdende zorg: impact op de (Belgische) gezondheidszorg', 17 *Tijdschrift voor Gezondheidsrecht/Revue Droit de la Santé* 412 (2011–2012).
442. *Supra* n. 405, 326.
443. *Supra* n. 367, 509–517.
444. P. Kierkegaard, 'Electronic Health Record: Wiring Europe's Healthcare', 27 *Computer Law & Security Review* 507 (2011).
445. *Supra* n. 356, 33–34.
446. Answer given by Ms Kyriakides on behalf of the European Commission to a written Parliamentary question of L. Pereira et al., State of implementation of Directive 2011/24, 17 Jul. 2020, E-001373/2020.
447. 'Medical records' means all the documents containing data, assessments and information of any kind on a patient's situation and clinical development throughout the care process (Art. 3m).

record.[448] De Grove regrets that the Directive remains vague as to the practical modalities of the medical record and the possible liability problems in this regard.[449] Whether the personal notes of the healthcare providers are part of the medical record (and thus may be accessed by the patient) is not clarified. According to de Ruijter, they 'presumably do fall within the context of the right to privacy under Article 7 CFREU'.[450] Neither is it clear whether the right to access the medical record also implies the right to access it in a direct way (right to consult; right to inspection). Article 5d is less ambivalent in this respect. It obliges the Member State of affiliation to ensure that patients who seek to receive or do receive cross-border healthcare have remote access to *or* have at least a copy of their medical records, in conformity with, and subject to, national measures implementing Union provisions on the protection of personal data (emphasis added).

360. Article 14 deals with e-Health. The Union shall support and facilitate cooperation and the exchange of information among Member States working within a voluntary network connecting national authorities responsible for e-Health designated by the Member States (Article 14.1). The objectives of the e-Health network are to: (a) work towards delivering sustainable economic and social benefits of European e-Health systems and services and interoperable applications, with a view to achieving a high level of trust and security, enhancing continuity of care and ensuring access to safe and high-quality healthcare; (b) draw up guidelines on: (i) a non-exhaustive list of data that are to be included in patients' summaries and that can be shared between health professionals to enable continuity of care and patient safety across borders; and (ii) effective methods for enabling the use of medical information for public health and research; (c) support Member States in developing common identification and authentication measures to facilitate transferability of data in cross-border healthcare. The objectives referred to in points (b) and (c) shall be pursued in due observance of the principles of data protection (Article 14.2). The Commission adopts, in accordance with the regulatory procedure referred to in Article 16(2), the necessary measures for the establishment, management and transparent functioning of this network (Article 14.3).[451] The European Commission adopted on 6 February 2019 a Recommendation on a European Electronic Health Record Exchange Format (EEHRxF) seeking to facilitate cross-border interoperability of health data.[452] Such a recommendation is not legally binding, and not all Member States have implemented such format in their national

448. *Supra* n. 279, 75, footnote 307.
449. *Supra* n. 405, 326.
450. *Supra* n. 5, 174.
451. Commission Implementing Decision 2019/1765 of 22 Oct. 2019 providing the rules for the establishment, the management and the functioning of the network of national authorities responsible for e-Health, and repealing Implementing Decision 2011/890/EU, *OJ L* 270 of 24 Oct. 2019; N. De Grove-Valdeyron, '*De l'espace européen de la santé en ligne à l'espace européen des données de la santé: le numérique au service de la construction d'une Union Européenne de la santé [From the European e-Health Space to the European Health Data Space: Digital Technology for the Construction of a European Health Union]*', *Revue des Affaires Européennes/Law and European Affairs* 337–338 (2021); K. Misheva & M. Ampovska, 'The Legal Aspects of Telehealth', *EU and Comparative Issues and Challenges* 393–409 (2022).
452. *OJ* L 39, 11 Feb. 2019, 18.

processing.[453] The Commission can also contribute to further developing the e-Health Digital Service Infrastructure (eHDSI) that allows exchanging e-prescriptions and summaries of patient health records between Member States.[454] The Commission also supports Member States in exchanging e-Health data (currently e-prescription and patient summaries) across borders using the eHDSI. Twenty-two Member States have committed to start exchanging health data by mid-2022 through the eHDSI.[455] In April 2020, seven Member States started exchanging health records between health professionals across borders, electronic Patient Summaries (PS) and/or e-Prescriptions (eP).[456] The Commission does not intend to propose the way in which medical terms are recorded and presented to patients within an EU Member State, nor does it have competence in this area.[457]

§8. The Patients' Right to Recognition of a Prescription for a Medicinal Product

361. If a medicinal product is authorized to be marketed on their territory, Member States ensure that prescriptions issued for such a product in another Member State for a named patient can be dispensed on their territory in compliance with their national legislation in force and that any restrictions on recognition of individual prescriptions are prohibited. Such restrictions are only lawful if they are: (a) limited to what is necessary and proportionate to safeguard human health and non-discriminatory; or (b) based on legitimate and justified doubts about the authenticity, content or comprehensibility of an individual prescription. The recognition of prescriptions does not affect a pharmacist's right, by virtue of national rules, to refuse, for ethical reasons, to dispense a product that was prescribed in another Member State, where the pharmacist would have the right to refuse to dispense, had the prescription been issued in the Member State of affiliation (Article 11.1.).[458] The Directive does not cover remote prescribing.[459]

453. Answer given by Ms Kyriakides on behalf of the European Commission to a written Parliamentary question of J. Kopcinka, European Electronic Health Record Exchange format, 10 Nov. 2021, E-004159/2021.
454. Answer given by Ms Gabriel on behalf of the European Commission to a written Parliamentary question of A. Guoga, Status of legislative initiatives on digital health, 17 Jun. 2019, P-001704/2019.
455. Answer given by Mr Andriukaitis on behalf of the European Commission to a written Parliamentary question of A-I. Valean, Cross-border standardization in healthcare, 20 Mar. 2019, P-000686/2019.
456. Answer given by Ms Kyriakides on behalf of the European Commission to a written Parliamentary question of P. Arimont, Cross-border interoperability of electronic health record systems, 23 Apr. 2020, E-000478/2020.
457. Answer given by Vice-President Katainen on behalf of the European Commission to a written Parliamentary question of M. Kyllönen, Harmonising laboratory test reporting practices within the EU, 3 Apr. 2019, E-000644/2019.
458. *See* Commission Implementing Directive 2012/52/EU of 20 Dec. 2012 laying down measures to facilitate the recognition of medical prescriptions issued in another Member State, *OJ* 2012, L 356/68-70.
459. T. Hervey & S. Sheldon, 'Abortion by Telemedicine in the European Union', 145 *International Journal Gynecology Obstet* 127 (2018).

Part V. The Physician-Patient Relationship in Specific Terms in EU Law

Chapter 1. Clinical Trials on Medicinal Products for Human Use

§1. Introduction

362. Clinical trials are regulated in Regulation (EU) No. 536/2014 of the European Parliament and of the Council of 16 April 2014 on clinical trials on medicinal products from human use, and repealing Directive 2001/20/EC on the approximation of the laws, regulations and administrative provisions of the Member States relating to good clinical practice in the conduct on medicinal products for human use.[460]

363. Directive 2001/20/EC (the Clinical Trials Directive) aimed to simplify and harmonize the administrative provisions governing clinical trials in the Union. However, experience has shown that a harmonized approach to the regulation of clinical trials has only been partially achieved. This made it particularly difficult to perform a given clinical trial in several Member States (Recital 4 in the Preamble to Regulation No. 536/2014 [the Clinical Trials Regulation]). Experience has also indicated that the legal form of a Regulation would present advantages for sponsors and investigators, for example, in the context of clinical trials taking place in more than one Member State, since they will be able to rely on its provisions directly. Divergences of approach among different Member States will, therefore, be kept to a minimum (Recital 5 in the Preamble to the Clinical Trials Regulation).[461] In the past two decades, the EU legislative institutions transformed dozens of directives into regulations.[462] Another example relevant to health law is the Clinical Trials Regulation.

364. The Clinical Trials Regulation entered into force on 16 June 2014. It shall apply from six months after the publication of the notice referred to in Article 82(3)

460. *OJ* 2014, L 158/1-76.
461. M.L. Flear, 'The EU Clinical Trials Regulation: Key Priorities, Purposes and Aims and the Implications for Public Health', 42 *Journal Medical Ethics* 193–194 (2016).
462. F. Krepelka, 'Transformations of Directives into Regulations: Towards a More Uniform Administrative Law', 27 *European Public Law* 781–806 (2021).

(Article 99). It became applicable on 31 January 2022. The Regulation applies from that date onwards to all clinical trials conducted in the EU that have been authorized under its principles.[463]

§2. Field of Application of the Clinical Trials Regulation

365. The Clinical Trials Regulation applies to all clinical trials conducted in the Union (Article 1). Although there appears to be some uncertainty as to the application of the Clinical Trials Regulation in relation to clinical trials conducted only within one Member State,[464] it follows from different Articles of the Clinical Trials Regulation that it is also applied to clinical trials conducted only within one Member State. For instance, Article 5.1(4) provides that if the clinical trial involves only one Member State, that Member State shall be the reporting Member State. *See also* Article 30 in this regard (*see* paragraph 396).

366. A 'clinical trial' means a clinical study which fulfils any of the following conditions: (a) the assignment of the subject to a particular therapeutic strategy is decided in advance and does not fall within normal clinical practice of the Member State concerned; (b) the decision to prescribe the investigational medicinal products is taken together with the decision to include the subject in the clinical study; or (c) diagnostic or monitoring procedures in addition to normal clinical practice are applied to the subjects (Article 2.2(2)).[465] A 'clinical study' means any investigation in relation to humans intended: (a) to discover or verify the clinical, pharmacological or other pharmacodynamic effects of one or more medicinal products; (b) to identify any adverse reactions to one or more medicinal products; or (c) to study the absorption, distribution, metabolism and excretion of one or more medicinal products, with the objective of ascertaining the safety and/or efficacy of those medicinal products (Article 2.2(1)). 'Normal clinical practice' means the treatment regime typically followed to treat, prevent, or diagnose a disease or a disorder (Article 2.2(6)).

367. Low-intervention clinical trials fall within the field of application of the Clinical Trials Regulation but are subjected to less stringent rules because they pose only a minimal additional risk to the subject's safety compared to normal clinical practice (Recital 11 in the Preamble). 'Low-intervention clinical trial' means a clinical trial which fulfils all of the following conditions: (a) the investigational medicinal products, excluding placebos, are authorized; (b) according to the protocol of the clinical trial: (i) the investigational medicinal products are used in accordance

463. Answer given by Ms Kyriakides on behalf the European Commission to a written priority Parliamentary question by M. Rivasi, The Application of Regulation 536/2014 to COVID-19 Vaccines, 13 Jan. 2022, P-005425/2021.

464. J.V. McHale, 'Reforming the EU Clinical Trials Directive: Streamlining Processes of a Radical "New" Agenda?', 20 *European Journal of Health Law* 368 (2013); *supra* n. 3, 307.

465. T.Faltus & I. Miguel Berlain, 'The EU Legal Framework on Clinical Trials Directed to Therapeutic Germline Gene Alteration: A Critical and Systematic Analysis', 23 *Medical Law International* 44–69 (2023).

with the terms of the marketing authorization; or (ii) the use of the investigational medicinal products is evidence-based and supported by published scientific evidence on the safety and efficacy of those investigational medicinal products in any of the Member States concerned; and (c) the additional diagnostic or monitoring procedures do not pose more than minimal additional risk or burden to the safety of the subjects compared to normal clinical practice in any Member State concerned (Article 2.2(3)).

368. The Clinical Trials Regulation does not apply to non-interventional studies (Article 1). A 'non-interventional study' means a clinical study other than a clinical trial (Article 2.2(4)). The precise scope of the Clinical Trials Regulation in this respect is not very clear.[466]

§3. The Protection of Subjects in Clinical Trials

369. A 'subject' means an individual who participates in a clinical trial, either as a recipient of an investigational medicinal product or as a control (Article 2.2.17). Regarding development of medicines depending on gender, the Clinical Trials Regulation includes provisions related to the justification for the gender allocation of subjects. The Commission evaluates the evolution of clinical research in Europe with a series of metrics collected through the Clinical Trials Information System (CTIS). One key performance indicator is gender representation in clinical trials: male/female/both gender categories. When looking at clinical trials authorized since 31 January 2022, at the end of September 2023, the gender of subjects was distributed as follows: 70 clinical trials (5%) with only women, 88 clinical trials (7%) with only men, and 1,140 clinical trials (88%) with both genders.[467]

370. Human cells and human tissues that in clinical trials are applied to the human body should comply with the quality and safety standard laid down in Directive 2004/23/EC of the European Parliament and of the Council of 31 March 2004 on setting standards of quality and safety for the donation, procurement, testing, processing, preservation, storage and distribution of human tissues and cells (Recital 11 in the Preamble of Directive 2004/23/EC).

371. The rules for clinical trials in Europe require the sponsors of such clinical trials to respect the principles of good clinical practice. These principles are a set of internationally recognized ethical and scientific quality requirements which must be observed for designing, conducting, recording and reporting clinical trials that

466. J. Herringa & J. Dute, 'The Proposed EU-Regulation on Clinical Trials on Medicinal Products', 20 *European Journal of Health Law* 349 (2013).

467. Answer given by Ms Kyriakides on behalf of the European Commission to a written Parliamentary question of E. De Blasis and P.Fiocchi, Gender medicine in European health systems, 5 Apr. 2024, E-003561/2023.

involve the participation of human species. Compliance with this good practice provides assurance that the rights, safety and well-being of those participating in clinical trials are protected and that the results of the clinical trials are credible. The principles of good clinical practice need to be respected in every clinical trial that is part of an authorization to market a medicinal product in the EU, even when the trial itself does not take place in the EU.[468]

I. Prior Authorization

372. According to Article 4, first sentence, a clinical trial has to be subjected to scientific and ethical review and authorized in accordance with the Clinical Trials Regulation. In order to obtain authorization, the sponsor has to submit an application dossier to the intended Member States concerned through the portal referred to in Article 80 (the 'EU portal') (Article 5.1). 'Sponsor' means an individual, company, institution or organization which takes responsibility for the initiation, management and financing of the clinical trial (Article 2.2(14)). The sponsor proposes one of the Member States concerned as reporting Member State (Article 5.1). Within ten days from the submission of the application dossier, the reporting Member State validates the application, taking into account considerations expressed by the other Member States concerned (Article 5.3). The date on which the sponsor is notified that the application is validated by the reporting state is the validation date of the application (Article 5.6).

373. The ethical review and the authorization referred to in Article 4 are both the responsibility of the reporting Member State and the Member State concerned. This shared responsibility is clarified in Recital 6 in the Preamble as follows: 'The Member States concerned should cooperate in assessing a request for authorisation of a clinical trial. This cooperation should not include aspects of an intrinsically national nature, such as informed consent.'

374. Unlike that in the Clinical Trials Directive, an ethical review by an ethics committee is not an obligation. In the proposed Clinical Trials Regulation, the concept of an ethics committee was not mentioned at all.[469] The Clinical Trials Regulation leaves it to the Member States to determine which body is competent for the ethical review and the authorization. Recital 18 in the Preamble states the following in this respect: 'It should be left to the Member State concerned to determine the appropriate body or bodies to be involved in the assessment of the application to conduct a clinical trial and to organise the involvement of ethics committees within the timelines for the authorisation of that clinical trial as set out in this Regulation.

---

468. *Supra* n. 463.

469. H. Nys, 'New European Rules Regarding the Approval of Clinical Trials, the Role of Ethics Committees and the Protection of Subjects', 30 *Archives Immunology Experimental Therapy* 409 (2012); *supra* n. 446, 347–362; C. Pertini, 'What is the role of ethics committees after Regulation (EU) 536/2014?', 42 *Journal Medical Ethics* 186–188 (2016); I. De Miguel Beriain et al., 'An EU Comparative Analysis of the Regulation of Clinical Trials Supervising Bodies in the Aftermath of Regulation 536/2014', 26 *European Public Law* 307–330 (2020).

Such decisions are a matter of internal organisation for each Member State.' At first sight, this is in contradiction with Article 4, second sentence that begins as follows: 'The ethical review shall be performed by an ethics committee in accordance with the law of the Member State concerned.' That seems to imply the obligation for Member States to delegate the ethical review to an ethics committee. However, the second sentence of Article 4 goes as follows: 'The review by the ethics committee *may* encompass aspects addressed in Part I of the assessment report for the authorisation of a clinical trial as referred to in Article 6 and in Part II of that assessment report as referred to in Article 7 as appropriate for each Member State concerned' (italics added). Those aspects form the core of the ethical review which may be evaluated by an ethics committee without being an obligation. In answer to a Parliamentary question, the European Commission, however, suggested that the ethical review by an ethics committee is an obligation: 'The authorisation of clinical trials in the EU is Member State responsibility after scientific assessment by national competent authorities and ethics committees to ensure participant's protection.'[470] According to Hervey and McHale, the need for research ethics committee approval for publication in journals is probably enough to secure the continued use of research ethics committees across the EU.[471]

375. The Clinical Trials Regulation defines an 'ethics committee' and contains provisions concerning the composition and the management of such a committee or the body that is responsible for the ethical review and the authorization. According to Article 2(11), an 'ethics committee' means an independent body established in a Member State in accordance with the law of that Member State and empowered to give opinions for the purposes of this Regulation, taking into account the views of laypersons, in particular patients or patients' organizations. Article 9 contains more detailed provisions concerning the persons who validate and assess the application without mentioning ethics committees. Member States have to ensure that these persons do not have conflicts of interest, are independent of the sponsor, of the clinical trial site and the investigators involved and of persons financing the clinical trial, as well as free of any other undue influence.[472] In order to guarantee independence and transparency, the Member States ensure that persons admitting and assessing the application as regards the aspects addressed in Parts I and II of the assessment report have no financial or personal interests which could affect their impartiality. These persons have to make an annual declaration of their financial interests (Article 9.1). Member States ensure that the assessment is done jointly by a reasonable number

470. Answer given by Ms Kyriakides on behalf of the European Commission to a written Parliamentary question of J. Kuhs, A recent Pfizer publication shows that it conducts clinical trials of COVID-19 vaccines on children, even children under five years of age, 6 Jan. 2022, E-004563/2021.
471. *Supra* n. 3, 315.
472. This condition may pose problems in small countries because it may be difficult to find independent researchers in the case of large multi-site trials, *see* Nordic Trial Alliance Working Group on Ethics, *Report on the Ethical Review Process for Clinical Trials in the Nordic Countries: The Challenges and Opportunities of the New Clinical Trials Regulation*, 2016, 30, http://nta.nordforsk.org/files/NordForsk_NTAREPORT_Ethics.pdf.

of persons who collectively have the necessary qualifications and experience (Article 9.2). At least one layperson has to participate in the assessment (Article 9.3).

376. The reporting Member State has to assess, among other aspects, the compliance with Chapter V of the Clinical Trials Regulation with respect to the anticipated therapeutic and public health benefits and the risks and conveniences for the subject (Article 6.1a(i) and (ii)). Both, but especially the second one, are very important in view of the protection of the subject. This is also highlighted by the title of Chapter V: 'Protection of subjects and informed consent'. After the assessment of these and other aspects, the reporting Member State draws up an assessment report. The assessment of these aspects constitutes Part I of the assessment report (Article 6.2). Given the themes treated in Part I, it is obviously not correct to state that Part I is merely scientific.[473] The reporting Member State submits, through the EU portal, the final Part I of the assessment report, including its conclusion (acceptable; acceptable subject to compliance with specific conditions; not acceptable, *see* Article 6.3) to the sponsor and the other Member States concerned within forty-five days from the validation date (Article 6.4).

377. For clinical trials involving more than one Member State, the assessment process includes three phases: (a) an initial assessment phase performed by the reporting Member State within twenty-six days from the validation date. During this phase, the reporting Member State develops a draft Part I of the assessment report and circulates it to all other Member States concerned; (b) a coordinated review phase performed within twelve days from the end of the initial assessment phase involving all Member States concerned. During this phase, all Member States concerned jointly review the application based on the draft Part I of the assessment report and share any considerations relevant to the application; (c) a consolidation phase performed by the reporting Member State within seven days from the end of the coordinated review phase. During this phase, the reporting Member State takes due account of the considerations of the other Member States concerned when finalizing Part I of the assessment report and records how all such considerations have been dealt with. The reporting Member State submits the final Part I of the assessment report to the sponsor and all other Member States concerned within forty-five days from the validation date (Article 6.5). The date on which the final part of the assessment is submitted is the reporting date (Article 6.6). Between the validation date and the reporting date, only the reporting Member State may request additional information from the sponsor. For the purpose of obtaining and reviewing this additional information from the sponsor, the reporting Member State may extend the period referred to in paragraph 4 by a maximum of thirty-one days (Article 6.8).

---

473. I. Vranken, 'Krachtlijnen van de Europese Verordening klinische proeven', 20 *Tijdschrift Gezondheidsrecht/Revue droit de la santé* 264 (2014–2015); Shaw & Townend also state that 'ethics committees can also consider part 1 issues in their deliberation', D. Shaw & D. Townend, 'Division and Discord in the Clinical Trials Regulation', 42 *Journal Medical Ethics* 729 (2016). *See also* at p. 731: 'While the Clinical Trials Regulation does allow ethics committees to consider part 1 issue, they should really be listed as a specific responsibility of the ethics committee.'

378. Each Member State concerned assesses, for its own territory, the application with respect to the following aspects: (a) compliance with the requirements for informed consent as set out in Chapter V (*see* paragraphs 386 et seq.); (b) compliance of the arrangements for rewarding or compensating subjects with the requirements set out in Chapter V and investigators; compliance of the arrangements for recruitment of subjects with the requirements set out in Chapter V; (d) compliance with Directive 95/46/EC (protection of personal data, *see* paragraph 403); (e) compliance with Article 49 (suitability of individuals involved in conducting the clinical trials); (f) compliance with Article 50 (suitability of clinical trials sites); (g) compliance with Article 76 (damage compensation, *see* paragraph 401); (h) compliance with the applicable rules for the collection, storage and future use of biological samples of the subject. The assessment of the aspects referred to constitutes Part II of the assessment report (Article 7.1). Each Member State concerned completes its assessment within forty-five days from the validation date and submits, through the EU portal, Part II of the assessment report, including its conclusion, to the sponsor. Each Member State concerned may request, with justified reasons, additional information from the sponsor regarding the aspects referred to in Article 7.1 only within the period of forty-five days (Article 7.2). For the purpose of obtaining and reviewing this additional information, the Member State concerned may extend the period of forty-five days by a maximum of thirty-one days (Article 7.3). Regarding the period within the ethical review has to be finished, one also has to take into account of Article 4 that provides that Member States ensure that the timelines and procedures for the review by the ethics committees are compatible with the timelines and procedures set out in this Regulation for the assessment of the application for authorization of a clinical trial.

379. Each Member State concerned notifies the sponsor through the EU portal as to whether the clinical trial is authorized, whether it is authorized subject to conditions, or whether authorization is refused. Notification has to be done by way of one single decision within five days from the reporting date (Article 8.1). Where the Member State concerned has not notified the sponsor of its decision within this period, the conclusion on Part I of the assessment report is deemed to be the decision of the Member State concerned on the application for authorization of the clinical trial (Article 8.6).

380. Where the conclusion of the reporting Member State as regards Part I of the assessment report is that the conduct of the clinical trial is acceptable or acceptable subject to compliance with specific conditions, that conclusion is deemed to be the conclusion of the Member State concerned. Notwithstanding this, a Member State concerned may disagree with the conclusion of the reporting Member State as regards Part I of the assessment report only on the following grounds: (a) when it considers that participation in the clinical trial would lead to a subject receiving an inferior treatment than in normal clinical practice in the Member State concerned; (b) infringement of its national law as referred to in Article 90 (specific requirements for special groups of medicinal products); (c) considerations as regards subject safety and data reliability and robustness (Article 8.2).

381. A Member State concerned refuses to authorize a clinical trial if it disagrees with the conclusion of the reporting Member State as regards Part I of the assessment report on any of the grounds referred to in the previous paragraph or if it finds, on duly justified grounds, that the aspects addressed in Part II of the assessment report are not complied with, or where an ethics committee has issued a negative opinion which in accordance with the law of the Member State concerned is valid for that entire Member State. That Member State has to provide for an appeal procedure in respect of such refusal (Article 8.4).

382. Where the conclusion of the reporting Member State as regards Part I of the assessment report is that the clinical trial is not acceptable, that conclusion is deemed to be the conclusion of all Member States concerned (Article 8.5).

383. If no subject has been included in the clinical trial in a Member State concerned within two years from the notification date of the authorization, the authorization expires in that Member State concerned unless an extension, on request of the sponsor, has been approved following the procedure set out in Chapter III (Article 8.9).

II. General Provisions for the Protection of Subjects

A. General Principle

384. A clinical trial may be conducted only if the rights, safety, dignity and well-being of subjects are protected and prevail over all other interests and if it is designed to generate reliable and robust data (Article 3). Recital 27 in the Preamble explicitly refers to the Charter of Fundamental Rights of the EU (*see* paragraphs 236 et seq.): 'Human dignity and the right to the integrity of the person are recognised in the Charter of Fundamental Rights of the European Union (the 'Charter'). In particular, the Charter requires that any intervention in the field of biology and medicine cannot be performed without free and informed consent of the person concerned.' Moreover, 'Directive 2001/20/EC contains an extensive set of rules for the protection of subjects. These rules should be upheld.'

B. Proportionality Requirement (Balance Benefits-Risks)

385. A clinical trial may be conducted only where the anticipated benefits to the subjects or to public health justify the foreseeable risks and inconveniences, and compliance with this condition is constantly monitored (Article 28.1a).

C. Informed Consent

386. The Clinical Trials Regulation contains the following definition of informed consent: 'a subject's free and voluntary expression of his or her willingness to participate in a particular clinical trial, after having been informed of all aspects of the clinical trial that are relevant to the subject's decision to participate or, in case of minors and of incapacitated subjects, an authorisation or agreement from their legally designated representative to include them in the clinical trial' (Article 2.2.26). In order to certify that informed consent is given freely, the investigator should take into account all relevant circumstances which might influence the decision of a potential subject to participate in a clinical trial, in particular, whether the potential subject belongs to an economically or socially disadvantaged group or is in a situation of institutional or hierarchical dependency that could inappropriately influence her or his decision to participate (Recital 31 in the Preamble).

1. Express Informed Consent as a Rule

a. Prior Information

i. Basic Rule

387. The subjects have to be informed in accordance with Article 29.2–6 (Article 28.1b).

ii. Contents of the Information

388. Information given to the subject has to enable the subject to understand: (i) the nature, objectives, benefits, implications, risks and inconveniences of the clinical trial; (ii) the subject's rights and guarantees regarding his or her protection, in particular, his or her right to refuse to participate and the right to withdraw from the clinical trial at any time without any resulting detriment and without having to provide any justification; (iii) the conditions under which the clinical trial is to be conducted, including the expected duration of the subject's participation in the clinical trial; and (iv) the possible treatment alternatives, including the follow-up measures if the participation of the subject in the clinical trial is discontinued (Article 29.2a).

389. The information has to include information about the applicable damage compensation system referred to in Article 76.1. and has to include the EU trial number and information about the availability of the clinical trial results (Article 29.2d and 2e).

390. The subject has to be informed that the summary of the results of the clinical trial and a summary presented in terms understandable to a layperson will be made available in the EU database, referred to in Article 81 (the 'EU database'), pursuant to Article 37.4., irrespective of the outcome of the clinical trial, and, to the extent possible, when the summaries become available (Article 29.6.).

391. The subject has to be provided with the contact details of an entity where further information can be received in case of need (Article 28.1g).

iii. Understandable to a Layperson

392. The information has to be kept comprehensive, concise, clear, relevant, and understandable to a layperson (Article 29.2b).

iv. Provided in a Prior Interview

393. The information has to be provided in a prior interview with a member of the investigating team who is appropriately qualified according to the law of the Member State concerned (Article 29.2c). In this interview, special attention has to be paid to the information needs of specific patient populations and individual subjects, as well as to the methods used to give the information. In this interview, it has to be verified that the subject has understood the information (Article 29.4. and 29.5.).

v. In Writing and Available to the Subject

394. The information has to be prepared in writing and be available to the subject (Article 29.3.).

b. Express (Written, Documented and Well-Considered) Consent

395. Informed consent has to be written, dated and signed by the person performing the interview referred to in paragraph 393 and by the subject after having been duly informed in accordance with Article 29.2. Where the subject is unable to write, consent may be given and recorded through appropriate alternative means in the presence of at least one impartial witness. In that case, the witness signs and dates the informed consent document (Article 29.1.). According to Recital 30 in the Preamble, appropriate alternative means are, for instance, audio or video recorders. There are no rules regarding the length of an informed consent form. Some expressed concerns about the increasing length and complexity of informed consent forms for clinical trials. The longer the form, the more challenging it can be for the patient to process information necessary to make an informed decision about participation in a clinical trial. Key considerations are whether the information is necessary, understandable, relevant and appropriate for lay people. Long, complex and unclear forms may prevent potential participants from fully understanding the nature and purpose of the research. Therefore, when presenting informed consent to patients who are eligible to participate in a clinical trial, we find it important that the consent form does not exceed 1,000 words.[474] The Council for International

474. *Recommendations of the Coalition for Reducing Bureaucracy in Clinical Trials,* 7 Nov. 2021.

Organizations of Medical Sciences (CIOMS) international guidelines for health-related research involving humans, developed in collaboration with the WHO, stipulate that the information leaflet going to all recruits should ideally not be longer than two to three pages.[475]

396. The subject has to be provided with a copy of the document (or the record) by which informed consent has been given. The informed consent has to be documented. Adequate time has to be given for the subject to consider his or her decision to participate in the clinical trial (Article 29.1.). This consent must not be confused with the notion of consent as a legal ground for the processing of personal data under the GDPR (*see* paragraph 530).[476]

2. Implicit Informed Consent for Cluster Trials

397. Article 30.3. Clinical Trials Regulation determines the conditions following which informed consent can be obtained for so-called cluster trials that are conducted exclusively in one Member State. The Clinical Trials Regulation does not define cluster trials, but from Recital 33 of the Preamble, it can be deduced that these are clinical trials where the methodology of the trial requires that groups of subjects rather than individual subjects are allocated to receive different investigational medicinal products. In those clinical trials, the investigational medicinal products are used in accordance with the marketing authorizations, and the individual subject receives a standard treatment regardless of whether he or she accepts or refuses to participate in the clinical trial or withdraws from it so that the only consequence of non-participation is that data relating to him or her are not used for the clinical trial. Such clinical trials serve to compare established treatments. It is appropriate to allow informed consent to be obtained by simplified means for such clinical trials.

398. The simplified means to obtain informed consent for such clinical trials means that informed consent is deemed to have been obtained if the information is required by Article 29.2. has been given, and this information makes clear, in particular, that the subject can refuse to participate in, or withdraw at any time from, the clinical trial without any resulting detriment and the potential subject, after being informed, does not object to participating in the clinical trial (Article 30.2.).

---

475. Council for International Organizations of Medical Sciences (CIOMS), *International Ethical Guidelines for Health-related Research Involving Humans,* 2016, Ed. 4, Geneva, 34, Guideline 9.

476. European Data Protection Board, *Opinion 3/2019 Concerning the Questions and Answers on the Interplay between the Clinical Trial Regulation (CTR) and the General Data Protection Regulation (GDPR) (Article 70.1b)*, 5, para. 15 (23 Jan. 2019); European Data Protection Supervisor (EDPS), *A Preliminary Opinion on Data Protection and Scientific Research*, 19 (6 Jan. 2020); W. Long & F. Blythe, 'Continued Uncertainty for the GDPR and Clinical Trials', 3 *European Pharmaceutical Law Review* 82–85 (2019); G. Verhenneman et al., 'How GDPR Enhances Transparency and Fosters Pseudonymisation in Academic Medical Research', 27 *European Journal of Health Law* 47 (2020).

This is called implicit, tacit or non-verbal consent. It is not a presumed consent because the will of the subject is known.

399. Informed consent may be obtained by this simplified means if all the following conditions are fulfilled: (a) it does not contradict national law in the Member State concerned;[477] (b) the methodology of the clinical trial requires that groups of subjects rather than individual subjects are allocated to receive different investigational medicinal products in a clinical trial; (c) the clinical trial is a low-intervention clinical trial (*see* paragraph 358), and the investigational medicinal products are used in accordance with the terms of the marketing authorization; (d) there are no interventions other than the standard treatment of the subjects concerned; (e) the protocol justifies the reasons for obtaining informed consent with simplified means and describes the scope of information provided to the subjects, as well as the ways of providing information (Article 30.3.).

400. The investigator has to document all refusals and withdrawals and has to ensure that no data for the clinical trial are collected from subjects that refuse to participate in or have withdrawn from the clinical trial (Article 30.4.).

3. Withdrawal of Informed Consent

401. Any subject may, without any resulting detriment and without having to provide any justification, withdraw from the clinical trial at any time by revoking his or her informed consent. Without prejudice to Directive 95/46/EC, the withdrawal of the informed consent will not affect the activities already carried out and the use of data obtained based on informed consent before its withdrawal (Article 28.3. and Recital 76). The European Data Protection Board (EDPB) considered that this withdrawal of consent shall not be confused with the withdrawal of the informed consent under the GDPR.[478]

402. The fact that withdrawal is not retrospective has to be included in the consent process so that subjects are aware of it.[479]

D. Respect for the Rights to Physical and Mental Integrity, Privacy and Data Protection

403. The rights of the subjects to physical and mental integrity, privacy and the data protection of the data concerning them in accordance with Directive 95/46/EC

477. In some Member States the law explicitly prohibits to obtain informed consent for cluster trials by simplified means, *see*, e.g., H. Nys, *Medical Law in Belgium* 181 (Alphen aan den Rijn: Wolters Kluwer 2017). However in Belgium the law has been revised in 2018 and this is now allowed, H. Nys, *Medical Law in Belgium* 213 (Alphen aan den Rijn: Kluwer Law International 9th ed. 2024).
478. *Supra* n. 454, 6 para. 22.
479. *Supra* n. 444, 375.

(repealed by the GDPR) are safeguarded (Article 28.1d). Without prejudice to Directive 95/46/EC, the sponsor may ask the subject or, where the subject is not able to give informed consent, his or her legally designated representative at the time when the subject or the legally designated representative gives his or her informed consent to participate in the clinical trial to consent to the use of his or her data outside the protocol of the clinical trial exclusively for scientific purposes. That consent may be withdrawn at any time by the subject or his or her legally designated representative. The scientific research making use of data outside the protocol of the clinical trial shall be conducted in accordance with the applicable law on data protection (Article 28.2.). All clinical trial information has to be recorded, processed, handled, and stored by the sponsor or investigator, as applicable, in such a way that it can be accurately reported, interpreted and verified while the confidentiality of records and the personal data of the subjects remain protected in accordance with the applicable law on personal data protection. Appropriate technical and organizational measures have to be implemented to protect information and personal data processed against unauthorized or unlawful access, disclosure, dissemination, alteration, destruction or accidental loss, in particular where the processing involves the transmission over a network (Article 56). Member States have to apply Directive 95/46/EC to the processing of personal data carried out in the Member States pursuant to the Clinical Trials Regulation (Article 93.1.).

E. As Little Pain, Discomfort, Fear and Any Other Foreseeable Risk

404. The clinical trial has to be designed to involve as little pain, discomfort, fear and any other foreseeable risk as possible for the subjects, and both the risk threshold and the degree of distress have to be specifically defined in the protocol and constantly monitored (Article 28.1e).

F. Medical Care under the Responsibility of an Appropriately Qualified Medical Doctor/Dental Practitioner

405. The medical care provided to the subjects is the responsibility of an appropriately qualified medical doctor or, where appropriate, a qualified dental practitioner (Article 28.1f).

G. No Undue Influence

406. No undue influence, including that of a financial nature, is exerted on subjects to participate in the clinical trial (Article 28.1h).

H. Protection of Subjects During the Clinical Trial

1. Conduct in Accordance with the Protocol and Good Clinical Practice Principles

407. The sponsor of a clinical trial and the investigator ensure that the clinical trial is conducted in accordance with the protocol and with the principles of good clinical practice (Article 47).

2. Adequate Monitoring of the Conduct of the Clinical Trial

408. In order to verify that the rights, safety and well-being of subjects are protected, that the reported data are reliable and robust and that the conduct of the clinical trial is in compliance with the requirements of the Clinical Trials Regulation, the sponsor adequately monitors the conduct of a clinical trial. The extent and nature of the monitoring is determined by the sponsor on the basis of an assessment that takes into consideration all characteristics of the clinical trial, including the following characteristics: (a) whether the clinical trial is a low-intervention clinical trial; (b) the objective and methodology of the clinical trial; and (c) the degree of deviation of the intervention from normal clinical practice (Article 48).

3. Qualified Investigator

409. The investigator has to be a medical doctor as defined in national law, or a person following a profession which is recognized in the Member State concerned as qualifying for an investigator because of the necessary scientific knowledge and experience in patient care. Other individuals involved in conducting a clinical trial have to be suitably qualified by education, training and experience to perform their tasks (Article 49).

4. Suitable Facilities

410. The facilities where the clinical trial is conducted have to be suitable for the conduct of the clinical trial in compliance with the requirements of the Clinical Trials Regulation (Article 50).

5. Notification of Serious Breaches of Safety and Rights of a Subject

411. The sponsor has to notify the Member States concerned about a serious breach of the Clinical Trials Regulation or of the version of the protocol applicable at the time of the breach through the EU portal without undue delay but not later than seven days of becoming aware of that breach. For the purposes of this Article, a 'serious breach' means a breach likely to affect to a significant degree the safety and rights of a subject or the reliability and robustness of the data generated in the clinical trial (Article 51).

6. No Costs to Be Borne by the Subject

412. Without prejudice to the Member States' competence for the definition of their health policy and for the organization and delivery of health services and medical care, the costs for investigational medicinal products, auxiliary medicinal products, medical devices used for their administration and procedures specifically required by the protocol are not to be borne by the subject, unless the law of the Member State concerned provides otherwise (Article 92).

I. Damage Compensation

413. Member States ensure that systems for compensation for any damage suffered by a subject resulting from participation in a clinical trial conducted on their territory are in place in the form of insurance, a guarantee, or a similar arrangement that is equivalent as regards its purpose and which is appropriate to the nature and the extent of the risk. The sponsor and the investigator make use of that system in the form appropriate for the Member State concerned where the clinical trial is conducted. Member States may not require any additional use of that system for low-intervention clinical trials if any possible damage that could be suffered by a subject resulting from the use of the investigational medicinal product in accordance with the protocol of that specific clinical trial on the territory of that Member State is covered by the applicable compensation system already in place (Article 76).[480]

J. Summary of the Results of the Clinical Trial Within One Year

414. Irrespective of the outcome of a clinical trial, within one year from the end of a clinical trial in all Member States concerned, the sponsor has to submit to the EU database a summary of the results of the clinical trial (*see* for the content of that summary Annex IV to the Clinical Trials Regulation). It has to be accompanied by a summary written in a manner that is understandable to laypersons (*see* Annex V to the Clinical Trials Regulation for the content of that summary). However, where, for scientific reasons detailed in the protocol, it is not possible to submit a summary of the results within one year, the summary of results has to be submitted as soon as it is available. In this case, the protocol has to specify when the results are going

480. *See* for the state of affairs under the Clinical trials Directive, E. Gaspari, 'Sponsoring a Clinical Trial: Pharmaceutical Companies' Liability under the Scrutiny of the Italian Supreme Court', 5 *European Pharmaceutical Law Review* 100–101 (2021).

to be submitted, together with a justification (Article 37.4.). If sponsors fail to submit a summary of the results of the clinical trial, Member States can impose penalties (Article 93). The overall transparency of clinical trials will be enhanced when the related provisions in the Clinical Trials Regulation are fully implemented. The European Commission is aware of the low reporting rate of clinical trials in the EU, especially among academic sponsors. The Commission, with the European Medicine Agency (EMA) and Heads of Medicine Agencies, published a joint letter to sponsors about their reporting duties. As a result, reporting rates among academic sponsors improved considerably.[481]

III. Clinical Trials on Incapacitated Subjects

A. *Incapacitated Subject*

415. An incapacitated subject is a subject who is, for reasons other than the age of legal competence to give informed consent, incapable of giving informed consent according to the law of the Member State concerned (Article 2.2.19). For the purposes of the Clinical Trials Regulation, a subject which falls under the definition of both 'minor' and 'incapacitated subject' is deemed to be an incapacitated subject (Article 2.3). This explains why the Clinical Trials Regulation does not refer to adult incapacitated subjects.

416. In the case of incapacitated subjects who have not given, or have not refused to give, informed consent before the onset of their incapacity, a clinical trial may be conducted only where, in addition to the conditions set out in Article 28, all of the conditions provided for in Article 31 are met (Article 31.1.).

417. It follows from the wording of Article 31.1. that it is not applicable when an incapacitated person has given or refused informed consent before the onset of his or her incapacity. In that situation, the consent or refusal will remain valid.[482]

B. *Informed Consent of the Legally Designated Representative*

1. Basic Rule

418. The informed consent of the legally designated representative of the incapacitated person has to be obtained (Article 31.1a).

---

481. Answer by Ms Kyriakides on behalf of the European Commission to a written Parliamentary question of P. Beyer, Unpublished results of clinical trials on medicinal products, 6 Apr. 2020, E-000001/2020.
482. *Supra* n. 464, 375.

2. Legally Designated Representative

419. The rules concerning the determination of the legally designated representatives of incapacitated persons diverge in Member States. It is, therefore, left to the Member States to determine the legally designated representatives of incapacitated persons (*see* Recital 27 in the Preamble).

3. Participation and Signature of the Subject

420. The subject may, as far as possible, take part in the informed consent procedure (Article 31.3.). The Clinical Trials Regulation is without prejudice to national law requiring that both the signature of the incapacitated person and the signature of his or her legally designated representative may be required on the informed consent form (Article 29.7.).

C. Information to Be Provided to the Incapacitated Person

421. The incapacitated subjects must have received the information referred to in Article 29.2. in a way that is adequate in view of their capacity to understand it (Article 31.1b) (*see* paragraphs 387 et seq.). It is evident that the representative of this incapacitated person also has to receive all the information referred to in Article 29.2.

D. Respect for the Explicit Wish to Refuse or Withdraw Consent

422. The explicit wish of an incapacitated subject who is capable of forming an opinion and assessing the information referred to in Article 29.2. to refuse participation in, or to withdraw from, the clinical trial at any time has to be respected by the investigator (Article 31.1c). It is evident that this explicit will has also to be respected by the legally designated representative.

E. No Incentives or Financial Inducements

423. No incentives or financial inducements may be given to the subjects or their legally designated representatives, except for compensation for expenses and loss of earnings directly related to the participation in the clinical trial (Article 31.1d).

F. *Clinical Trial Is Essential and No Alternative*

424. The clinical trial has to be essential with respect to incapacitated subjects, and data of comparable validity cannot be obtained in clinical trials on persons able to give informed consent or by other research methods (Article 31.1e).

G. *Directly Related to the Medical Condition of the Subject*

425. The clinical trial has to relate directly to a medical condition from which the subject suffers (Article 31.1f). As a consequence, it is not possible to include in a clinical trial an incapacitated person who does not suffer from any medical condition or when the clinical trial does not directly relate to a medical condition the subject is suffering from.

H. *A Direct Benefit for the Subject ... Or ...*

426. There have to be scientific grounds for expecting that participation in the clinical trial will produce a direct benefit to the incapacitated subject, outweighing the risks and burdens involved (Article 31.1g(i)). As a consequence, an incapacitated subject cannot participate in a non-therapeutic clinical trial.

I. *Some Benefit for the Population Represented by the Subject and Directly Related to the Life-Threatening or Debilitating Medical Condition from Which the Subject Suffers*

427. If no direct benefit to the subject is to be expected, there have to be scientific grounds for expecting that his or her participation in the clinical trial will produce some benefit for the population represented by the incapacitated subject concerned. In that case, the clinical trial has to relate directly to the life-threatening or debilitating medical condition from which the subject suffers, and the trial may pose only minimal risk to and may impose only minimal burden on, the incapacitated subject concerned in comparison with the standard treatment of the incapacitated subject's condition (Article 31.1g(ii)).

428. Unlike the Clinical Trials Directive, that did not allow for non-therapeutic clinical trials on incapacitated persons,[483] the Clinical Trials Regulation does allow for such trials under strict conditions. This is remarkable, more so, as the draft Clinical Trials Regulation did not differ from the Clinical Trials Directive in this

483. And this was severely criticized, *see* H. Visser, 'Non-therapeutic Research in the EU in Adults Incapable of Giving Consent', *The Lancet* 818–819 (2001); *see also* A.E. Westra, 'Ambiguous Articles in the New EU Regulation May Lead to Exploitation of Vulnerable Research Subjects', 42 *Journal Medical Ethics* 189 (2016): 'A total ban on so called non-therapeutic with incompetent subjects would make it impossible to improve healthcare for these groups.'

respect.[484] Only one Recital in the Preamble is devoted to this fundamental change and in a rather superficial way: 'In order to improve treatments available for vulnerable groups, such as frail or older people, people suffering from multiple chronic conditions, and people affected by mental health disorders, medicinal products which are likely to be of significant clinical value should be fully and appropriately studied for their effects in these specific groups, including as regards requirements related to their specific characteristics and the protection of the health and well-being of subjects belonging to these groups.' (Recital 15 in the Preamble)

429. The criterion of minimal risk and minimal burden appears in many guidelines and regulations and is generally accepted. However, the Clinical Trials Regulation adds to this 'in comparison with the standard treatment of the subject's condition'. Westra argues correctly that this condition can be interpreted in a way that may lead to exploitation of vulnerable research subjects. The added wording sets a relative standard for the concepts of minimal risk and minimal burden: the meaning of 'minimal' depends on the severity of the standard treatment: if, for example, the standard treatment for the subjects' condition includes muscle biopsies, the risk and burdens of such biopsies for these subjects may be regarded as minimal.[485]

430. The ethical and legal delicateness of this condition is highlighted in Article 31.2., that leaves without prejudice more stringent national rules prohibiting the conduct of those clinical trials on incapacitated subjects, where there are no scientific grounds to expect that participation in the clinical trial will produce a direct benefit to the subject outweighing the risks and burdens involved.[486]

J. Ethical Assessment on the Basis of Expertise in the Relevant Disease

431. Specific consideration has to be given to the assessment of the application for authorization of a clinical trial on the basis of expertise in the relevant disease and the patient population concerned or after taking advice on clinical, ethical and psychosocial questions in the field of the relevant disease and the patient population concerned (Article 10.2.).

IV. Clinical Trials on Minors

432. A minor is a subject who is, according to the law of the Member State concerned, under the age of legal competence to give informed consent (Article 2.2(18)).

484. *Supra* n. 464, 376.
485. *Supra* n. 483, 189–190.
486. For example, Belgian law does not allow for this kind of clinical trials, *see supra* n. 455, 196.

A. Basic Rule

433. In the case of minors, a clinical trial may be conducted only where, in addition to the conditions set out in Article 28, all of the conditions provided for in Article 32 are met (Article 32.1.).[487]

B. Informed Consent

1. Informed Consent of the Legally Designated Representative

434. The informed consent of the legally designated representative has to be obtained (Article 32.1a). As the rules concerning the determination of the legally designated representatives of minors diverge in the Member States, it is left to the Member States to determine the legally designated representatives of minors (*see* Recital 27 in the Preamble).

2. Participation of the Minor

435. The minor has to take part in the informed consent procedure in a way adapted to his or her age and mental maturity (Article 32.2.).

3. Assent of the Minor

436. The Clinical Trials Regulation is without prejudice to national law requiring that, in addition to the informed consent given by the legally designated representative, a minor who is capable of forming an opinion and assessing the information given to him or her also has to assent in order to participate in a clinical trial (Article 29.8.).

4. Informed Consent of the Minor When He Reaches the Age of Legal Competence

437. If, during a clinical trial, the minor reaches the age of legal competence to give informed consent as defined in the law of the Member State concerned, his or

487. Paragraph 5 of the European Parliament Resolution of 15 Dec. 2016 on the regulation on paediatric medicines (2016/2902(RSP)) stresses the importance of cross-border trials for research into many paediatric and rare illnesses and therefore welcomes Regulation 536/2014; para. 26 of the European Parliament Resolution of 14 Feb. 2017 on promoting gender equality in mental health and clinical research (2016/2096(INI)) 'suggests that clinical trials should also take account of specific vulnerable population groups such as paediatric and geriatric patients and persons from ethnic minorities'.

her express informed consent has to be obtained before that subject can continue to participate in the clinical trial (Article 32.3.).

C. Information to Be Provided to the Minor

438. The minors have to receive the information referred to in Article 29.2. in a way adapted to their age and mental maturity and from investigators or members of the investigating team who are trained or experienced in working with children (Article 32.1b).

D. Explicit Wish to Refuse Is Respected

439. The explicit wish of a minor who is capable of forming an opinion and assessing the information referred to in Article 29.2. to refuse participation in, or to withdraw from, the clinical trial at any time has to be respected by the investigator (Article 32.1c).

E. No Incentives or Financial Inducements

440. No incentives or financial inducements should be given to the subject or his or her legally designated representative except for compensation for expenses and loss of earnings directly related to the participation in the clinical trial (Article 32.1d).

F. A Medical Condition That Only Occurs in Minors … Or …

441. The clinical trial has to be intended to investigate treatments for a medical condition that only occurs in minors (Article 32.1e). In this respect, the question arises of how this provision relates to Article 32.3. of the Clinical Trials Regulation (*see* paragraph 437). Probably, the answer is that the clinical trial has to be halted once the minor has reached the age of legal competence to give informed consent.

G. … Essential to Validate Alternatives

442. If the clinical trial does not have the intention to investigate treatments for a medical condition that only occurs in minors, the clinical trial has to be essential with respect to minors to validate data obtained in clinical trials on persons able to give informed consent or by other research methods (Article 32.1e).

H. Directly Related to the Medical Condition of the Minor or No Alternative but Minors

443. The clinical trial either has to relate directly to a medical condition from which the minor concerned suffers or has to be of such a nature that it can only be carried out on minors (Article 32.1f).

I. A Direct Benefit for the Minor ... Or ...

444. There have to be scientific grounds for expecting that participation in the clinical trial will produce a direct benefit to the minor concerned outweighing the risks and burdens involved (Article 32.1g(i)). This means that a minor cannot participate in a non-therapeutic clinical trial.

J. ... Some Benefit for the Population Represented by the Minor

445. If there are no scientific grounds for expecting that participation will produce a direct benefit to the minor, there have to be scientific grounds for expecting that participation in the clinical trial will produce some benefit for the population represented by the minor concerned. Moreover, the clinical trial should pose only minimal risk to, and should impose minimal burden on, the minor concerned in comparison with the standard treatment of the minor's condition (Article 32.1g(ii)).[488]

446. Compared with the conditions for such a clinical trial with adult incapacitated persons, it is remarkable that the condition regarding life-threatening or debilitating medical condition from which the subject suffers is not provided here (*see* paragraph 427). The Clinical Trials Directive was already more flexible for non-therapeutic clinical trials on minors than on incapacitated persons. This possibly explains why, for clinical trials on minors, a provision analogous to Article 31.1g(ii) is lacking.

K. Ethical Assessment on the Basis of Paediatric Expertise

447. Specific consideration has to be given to the assessment of the application for authorization of a clinical trial on the basis of paediatric expertise or after taking advice on clinical, ethical and psychosocial problems in the field of paediatrics (Article 10.1.).

488. K. Wade, 'Defining the Threshold of Permissible Risk for Non-therapeutic Clinical Trials with Children in Europe', 24 *European Journal of Health Law* 414–431 (2017).

V. Clinical Trials on Pregnant or Breastfeeding Women

448. A clinical trial on pregnant or breastfeeding women may be conducted only where, in addition to the conditions set out in Article 28 (*see* paragraphs 385 et seq.), the following conditions are met: (a) the clinical trial has the potential to produce a direct benefit for the pregnant or breastfeeding woman concerned, or her embryo, foetus or child after birth, outweighing the risks and burdens involved; or (b) if such clinical trial has no direct benefit for the pregnant or breastfeeding woman concerned, or her embryo, foetus or child after birth, it can be conducted only if: (i) a clinical trial of comparable effectiveness cannot be carried out on women who are not pregnant or breastfeeding; (ii) the clinical trial contributes to the attainment of results capable of benefitting pregnant or breastfeeding women or other women in relation to reproduction or other embryos, foetuses or children; and (iii) the clinical trial poses a minimal risk to, and imposes a minimal burden on, the pregnant or breastfeeding woman concerned, her embryo, foetus or child after birth; (c) where research is undertaken on breastfeeding women, particular care is taken to avoid any adverse impact on the health of the child; and (d) no incentives or financial inducements are given to the subject except for compensation for expenses and loss of earnings directly related to the participation in the clinical trial (Article 33).

449. Specific consideration has to be given to the assessment of the application for authorization of a clinical trial on the basis of expertise in the relevant condition and the population represented by the subject concerned (Article 10.3.).

VI. Clinical Trials on Other Vulnerable Subjects

450. Member States may maintain additional measures regarding persons performing mandatory military service, persons deprived of liberty, persons who, due to a judicial decision, cannot take part in clinical trials, or persons in residential care institutions (Article 34). Residential care institutions are accommodations providing uninterrupted assistance for persons who necessitate such assistance.

451. These four categories of persons have in common that they are in a situation of subordination or factual dependency and, therefore, may require specific protective measures (*see* Recital 35 in the Preamble).

452. It is not clear which additional measures can be provided for persons who, due to a judicial decision, cannot take part in clinical trials because, by definition, they cannot take part in a clinical trial.

453. Article 34 does not mention economically or socially disadvantaged groups and does not provide any specific protection for them.[489]

489. E. Gennet, R. Andorno & B. Elger, 'Does the New EU Regulation on Clinical Trials Adequately Protect Vulnerable Research Participants', 119 *Health Policy* 928 (2015).

454. If, according to the protocol, a clinical trial provides for the participation of specific groups or subgroups of subjects, where appropriate, specific consideration has to be given to the assessment of the application for authorization of that clinical trial on the basis of expertise in the population represented by the subjects concerned (Article 10.4.).

VII. Clinical Trials in Emergency Situations

455. By way of derogation from Article 28.1b (information to the subject or his legal representative) and Article 28.1c (informed consent), Article 31.1a and 1b (obligation to inform and obtain informed consent for a clinical trial on an incapacitated person) and Article 32.1a and 1b (obligation to inform and obtain informed consent for a clinical trial on a minor), informed consent to participate in a clinical trial may be obtained, and information on the clinical trial may be given, after the decision to include the subject in the clinical trial, provided that this decision is taken at the time of the first intervention on the subject, in accordance with the protocol for that clinical trial and that all of the following conditions are fulfilled:

(a) due to the urgency of the situation, caused by a sudden life-threatening or other sudden serious medical condition, the subject is unable to provide prior informed consent and to receive prior information on the clinical trial;
(b) there are scientific grounds to expect that participation of the subject in the clinical trial will have the potential to produce a direct clinically relevant benefit for the subject, resulting in a measurable health-related improvement alleviating the suffering and/or improving the health of the subject, or in the diagnosis of its condition;
(c) it is not possible within the therapeutic window to supply all prior information to and obtain prior informed consent from his or her legally designated representative;
(d) the investigator certifies that he or she is not aware of any objections to participating in the clinical trial previously expressed by the subject;
(e) the clinical trial relates directly to the subject's medical condition because of which it is not possible within the therapeutic window to obtain prior informed consent from the subject or from his or her legally designated representative and to supply prior information, and the clinical trial is of such a nature that it may be conducted exclusively in emergency situations;
(f) the clinical trial poses a minimal risk to and imposes a minimal burden on the subject in comparison with the standard treatment of the subject's condition (Article 35.1.).

456. Following an intervention pursuant to Article 35.1. informed consent in accordance with Article 29 has to be sought to continue the participation of the subject in the clinical trial, and information on the clinical trial has to be given in accordance with the following requirements:

(a) Regarding incapacitated subjects and minors, informed consent has to be sought by the investigator from his or her legally designated representative without undue delay and the information referred to in Article 29.2. has to be given as soon as possible to the subject and to his or her legally designated representative; some authors are nevertheless afraid that the Clinical Trials Regulation 'may not be completely apt for critical situations when relatives cannot be reached in time to give proxy consent'.[490]

(b) Regarding other subjects, informed consent has to be sought by the investigator without undue delay from the subject or his or her legally designated representative, whichever is sooner and the information referred to in Article 29.2. has to be given as soon as possible to the subject or his or her legally designated representative, whichever is sooner. Where informed consent has been obtained from the legally designated representative, informed consent to continue the participation in the clinical trial has to be obtained from the subject as soon as he or she is capable of giving informed consent (Article 35.2.).

457. If the subject or, where applicable, his or her legally designated representative does not give consent, he or she has to be informed of the right to object to the use of data obtained from the clinical trial (Article 35.3.).

458. In any application for authorization of a clinical trial in an emergency situation, specific consideration has to be given to the circumstances of the conduct of the clinical trial (Article 10.5.).

490. M. Timmers, et.al., 'Will the EU Data Protection Regulation 2016/679 Inhibit Critical Care Research?', 27 *Medical Law Review* 60 (2019).

Chapter 2. Clinical Investigations on Medical Devices

459. Clinical investigations on medical devices are regulated in Chapter VI of Regulation (EU) 2017/745 of the European Parliament and of the Council of 5 April 2017 on medical devices, amending Directive 2001/83/EC, Regulation (EC) No. 178/2002 and Regulation (EC) No. 1223/2009 and repealing Council Directives 90/385/EEC and 93/42/EEC (the Medical Devices Regulation (MDR)).[491] The MDR entered into force on 5 May 2017 (Article 123.1) and became fully applicable on 26 May 2021.[492] The Commission acknowledged that implementing the MDR is challenging.[493] In 2024, the Commission will start a preparatory work for a targeted evaluation of the MDR. The evaluation will assess how the legislation is affecting the availability of devices, in particular for devices with specific characteristics (e.g., paediatrics, orphan and innovative devices). In the assessment, special attention will also be given to costs and administrative burdens stemming from the implementation of legislation, especially for small and medium-sized enterprises. The potential of digitalization in this exercise will be part of this assessment.[494]

§1. Field of Application

460. The MDR applies to clinical investigations concerning medical devices for human use and accessories for such devices conducted in the Union (Article 1) (*see* for the definition of medical devices, *supra* paragraph 44).[495] It does not apply to in vitro diagnostic medical devices covered by Regulation 2017/746 (*see* Chapter 3). A clinical investigation means any systematic investigation involving one or more human subjects undertaken to assess the safety or performance of a device (Article 2(45)). A subject is an individual who participates in a clinical investigation (Article 2(50)).

491. *Supra* n. 90; *see* I. Vinck et al., 'Market Introduction of Innovative High Risk Medical Devices: Towards a Recast of the Directive Concerning Medical Devices', 18 *European Journal of Health Law* 477–489 (2011).
492. Regulation (EU) 2020/561 of 23 Apr. 2020 amending the MDR, *OJ* 2020, L 130, 18–22.
493. Answer given by Ms Kyriakides on behalf of the European Commission to a written Parliamentary question of J. Van Overtveldt and G. Bourgeois, Implementation of the Regulation on medical devices, 1 Apr. 2020, E-004441/2019; comparable answer given by Ms Kyriakides on behalf of the European Commission to a written Parliamentary question of A. Glück, Ongoing problems with the implementation of the Medical Device Regulation, 19 Jul. 2022, E-001920/2022; K. Shatrov and C.R. Blankart, 'After the Four-Year Transition Period: Is the European Union's Medical Device Regulation of 2017 Likely to Achieve Its Main Goals?', 126 *Health Policy* 1233–1240 (2022).
494. Answer given by Ms Kyriakides on behalf of the European Commission to a written Parliamentary question of K Van Brempt, Allowing electronic instructions for use for medical devices to be issued to patients, 4 Apr. 2024, E-000535/2024.
495. C. McMillan, 'Rethinking the Regulation of Digital Contraception under the Medical Devices Regime', 23 *Medical Law International* 3–25 (2023).

§2. CONDITIONS TO CONDUCT A CLINICAL INVESTIGATION

I. Generally Applicable Conditions

461. The rules on clinical investigations should be in line with well-established international guidance in this field, such as the international standard ISO 14155:2011 on good clinical practice for clinical investigations of medical devices for human subjects, so as to make it easier for the results of clinical investigations conducted in the Union to be accepted as documentation outside the Union and to make it easier for the results of clinical investigations conducted outside the Union in accordance with international guidelines to be accepted within the Union. In addition, the rules should be in line with the most recent version of the World Medical Association Declaration of Helsinki on Ethical Principles for Medical Research Involving Human Subjects (*see* Recital 64 in the Preamble). McHale rightly argues 'that clinical trials concerning drugs are simply and inevitably practically different – put bluntly, it is easier to stop a participant taking a trial drug than to remove an implant'.[496]

462. Moreover, the MDR respects the fundamental rights and observes the principles recognized in particular by the Charter of Fundamental Rights and in particular human dignity, the integrity of the person, the protection of personal data, the freedom of art and science, the freedom to conduct business and the right to property. The MDR has to be applied by the Member States in accordance with those rights and principles (*see* Recital 89 in the Preamble).

463. Clinical investigations have to be designed and conducted in a way that the rights, safety, dignity and well-being of the subjects participating in a clinical investigation are protected and prevail over all other interests, and the clinical data generated are scientifically valid, reliable and robust. Clinical investigations have to be subject to scientific and ethical review. The ethical review has to be performed by an ethics committee in accordance with national law. Member States ensure that the procedures for review by ethics committees are compatible with the procedures set out in the MDR for the assessment of the application for authorization of a clinical investigation. At least one layperson has to participate in the ethical review (Article 62.3.).

A. Authorization

464. The clinical investigation is the subject of authorization by the Member State(s) in which the clinical investigation is to be conducted in accordance with the MDR unless otherwise stated (Article 62.4a). The application procedure is further regulated in Article 71 (Assessment by Member States). It should be left to the Member State where a clinical investigation is to be conducted to determine the

496. *Supra* n. 325, 202.

appropriate authority to be involved in the assessment of the application to conduct a clinical investigation (*see* Recital 65 in the Recital).

B. No Negative Opinion of an Ethics Committee

465. An ethics committee, set up in accordance with national law, has not issued a negative opinion in relation to the clinical investigation, which is valid for that entire Member State under its national law (Article 62.4b). An ethics committee is an independent body established in a Member State in accordance with the law of that Member State and empowered to give opinions for the purposes of the MDR, taking into account the views of laypersons, in particular patients or patients' organizations (Article 2(56)). 'Lay person' means an individual who does not have formal education in a relevant field of healthcare or medical discipline (Article 2.38). It should be left to the Member States to organize the involvement of ethics committees within the timelines for the authorization of that clinical investigation as set out in the MDR. Such decisions are a matter of internal organization for each Member State. In that context, Member States should ensure that the necessary expertise is available in an ethics committee (Recital 65 of the Preamble).

466. There are some remarkable differences concerning the role of an ethics committee in the Clinical Trials Regulation and the MDR. First of all, while an ethical review and an opinion by an ethics committee is no explicit obligation in the Clinical Trials Regulation (*see* paragraph 374), such an obligation is provided for in the MDR. Second, while the Clinical Trials Regulation requires Member States to provide for an appeal procedure in case of the refusal of an authorization based on a negative opinion of an ethics committee (Article 8.4) (*see* paragraph 381), this is not the case in the MDR. However, neither the Clinical Trials Regulation nor the MDR explicitly require a favourable opinion from an ethics committee. It suffices that the opinion is not a negative one.

C. Sponsor Established in the EU

467. The sponsor, its legal representative or a contact person is established in the Union (Article 62.4c).

D. Proportionality Requirement (Balance Benefits-Risks)

468. The anticipated benefits to the subjects or to public health justify the foreseeable risks and inconveniences, and compliance with this condition is constantly monitored (Article 62.4e).

E. Informed Consent of the Subject

469. The subject has given informed consent in accordance with Article 63 (Article 62.4f). Informed consent means a subject's free and voluntary expression of his or her willingness to participate in a particular clinical yinvestigation after having been informed of all aspects of the clinical investigation that are relevant to the subject's decision to participate or, in the case of minors and of incapacitated subjects, an authorization or agreement from their legally designated representative to include them in the clinical investigation (Article 2(55). This is exactly the same definition as in Article 2.2.26 Clinical Trials Regulation) (*see* paragraph 383).

470. Informed consent has to be written, dated and signed by the person performing the interview referred to in paragraph 2c of this article and by the subject or where the subject is unable to write, consent may be given and recorded through appropriate alternative means in the presence of at least one impartial witness. In that case, the witness has to sign and date the informed consent document. The subject has to be provided with a copy of the document or the record, as appropriate, by which informed consent has been given. The informed consent has to be documented. Adequate time has to be given for the subject to consider his or her decision to participate in the clinical investigation (Article 63.1.).

471. Information given to the subject for the purposes of obtaining his or her informed consent: (a) has to enable the subject to understand: (i) the nature, objectives, benefits, implications, risks and inconveniences of the clinical investigation; (ii) the subject's rights and guarantees regarding his or her protection, in particular his or her right to refuse to participate and the right to withdraw from the clinical investigation at any time without any resulting detriment and without having to provide any justification; (iii) the conditions under which the clinical investigation is to be conducted, including the expected duration of the subject's participation in the clinical investigation; and (iv) the possible treatment alternatives, including the follow-up measures if the participation of the subject in the clinical investigation is discontinued; (b) has to be kept comprehensive, concise, clear, relevant and understandable to the subject; (c) has to be provided in a prior interview with a member of the investigating team who is appropriately qualified under national law; (d) has to include information about the applicable damage compensation system referred to in Article 69; and (e) has to include the Union-wide unique single identification number of the clinical investigation referred to in Article 70.1. and information about the availability of the clinical investigation results in accordance with paragraph 6 of this Article (Article 63.2.).

472. This information has to be prepared in writing and be available to the subject (Article 63.3.). In the interview referred to in point (c), special attention has to be paid to the information needs of specific patient populations and individual subjects, as well as to the methods used to give the information. In this interview, it has to be verified that the subject has understood the information (Article 63.4. and 63.5.). The subject has to be informed that a clinical investigation report and a summary presented in terms understandable to the intended user will be made available pursuant to Article 77.4., irrespective of the outcome of the clinical investigation, and, to the extent possible, when they have become available (Article 63.6.).

473. Any subject may, without any resulting detriment and without having to provide any justification, withdraw from the clinical investigation at any time by revoking his or her informed consent. Without prejudice to Directive 95/46/EC, the withdrawal of the informed consent will not affect the activities already carried out and the use of data obtained based on informed consent before its withdrawal (Article 62.5.).

F. Contact Details for Further Information

474. The subjects have to be provided with the contact details of any entity where further information can be received in case of need (Article 62.4g).

G. Respect for the Rights to Physical and Mental Integrity, to Privacy and to Data Protection

475. The rights of the subject to physical and mental integrity, privacy and the protection of the data concerning him or her in accordance with Directive 95/46/EC are safeguarded (Article 62.4h).

H. As Little Pain, Discomfort, Fear and Any Other Foreseeable Risk

476. The clinical investigation has to be designed to involve as little pain, discomfort, fear and any other foreseeable risk as possible for the subjects, and both the risk threshold and the degree of distress have to be specifically defined in the clinical investigation plan and constantly monitored (Article 62.4i).

I. Medical Care under the Responsibility of an Appropriately Qualified Medical Doctor/Dental Practitioner

477. The medical care provided to the subjects is the responsibility of an appropriately qualified medical doctor or, where appropriate, a qualified dental practitioner or any other person entitled by national law to provide the relevant patient care under clinical investigation conditions (Article 62.4j).

J. No Undue Influence

478. No undue influence, including that of a financial nature, is exerted on subjects to participate in the clinical investigation (Article 63.4k).

K. The Investigational Device Conforms to the Applicable General Safety and Performance Requirements

479. The investigational device(s) in question conform(s) to the applicable general safety and performance requirements set out in Annex I of the MDR, apart from the aspects covered by the clinical investigation; with regard to those aspects, every precaution has been taken to protect the health and safety of the subjects. This includes, where appropriate, technical and biological safety testing and pre-clinical evaluation, as well as provisions in the field of occupational safety and accident prevention, taking into consideration state of the art (Article 62.4l).

L. Carried Out in Accordance with Recognized Ethical Principles

480. The requirements of Annex XV to the MDR are fulfilled (Article 62.4m). Chapter I of Annex XV contains some general requirements with regard to clinical investigations. The first of these requirements is 'Ethical Principles': Each step in the clinical investigation, from the initial consideration of the need for and justification of the study to the publication of the results, has to be carried out in accordance with recognized ethical principles.

M. Qualified Investigator and Other Personnel

481. The investigator has to be a person exercising a profession which is recognized in the Member State concerned as qualifying for the role of the investigator on account of having the necessary scientific knowledge and experience in patient care. Other personnel involved in conducting a clinical investigation have to be suitably qualified, by education, training or experience in the relevant medical field and in clinical research methodology, to perform their tasks (Article 62.6.).

N. Suitable Facilities

482. The facilities where the clinical investigation is to be conducted have to be suitable for the clinical investigation and similar to the facilities where the device is intended to be used (Article 62.7.).

O. Damage Compensation

483. Member States ensure that systems for compensation for any damage suffered by a subject resulting from participation in a clinical investigation conducted on their territory are in place in the form of insurance, a guarantee, or a similar arrangement that is equivalent as regards its purpose and which is appropriate to the nature and the extent of the risk. The sponsor and the investigator make use of this system in the form appropriate for the Member State in which the clinical investigation is conducted (Article 69).

II. Clinical Investigations on Incapacitated Subjects

484. Unlike the Clinical Trials Regulation (Article 2.2(19)) (*see* paragraph 415), the MDR does not contain a definition of incapacitated subjects. In the case of incapacitated subjects who have not given, or have refused to give, informed consent before the onset of their incapacity, a clinical investigation may be conducted only where, in addition to the conditions set out in Article 62.4., all of the following conditions are met:

(a) The informed consent of their legally designated representative has been obtained (Article 64.1a). It is left to the Member States to determine the legally designated representatives of incapacitated subjects (*see* Recital 72 in the Preamble). The subject has as much as possible to take part in the informed consent procedure (Article 64.2.).
(b) The incapacitated subjects have received the information referred to in Article 63.2. in a way that is adequate in view of their capacity to understand it (Article 64.1b).
(c) The explicit wish of an incapacitated subject who is capable of forming an opinion and assessing the information referred to in Article 63.2. to refuse participation in, or to withdraw from, the clinical investigation at any time is respected by the investigator (Article 64.1c).
(d) No incentives or financial inducements are given to subjects or their legally designated representatives, except for compensation for expenses and loss of earnings directly related to the participation in the clinical investigation (Article 64.1d).
(e) The clinical investigation is essential with respect to incapacitated subjects, and data of comparable validity cannot be obtained in clinical investigations on persons able to give informed consent or by other research methods (Article 64.1e).
(f) The clinical investigation relates directly to a medical condition from which the subject suffers (Article 64.1f).
(g) There are scientific grounds for expecting that participation in the clinical investigation will produce a direct benefit to the incapacitated subject outweighing the risks and burdens involved (Article 64.1g).

III. Clinical Investigations on Minors

485. Unlike the Clinical Trials Regulation (Article 2.2(18)) (*see* paragraph 432), the MDR does not contain a definition of a minor. A clinical investigation on minors may be conducted only where, in addition to the conditions set out in Article 62.4., all of the following conditions are met:

(a) The informed consent of their legally designated representative has to be obtained (Article 65a). It is left to the Member States to determine the legally designated representatives of minors (*see* Recital 72 in the Preamble). The minor has to take part in the informed consent procedure in a way adapted to his or her age and mental maturity (Article 65h). The explicit wish of a minor who is capable of forming an opinion and assessing the information referred to in Article 63.2. to refuse participation in, or to withdraw from, the clinical investigation at any time is respected by the investigator (Article 65c). If, during a clinical investigation, the minor reaches the age of legal competence to give informed consent as defined in national law, his or her express informed consent has to be obtained before that subject can continue to participate in the clinical investigation (Article 65i).
(b) The minors have to receive the information referred to in Article 63.2. in a way adapted to their age and mental maturity and from investigators or members of the investigating team who are trained or experienced in working with children (Article 65b).
(c) No incentives or financial inducements have been given to the subject or his or her legally designated representative except for compensation for expenses and loss of earnings directly related to the participation in the clinical investigation (Article 65d).
(d) The clinical investigation is intended to investigate treatments for a medical condition that only occurs in minors, or the clinical investigation is essential with respect to minors to validate data obtained in clinical investigations on persons able to give informed consent or by other research methods (Article 65e).
(e) The clinical investigation either relates directly to a medical condition from which the minor concerned suffers or is of such a nature that it can only be carried out on minors (Article 65f).
(f) There are scientific grounds for expecting that participation in the clinical investigation will produce a direct benefit to the minor subject outweighing the risks and burdens involved (Article 65g).

IV. Clinical Investigations on Pregnant or Breastfeeding Woman

486. A clinical investigation on pregnant or breastfeeding women may be conducted only where, in addition to the conditions set out in Article 62.4., all of the following conditions are met: (a) the clinical investigation has the potential to produce a direct benefit for the pregnant or breastfeeding woman concerned, or her embryo, foetus or child after birth, outweighing the risks and burdens involved; (b) where research is undertaken on breastfeeding women, particular care is taken to avoid any adverse impact on the health of the child; (c) no incentives or financial inducements are given to the subject except for compensation for expenses and loss of earnings directly related to the participation in the clinical investigation (Article 66).

V. Clinical Investigations on Other Vulnerable Subjects

487. Member States may maintain additional measures regarding persons performing mandatory military service, persons deprived of liberty, persons who, due to a judicial decision, cannot take part in clinical investigations, or persons in residential care institutions (Article 67; *see also* Article 34 Clinical Trials Regulation and above paragraph 453).

VI. Clinical Investigations in Emergency Situations

488. Informed consent to participate in a clinical investigation may be obtained, and information on the clinical investigation may be given after the decision to include the subject in the clinical investigation, provided that that decision is taken at the time of the first intervention on the subject, in accordance with the clinical investigation plan for that clinical investigation and that all of the following conditions are fulfilled:

(a) due to the urgency of the situation, caused by a sudden life-threatening or other sudden serious medical condition, the subject is unable to provide prior informed consent and to receive prior information on the clinical investigation;
(b) there are scientific grounds to expect that participation of the subject in the clinical investigation will have the potential to produce a direct clinically relevant benefit for the subject, resulting in a measurable health-related improvement alleviating the suffering and/or improving the health of the subject, or in the diagnosis of its condition;
(c) it is not possible within the therapeutic window to supply all prior information to and obtain prior informed consent from his or her legally designated representative;
(d) the investigator certifies that he or she is not aware of any objections to participate in the clinical investigation previously expressed by the subject;
(e) the clinical investigation relates directly to the subject's medical condition because of which it is not possible within the therapeutic window to obtain prior informed consent from the subject or from his or her legally designated representative and to supply prior information, and the clinical investigation is of such a nature that it may be conducted exclusively in emergency situations;
(f) the clinical investigation poses a minimal risk to and imposes a minimal burden on the subject in comparison with the standard treatment of the subject's condition (Article 68.1.).

489. Following such an intervention, informed consent in accordance with Article 63 has to be sought to continue the participation of the subject in the clinical investigation, and information on the clinical investigation has to be given in accordance with the following requirements:

(a) regarding incapacitated subjects and minors, informed consent has to be sought by the investigator from his or her legally designated representative without undue delay and the information referred to in Article 63.2. has to be given as soon as possible to the subject and to his or her legally designated representative;

(b) regarding other subjects, informed consent has to be sought by the investigator without undue delay from the subject or his or her legally designated representative, whichever can be done sooner, and the information referred to in Article 63.2. has to be given as soon as possible to the subject or his or her legally designated representative, as applicable. Where informed consent has been obtained from the legally designated representative, informed consent to continue the participation in the clinical investigation has to be obtained from the subject as soon as he or she is capable of giving informed consent (Article 68.2.).

If the subject or, where applicable, his or her legally designated representative does not give consent, he or she has to be informed of the right to object to the use of data obtained from the clinical investigation (Article 68.3.).

Chapter 3. Performance Studies on In Vitro Diagnostic Medical Devices

490. Performance studies on in vitro diagnostic medical devices are regulated in Chapter VI of Regulation (EU) 2017/746 of the European Parliament and of the Council of 5 April 2017 on in vitro diagnostic medical devices and repealing Directive 97/79/EC and Commission Decision 2010/227/EU (the In Vitro Diagnostic Medical Devices Regulation (IVD MDR)).[497] The IVD MDR entered into force on 5 May 2017 (Article 123.1). The transitional provisions provided for in Regulation 2017/746 have been extended by Regulation (EU) 2022/112.[498]

§1. Field of Application

491. The IVD MDR applies to performance studies concerning in vitro diagnostic medical devices for human use and accessories for such devices in the Union (Article 1).

492. In vitro, diagnostic medical device means any medical device which is a reagent, reagent product, calibrator, control material, kit, instrument, apparatus, piece of equipment, software or system, whether used alone or in combination, intended by the manufacturer to be used in vitro for the examination of specimens, including blood and tissue donations, derived from the human body, solely or principally for the purpose of providing information on one or more of the following: (a) concerning a physiological or pathological process or state; (b) concerning congenital physical or mental impairments; (c) concerning the predisposition to a medical condition or a disease; (d) to determine the safety and compatibility with potential recipients; (e) to predict treatment response or reactions; (f) to define or monitor therapeutic measures (Article 2.2).

493. A performance study means a study undertaken to establish or confirm the analytical or clinical performance of a device (Article 2(42)). Subject means an individual who participates in a performance study and whose specimen(s) undergo in vitro examination by a device for performance study and/or by a device used for control purposes (Article 2(47)).

---

497. *Supra* n. 91.
498. *OJ* L 19, 28 Jan. 2022, 3. Answer given by Ms Kyriakides on behalf of the European Commission on a written Parliamentary question of A. Niebler, Additional Costs Arising from the Regulation on Medical Devices, 17 Feb. 2022, E-005564/2021.

§2. CONDITIONS TO CONDUCT A PERFORMANCE STUDY

I. General Requirements Regarding Performance Studies

494. Performance studies have to be designed and conducted in such a way that the rights, safety, dignity and well-being of the subjects participating in such performance studies are protected and prevail over all other interests, and the data generated are scientifically valid, reliable and robust. Performance studies, including performance studies that use left-over samples, have to be conducted in accordance with applicable law on data protection (Article 57.3.).

495. The rules on performance studies should be in line with well-established international guidance in this field, such as the international standard ISO 14155:2011 on good clinical practice for clinical investigations of medical devices for human subjects, so as to make it easier for the results of performance studies conducted in the Union to be accepted as documentation outside the Union and to make it easier for the results of performance studies conducted outside the Union in accordance with international guidelines to be accepted within the Union. In addition, the rules should be in line with the most recent version of the World Medical Association Declaration of Helsinki on Ethical Principles for Medical Research Involving Human Subjects (*see* Recital 66 in the Preamble).

496. Moreover, the IVD MDR respects fundamental rights and observes the principles recognized in particular by the Charter of Fundamental Rights of the EU (*see* paragraphs 2 et seq.) and in particular, human dignity, the integrity of the person, the protection of personal data, the freedom of art and science, the freedom to conduct business and the right to property. The IVD MDR has to be applied by the Member States in accordance with those rights and principles (*see* Recital 89 in the Preamble).

II. Additional Requirements for Certain (Invasive) Performance Studies

497. Any performance study in which surgically invasive sample-taking is done only for the purpose of the performance study, or that is an interventional clinical performance study or where the conduct of the study involves additional invasive procedures or other risks for the subjects of the studies, has, in addition to meeting the requirements set out in Article 57 and Annex XIII, be designed, authorized, conducted, recorded and reported in accordance with this article and Articles 59–77 and Annex XIV (Article 58.1.). An interventional clinical performance study means a clinical performance study where the test results may influence patient management decisions and/or may be used to guide treatment (Article 2(46)).

498. Performance studies involving companion diagnostics are subjected to the same requirements as the performance studies listed in the previous paragraph. This does not apply to performance studies involving companion diagnostics using only left-over samples. Such studies have to be notified to the competent authority

(Article 58.2.). Companion diagnostic means a device which is essential for the safe and effective use of a corresponding medicinal product to identify, before and/or during treatment, patients who are most likely to benefit from the corresponding medicinal product or to identify, before and/or during treatment, patients likely to be at increased risk of serious adverse reactions as a result of treatment with the corresponding medicinal product (Article 2(7)).

499. Such performance studies are subjected to scientific and ethical review. The ethical review has to be performed by an ethics committee in accordance with national law. Member States have to ensure that the procedures for review by ethics committees are compatible with the procedures set out in the IVD MDR for the assessment of the application for authorization of a performance study. At least one layperson has to participate in the ethical review. 'Lay person' means an individual who does not have formal education in a relevant field of healthcare or medical discipline (Article 2.31).

500. The great majority of requirements for these performance studies are provided for in Article 58.5. are literally the same as the conditions to conduct a clinical investigation (*see* paragraphs 461 et seq.). More, in particular, are the following: authorization (Article 58.5a), no negative opinion of an ethics committee (Article 58.5b), sponsor established in the EU (Article 58.5c), proportionality (Article 58.5e), informed consent (Article 58.5f), contact details for further information (Article 58.5g), respect for the rights to physical and mental integrity, to privacy and to data protection (Article 58.5h), as little pain, discomfort, fear and any other foreseeable risk (Article 58.5i), medical care under the responsibility of an appropriately qualified medical doctor/dental practitioner (Article 58.5j) and no undue influence (Article 58.5k).

501. Moreover, Article 58.5. adds the following requirements for performance studies:

(a) where appropriate, biological safety testing reflecting the latest scientific knowledge or any other test deemed necessary in the light of the device's intended purpose has been conducted (Article 58.5l);
(b) in the case of clinical performance studies, the analytical performance has been demonstrated, taking into consideration state of the art (Article 58.5m);
(c) in the case of interventional clinical performance studies, the analytical performance and scientific validity have been demonstrated, taking into consideration the state of the art; where, for companion diagnostics, the scientific validity is not established, the scientific rationale for the use of the biomarker shall be provided (Article 58.5n);
(d) the technical safety of the device with regard to its use has been proven, taking into consideration state of the art as well as provisions in the field of occupational safety and accident prevention (Article 58.5o).

502. The requirements in Annex XIV of the IVD MDR have to be fulfilled. According to Article 2.2 of this Annex, each step in the clinical performance study, from the initial consideration of the need and justification of the study to the publication of the results, has to be carried out in accordance with recognized ethical principles.

503. As for clinical investigations, the requirements of a qualified investigator (Article 58.7.), suitable facilities (Article 58.8.) and damage compensation (Article 65) are also applicable to performance studies.

III. Performance Studies on Incapacitated Subjects

504. Article 60.1. and 60.2. provide for exactly the same conditions for performance studies on incapacitated studies as do Article 64.1. and 64.2. MDR for clinical investigations on incapacitated subjects (*see* paragraph 484).

505. There is, however, one very important exception. Whereas Article 64.1g of the MDR only allows for clinical investigations that will produce a direct benefit to the incapacitated subject, Article 60.1g of the IVD MDR not only allows performance studies on incapacitated persons that will produce a direct benefit (Article 60.1g(i)) but also performance studies on incapacitated persons when there are scientific grounds for expecting that participation in the performance study will produce some benefit for the population represented by the incapacitated subject concerned when the performance study will pose only minimal risk to, and will impose minimal burden on, the incapacitated subject concerned in comparison with the standard treatment of the incapacitated subject's condition (Article 60.1g(ii)). This is exactly the same wording that is used in Article 32.1g(ii) of the Clinical Trials Regulation (*see* paragraphs 445–446) that allows for the participation of minors in non-therapeutic clinical trials (in the case of incapacitated subjects the Clinical Trials Regulation requires for an additional requirement: a life-threatening or debilitating medical condition). However, the Clinical Trials Regulation does not allow minors in Member States to follow more stringent rules, whereas Article 61.3. of the IVD MDR provides that Article 60.1g(ii) is without prejudice to more stringent national rules prohibiting the conduct of those performance studies on incapacitated subjects, where there are no scientific grounds to expect that participation in the performance study will produce a direct benefit to the subject outweighing the risks and burdens involved. In this case, the IVD MDR uses exactly the same wording as Article 31.2. of the Clinical Trial Regulation (CTR) concerning clinical trials with incapacitated persons.

IV. Performance Studies on Minors

506. Article 61.1. of the IVD MDR allows performance studies on minors under the same conditions as Article 65 of the MDR concerning clinical investigations on minors (*see* paragraph 482). Also, here is one important exception. Whereas Article 65(g) MDR only allows for clinical investigations on minors that may produce a direct benefit, Article 61.1g(ii) IVD MDR allows performance studies on minors when there are scientific grounds for expecting that participation in the performance study will produce some benefit for the population represented by the minor concerned when the performance study will pose only minimal risk to, and will impose minimal burden on, the minor concerned in comparison with the standard treatment of the minor's condition. This is in accordance with Article 31.1g(ii) Clinical Trials Regulation. Unlike the Clinical Trials Regulation, Article 61.2. IVD MDR allows for more stringent national rules prohibiting the conduct of those performance studies on minors, where there are no scientific grounds to expect that participation in the performance study will produce a direct benefit to the subject outweighing the risks and burdens involved.

V. Performance Studies on Pregnant or Breastfeeding Women

507. Article 62a, c and d IVD MDR allow performance studies on pregnant and breastfeeding women under the same conditions as Article 66a, b and c MDR allow clinical investigations on these women (*see* paragraph 483). Unlike the MDR, however, Article 62b IVD MDR allows a performance study that has no direct benefit for the pregnant or breastfeeding woman concerned or her embryo, foetus or child after birth if: (i) a performance study of comparable effectiveness cannot be carried out on women who are not pregnant or breastfeeding; (ii) the performance study contributes to the attainment of results capable of benefitting pregnant or breastfeeding women or other women in relation to reproduction or other embryos, foetuses or children; and (iii) the performance study poses a minimal risk to, and imposes a minimal burden on, the pregnant or breastfeeding woman concerned, her embryo, foetus or child after birth. Article 33 Clinical Trials Regulation allows under the same conditions non-therapeutic clinical trials on pregnant or breastfeeding women (*see* paragraph 448).

VI. Performance Studies on Other Vulnerable Subjects

508. Member States may maintain additional measures regarding persons performing mandatory military service, persons deprived of liberty, persons who, due to a judicial decision, cannot take part in performance studies, or persons in residential care institutions (Article 63).

VII. Performance Studies in Emergency Situations

509. Article 64 IVD MDR provides for the same conditions as Article 68 MDR regarding clinical investigations in emergency situations (*see* paragraph 488).

Chapter 4. Non-interventional Post-Authorization Safety Studies

510. Article 107m–107p of Directive 2001/83/EC on the Community code relating to medicinal products for human use,[499] amended by Directive 2010/84 of 15 December 2010 regulate post-authorization safety studies.[500] According to Recital 28 in the Preamble to Directive 2010/84, it is necessary to introduce harmonized guiding principles for, and regulatory supervision of, post-authorization safety studies that are requested by competent authorities and that are non-interventional, that are initiated, managed or financed by the marketing authorization holder, and that involve the collection of data from patients or healthcare professionals and that therefore fall outside of the scope of the Clinical Trials Directive.

511. A post-authorization safety study is any study relating to an authorized medicinal product conducted with the aim of identifying, characterizing or quantifying a safety hazard, confirming the safety profile of the medicinal product, or measuring the effectiveness of risk management measures (Article 1(15) Directive 2001/83/EC).

512. The rules only apply to non-interventional post-authorization safety studies which are initiated, managed or financed by the marketing authorization holder voluntarily or pursuant to obligations imposed in accordance with Article 21a or 22a and which involve the collection of safety data from patients or healthcare professionals (Article 107m1). They are without prejudice to national and Union requirements for ensuring the well-being and rights of participants in non-interventional post-authorization safety studies (Article 107m2).

513. A non-interventional post-authorization safety studies must not be performed where the act of conducting the study promotes the use of a medicinal product (Article 107m3). Payments to healthcare professionals for participating in a non-interventional post-authorization safety study have to be restricted to compensation for time and expenses incurred (Article 107m4).

499. *Supra* n. 86.
500. *Supra* n. 321.

Chapter 5. Use of Human Embryos for Purposes of Scientific Research

514. In *Brüstle v. Greenpeace*, the referring court asked whether the concept of 'uses of human embryos for industrial or commercial purposes' within the meaning of Article 6.2c of the Biotech Patent Directive (*see* paragraph 644) also covers the use of human embryos for purposes of scientific research. In that regard, the CJEU pointed out that the purpose of this Directive is not to regulate the use of human embryos in the context of scientific research. It is limited to the patentability of biotechnological inventions.[501] This was confirmed later by the Court: 'The judgment in *Brüstle* contains no finding by the Court that scientific research making use of human embryos could under no circumstances be funded by the Union.'[502]

501. CJEU, *Brüstle v. Greenpeace*, Case C-34/10, ECLI:EU:C:2011:669, paras 39 and 40; CJEU, *International Stem Cell Corporation,* Case C-364/13, ECLI:C:2014:2451, para. 22.
502. CJEU, *European Citizens' Initiative One of Us,* C-418/18 P, ECLI:EU:C:2019:1113, para. 107.

Chapter 6. Genetic Testing

515. With the IVD MDR, EU law disposes of a limited number of specific rules for genetic testing of individuals.[503] Article 4 IVD MDR which is a rather short provision is entitled: 'Genetic information, counselling and informed consent'.

516. Recital 9 in the Preamble contains a justification for this limited approach: 'It appears that it is possible that divergent national rules regarding the provision of information and counselling in relation to genetic testing might only have an impact on the smooth functioning of the internal market to a limited extent. Therefore, it is appropriate to lay down only limited requirements in this regard in this Regulation, having regard to the need to ensure constant respect of the principles of proportionality and subsidiarity.'[504]

517. Recital 10 in the Preamble makes it clear that all tests that provide information on the predisposition to a medical condition or a disease, such as genetic tests, and tests that provide information to predict treatment response or reactions, such as companion diagnostics, are in vitro diagnostic medical devices. *See* for a definition of companion diagnostics, above, paragraph 498.

518. Member States have to ensure that where a genetic test is used on individuals, in the context of healthcare as defined in Article 3a of the Cross-Border Healthcare Directive (*see* paragraph 12) for the medical purposes of diagnostics, improvement of treatment, predictive or prenatal testing, the individual being tested or, where applicable, his or her legally designated representative is provided with relevant information on the nature, the significance and the implications of the genetic test, as appropriate (Article 4.1).

519. In the context of the obligations referred to in Article 4.1, Member States have, in particular, to ensure that there is appropriate access to counselling in the case of the use of genetic tests that provide information on the genetic predisposition for medical conditions and/or diseases which are generally considered to be untreatable according to the state of science and technology (Article 4.2). However,

---

503. H. Roscam Abbing, 'Editorial: New EU Rules for in Vitro Diagnostic Genetic Tests, a First Step in the Right Direction', 24 *European Journal of Health Law* 132 (2017).
504. *See also* L. Kalokairinou et al., 'Legislation of Direct-to-Consumer Genetic Testing in Europe: A Fragmented Regulatory Landscape', Journal Community Genet published online 18 Nov. 2017; L. Kalokairinou, H. Howard & P. Borry, 'Current Developments in the Regulation of Direct-to-Consumer Genetic Testing in Europe', 15 *Medical Law International* 97–123 (2015); S. Slokenberga, 'Direct-to-Consumer Genetic Testing: Changes in the EU Regulatory Landscape', 20 *European Journal for Health Law* 463–480 (2015); S. Slokenberga, *European Legal Perspectives on Health-Related Direct-to-Consumer Genetic Testing* 374 (Stockholm: Jure 2016); D. Sprumont, P. Borry & M. Shabani, *Genetic Testing in Europe. An Overview of the Legal Framework*, in A. den Exter (ed.), *European Health Law* 384 (Antwerp: Maklu 2017).

access to counselling has not to be ensured where a diagnosis of a medical condition and/or a disease which the individual being tested is already known to have is confirmed by a genetic test or in cases where a companion diagnostic is used (Article 4.3).

520. Nothing in Article 4 prevents Member States from adopting or maintaining measures at the national level which are more protective of patients, more specific or which deal with informed consent (Article 4.4).

Chapter 7. The Processing of Data Concerning Health and Genetic Data

521. The processing of data concerning health and genetic data is governed by Regulation (EU) 2016/679 of the European Parliament and of the Council of 27 April 2016 on the protection of natural persons with regard to the processing of personal data and on the free movement of such data, and repealing Directive 95/46/EC (GDPR).[505] It entered into force on 24 May 2016 (Article 99.1.) and became applicable on 25 May 2018 (Article 99.2.). Although the GDPR provides a consistent set of data protection rules in the EU, it relies on Member State law to put in place safeguards that would allow the processing of special categories of personal data, such as health data. Consequently, there is a risk of fragmentation due to such national rules. The Commission is currently preparing the second report on the application of the GDPR, where it will take stock of the implementation, including, among other topics, of the level of fragmentation.[506]

522. The European Data Protection Supervisor (EDPS) established under Regulation (EU) 2018/1725[507] is the body responsible for ensuring that the fundamental rights and freedoms of natural persons, and in particular their right to data protection, are respected by Union institutions and bodies when they process personal data. The EDPS is not competent for supervising the processing of personal data by Member States' public authorities. Without prejudice to the powers of the Commission as guardian of the Treaties, the monitoring and enforcement of the GDPR fall primarily under the competence of national authorities and courts.[508] The effective and full independence of national data protection supervisory authorities is crucial for the implementation of the fundamental right to data protection, as underlined in the Charter and the settled case law of the Court of Justice.[509]

505. *OJ* 2016, L 119. The European case law established on the basis of Directive 95/46/EC will, as a matter of principle, remains a reference in the context of the application of the GDPR insofar as it concerns key notions, principles and rights that remain essentially the same in the Regulation, *see* answer given by Ms Jourova on behalf of the Commission on 25 Jan. 2018 on a written priority Parliamentary question by M. Boni on 20 Nov. 2017, P-007111/2017.
506. Answer given by Ms Kyriakides on behalf of the European Commission on a written Parliamentary question of L.Fourlas and S.Kympouropoulos, Proposal for the European Health Data Space, 23 Apr. 2024, E-000309/2024.
507. Regulation (EU) 2018/1725 of the European Parliament and of the Council of 23 Oct. 2018 on the protection of natural persons with regard to the processing of personal data by the Union institutions, bodies, offices and agencies and on the free movement of such data, and repealing Regulation (EC) No. 45/2001 and Decision No. 1247/2002/EC, *OJ* L 295, 21.11.2018, pp. 39–98.
508. Answer by Mr Reynders on behalf of the European Commission to a written Parliamentary question of D. Montserrat and F.J. Millan Mon, Breach of GDPR in the procedure for the allocation of places on specialist health training courses, 11 Aug. 2021, E-003090/2021.
509. Answer by Mr Reynders on behalf of the European Commission to a written Parliamentary question of S. Bricmont, *Belgian Compliance with the GDPR*, 20 Apr. 2021, E-000859/2021.

§1. FIELD OF APPLICATION

523. The GDPR applies to the processing of personal data wholly or partly by automated means and to the processing other than by automated means of personal data which form part of a filing system or are intended to form part of a filing system (Article 2.1).

524. Processing means any operation or set of operations which is performed on personal data or on sets of personal data, whether or not by automated means, such as collection, recording, organization, structuring, storage, adaptation or alteration, retrieval, consultation, use, disclosure by transmission, dissemination or otherwise making available, alignment or combination, restriction, erasure or destruction (Article 4(2)).

525. Personal data means any information relating to an identified or identifiable natural person ('data subject'); an identifiable natural person is one who can be identified, directly or indirectly, in particular by reference to an identifier, such as a name, an identification number, location data, an online identifier or to one or more factors specific to the physical, physiological, genetic, mental, economic, cultural or social identity of that natural person (Article 4(1)). The use of the expression 'any information' in the definition of the concept of 'personal data' reflects the aim of the EU legislature to assign a wide scope to that concept, which potentially encompasses all kinds of information, not only objective but also subjective, in the form of opinions and assessments, provided that it 'relates' to the data subject. Information relates to an identified or identifiable natural person where, by reason of its content, purpose or effect, it is linked to an identifiable person. The use by the EU legislature of the word 'indirectly' suggests that, in order to treat information as personal data, it is not necessary that that information alone allows the data subject to be identified.[510] While the GDPR does not protect emotions and thoughts *as such,* entities using neurotechnology to access them would have to comply with data protection rules in the processing of personal data obtained that way. This includes, among others, the requirements for a lawful basis (such as free and informed consent of the person concerned), transparency and security.[511]

526. Filing system means any structured set of personal data which is accessible according to specific criteria, whether centralized, decentralized or dispersed on a functional or geographical basis (Article 4(4)).

527. The GDPR does not apply to the personal data of deceased persons. Penosa et al. consider this 'as one possible weakness … Bearing in mind the fact that a

---

510. CJEU, *OC,* Case C-479/22, ECLI:EU:C:2024:215, paras 46–48.
511. Answer by Mr Reynders on behalf of the European Commission to a written Parliamentary question of E. Fragkos, *Legislation Against the Manipulation of the Human Brain Through Neuroscience*, 21 Dec. 2021, E-004810/2021.

significant part of biobanking research is carried out on biological material collected while a donor was alive, but used after the donor's death, or on material collected from human corpses, the lack of appropriate regulation seems to be an important legal loophole'.[512] Member States may provide for rules regarding the processing of personal data of deceased persons (*see* Recital 27 in the Preamble).[513] However, according to Chassang, 'the right to be forgotten, as a complement to the right to erasure regarding the digital environment, as well as the right to restriction of processing established under the GDPR are of interest when considering post-mortem privacy regulatory approaches because these rights empower the living data subjects with the control of their digital life by allowing them to decide about their digital death'.[514] De Miguel Beriain et al. has proposed a normative framework that is based on the opt-out system for non-personal data combined with the application of the GDPR to the relatives' personal data.[515]

§2. Processing of Data Concerning Health and Genetic Data

I. Prohibition of Processing of Data Concerning Health and Genetic Data

528. The processing of 'special categories of personal data' is prohibited by Article 9.1 GDPR. Recital 10 in the Preamble refers to such data as 'sensitive data'.[516] The special categories of personal data are personal data revealing racial or ethnic origin, political opinions, religious or philosophical beliefs, or trade union membership, *genetic data*, biometric data for the purpose of uniquely identifying a natural person, *data concerning health* or data concerning a natural person's sex life or sexual orientation (Article 9.1 GDPR, italics added).

529. Data concerning health means personal data related to the physical or mental health of a natural person, including the provision of healthcare services, which reveal information about his or her health status (Article 4(15)). According to

512. S. Penosa et al., 'The EU General Data Protection Regulation: How Will It Impact the Regulation of Research Biobanks? Setting the Legal Frame in the Mediterranean and Eastern European Area', 18 *Medical Law International* 246 (2018).
513. This has been confirmed in the answer given by Ms Jourova on behalf of the Commission on 20 Feb. 2018 to a Parliamentary question, E-007611/2017.
514. G. Chassang, *What About Post-Mortem Digital Privacy and Personal Health Data Protection?*, in *Deep Diving into Data Protection* 444–445 (J. Herveg ed., Larcier 2021); E. Harbinja, *Posthumus Medical Data Donation: The Case for a Legal Framework, in The Ethics of Medical Data Donation* 100–111 (J. Krutzinna & L. Floridi eds, Springer 2019).
515. I. de Miguel Beriain et al., 'What Can We Do with the Data of Deceased People? A Normative Proposal', 29 *European Review of Private Law* 785–806 (2021).
516. Paragraph 3 of the European Parliament Resolution of 14 Mar. 2017 on fundamental rights implications of big data: privacy, data protection, non-discrimination, security and law enforcement (2016/2225(INI)) point out that sensitive information about persons can be inferred from non-sensitive data, which blurs the line between sensitive and non-sensitive data; P. Quinn & G. Malgieri, 'The Difficulty of Defining Sensitive Data: The Concept of Sensitive Data in the EU Data Protection Framework', 22 *German Law Journal* 1583–1612 (2021); A. Michalowicz, 'How to Protect Information About Our Mental States? A Few Remarks on Processing of Mental Data Under the GDPR', 21 *European Journal of Consumer Law* 127–143 (2023).

Recital 35 in the Preamble, this information relates to the past, current or future physical or mental health status of the data subject and includes information about the natural person collected in the course of the registration for, or the provision of, healthcare services as referred to in the Cross-Border Healthcare Directive (*see* paragraph 12) to that natural person; a number, symbol or particular assigned to a natural person to uniquely identify the natural person for health purposes; information derived from the testing or examination of a body part or bodily substance, including from genetic data and biological samples; and any information on, for example, a disease, disability, disease risk, medical history, clinical treatment or the physiological or biomedical state of the data subject independent of its source, for example, from a physician or other health professional, a hospital, a medical device or an in vitro diagnostic test. In comparison with Directive 95/46/EC, the GDPR has extended the notion of personal data concerning health.[517] Some argue that the definition of 'data concerning health' leaves a grey zone for its scope. This grey zone concerns indirect information concerning health.[518]

530. Genetic data means personal data relating to the inherited or acquired genetic characteristics of a natural person which give unique information about the physiology or the health of that natural person and which result, in particular, from an analysis of a biological sample from the natural person in question (Article 4(13)), (in particular chromosomal, deoxyribonucleic acid [DNA] or ribonucleic acid [RNA] analysis, or from the analysis of another element enabling equivalent information to be obtained) (*see* Recital 34 in the Preamble).

II. Derogation from the Prohibition on Processing of Data Regarding Health and Genetic Data

A. *Compliance with the Principles Relating to Processing of Personal Data*

531. When processing personal data, the following principles always have to be respected: the principles of lawfulness, fairness and transparency (Article 5.1a); the principle of purpose limitation (Article 5.1b); the principle of data minimization (Article 5.1c); the principle of accuracy (Article 5.1d); the principle of storage limitation (Article 5.1e) and the principle of integrity and confidentiality (Article 5.1f).[519]

517. A.-M. Duguet & J. Herveg, *Safeguards and Derogations Relating to Processing for Scientific Purposes: Article 89 Analysis for Biobank Review, in GDPR and Biobanking. Individual Rights, Public Interest and Research Regulation Across Europe* 107 (S. Slokenberga, O. Tzortzatou & J. Reichel eds, Springer 2021).
518. W. Schäfke-Zell, 'Revisiting the Definition of Health Data in the Age of Digitalized Health Care', 12 *International Data Privacy Law* 33–34 (2022).
519. S. Lindstad & K.R. Ludvigsen, 'When is the Processing of Data from Medical Implants Lawful? The Legal Grounds for Processing Health-Related Data from ICT Implantable Medical Devices for Treatment Purposes under EU Data Protection Law', 31 *Medical Law Review* 317–339 (2023).

532. Moreover, the controller is responsible for and able to demonstrate compliance with these principles (principle of accountability, Article 5.2). Controller means the natural or legal person, public authority, agency or other body which, alone or jointly with others, determines the purposes and means of the processing of personal data (Article 4(7)).

B. One of the Following Justifications Applies

1. The Data Subject or the Holder of Parental Responsibility Has Given Explicit Consent

533. Data regarding health or genetic data may be processed for one or more specified purposes if the data subject has given explicit consent, except where EU law or Member State law provides that the prohibition to process such data may not be lifted by the data subject (Article 9.2a).[520] In Greece, for instance, processing genetic data for health and life insurance purposes is prohibited even with the data subject's consent.[521] The GDPR does not define 'explicit' consent, nor is it explained in the Preamble (also, Recital 51 in the Preamble merely refers to explicit consent). According to Article 29 WP: 'the term *explicit* refers to the way consent is expressed by the data subject. It means that the data subject must give an express statement of consent. An obvious way to make sure consent is explicit would be to expressly confirm consent in a written statement'.[522] Explicit consent was also required by Article 8.1 of the Directive. Although the Directive did not require this consent to be in writing, some Member States, such as Belgium and Germany, required this.[523] An oral consent can also be considered explicit consent. Article 8 is entitled: Conditions applicable to a child's consent in relation to information society services. It provides that in relation to the offer of information society services directly to a child, the processing of the personal data of a child is lawful where the child is at least 16 years old. Where the child is below the age of 16 years, such processing is lawful only if and to the extent that consent is given or authorized by the holder of parental responsibility over the child. Member States may provide by law for a lower age for those purposes provided that such lower age is not below 13

520. Article 29 Data Protection Working Party, *Guidelines on Consent under Regulation 2016/679*, 28 Nov. 2017, WP259 and as last revised and adopted on 10 Apr. 2018.
521. A. Kiseleva & P. De Hert, 'Creating a European Health Data Space: Obstacles in Four Key Legal Areas', 26 *European Pharmaceutical Law Review* (2021).
522. *Supra* n. 520, 18.
523. P. Quinn, 'The Anonymisation of Research Data: A Pyric Victory for Privacy That Should Not Be Pushed Too Hard by the EU Data Protection Framework', 24 *European Journal of Health Law* 355 (2017).

years.[524] The GDPR does not define information society services. The Regulation does not contain a provision for consent for incompetent adults.[525]

534. Consent for processing of non-special categories of personal data (Article 6.1a) is defined as any freely given, specific, informed and unambiguous indication of the data subject's wishes by which he or she, by a statement or by a clear affirmative action, signifies agreement to the processing of personal data relating to him or her (Article 4(11)).

535. Article 7 of GDPR defines the conditions for consent. The controller has to be able to demonstrate that the data subject has consented to processing of his or her data (Article 7.1). If the data subject's consent is given in the context of a written declaration which also concerns other matters, the request for consent has to be presented in a manner which is clearly distinguishable from the other matters, in an intelligible and easily accessible form, using clear and plain language. Any part of such a declaration which constitutes an infringement of the GDPR is not binding (Article 7.2).

536. The data subject has the right to withdraw his or her consent at any time. The withdrawal of consent does not affect the lawfulness of processing based on consent before its withdrawal. Prior to giving consent, the data subject has to be informed thereof. It has to be as easy to withdraw as to give consent (Article 7.3).[526]

2. Necessity to Protect the Vital Interests of the Data Subject or of Another Natural Person

537. Data regarding health or genetic data may be processed in order to protect the vital interests of the data subject or of another natural person where the data subject is physically or legally incapable of giving consent (Article 9.2b). According to Recital 46 in the Preamble, a vital interest is an interest 'which is essential for the life'. Processing of personal data based on the vital interest of another natural person should, in principle, take place only where the processing cannot be manifestly based on another legal basis (*see* Recital 46 in the Preamble).[527]

---

524. *See* M. Taylor et al., 'When the Child Speaks for Herself? The Limits of Parental Consent in Data Protection Law for Health Research', 26 *Medical Law Review* 377–382 (2018); answer given by Ms Jourova on behalf of the Commission to a written Parliamentary question by A. Cadec, Digital age of consent in the EU, 6 Jul. 2018, E-002022/2018: 'The General Data Protection Regulation recognises that children merit specific protection with regard to their personal data.'.

525. *Supra* n. 490, 72.

526. M. Florea, 'Withdrawal of Consent for Processing Personal Data in Biomedical Research', 13 *International Data Privacy Law* 107–122 (2023).

527. The concept of 'vital interest' was already present in the text of Directive 95/46/EC. The Art. 29 Working Party has provided clarifications on the concept of 'vital interests' in its Opinion 06/2014 on the notion of legitimate interests of the data controller (WP 217). The national data protection authorities are as of May 2018 responsible for monitoring and enforcing the provisions of the GDPR. Questions regarding the application of the 'vital interest' legal basis in a specific case

3. Necessary for Reasons of Substantial Public Interest

538. Data regarding health or genetic data may be processed when this is necessary for reasons of substantial public interest, on the basis of Union or Member State law which has to be proportionate to the aim pursued, respect the essence of the right to data protection and provide for suitable and specific measures to safeguard the fundamental rights and the interests of the data subject (Article 9.2g). According to Recital 52 in the Preamble, one of the reasons for substantial public interest is health security, monitoring and alert purposes, and the prevention or control of communicable diseases and other serious threats to health. And the Recital continues: 'Such a derogation may be made for health purposes, including public health and the management of health-care services, especially in order to ensure the quality and cost-effectiveness of the procedures used for settling claims for benefits and services in the health insurance system.'

4. Necessary for Health-Related Purposes

539. Data regarding health or genetic data may be processed when this is necessary for the purposes of preventive or occupational medicine, for the assessment of the working capacity of the employee, medical diagnosis, the provision of health or social care or treatment or the management of health or social care systems and services on the basis of Union or Member State law or pursuant to contract with a health professional and subject to the conditions and safeguards referred to in Article 9.3 (Article 9.2h). Recital 53 in the Preamble calls this the processing for health-related purposes. This Recital specifies that such processing should be necessary to achieve those purposes for the benefit of natural persons and society as a whole, particularly in the context of the management of health or social care services and systems, including processing by the management and central national health authorities of such data for the purpose of quality control, management information and the general national and local supervision of the health or social care system, and ensuring continuity of health or social care and cross-border healthcare or health security, monitoring and alert purposes based on Union or Member State law which has to meet an objective of public interest.

540. Article 9.3 requires that the data are processed by or under the responsibility of a professional subject to the obligation of professional secrecy under Union or Member State law or rules established by national competent bodies or by another person also subject to an obligation of secrecy under Union or Member State law or rules established by national competent bodies.

---

should in the first place addressed to them; *see* Answer given by Ms Jourova on behalf of the Commission on 11 Jan. 2018 to a Parliamentary question by R. Sulik on 11 Oct. 2017, E-006389-2017.

5. Necessary for Reasons of Public Interest in the Area of Public Health

541. Data regarding health or genetic data may be processed if it is necessary for reasons of public interest in the area of public health, such as protecting against serious cross-border threats to health or ensuring high standards of quality and safety of healthcare and medicinal products or medical devices, on the basis of Union or Member State law which provides for suitable and specific measures to safeguard the rights and freedoms of the data subject, in particular professional secrecy (Article 9.2i). Recital 54 in the Preamble emphasizes that in such a case, the processing is possible without consent of the data subject. This is remarkable because this is also the case in the situation mentioned in sections 2, 3 and 4 above. Public health should be interpreted as defined in Regulation (EC) No. 1338/2008 of the European Parliament and of the Council on Community Statistics on public health and health and safety at work,[528] namely all elements related to health, namely health status, including morbidity and disability, the determinants having an effect on that health status, healthcare needs, resources allocated to healthcare, the provision of, and universal access to, healthcare as well as healthcare expenditure and financing, and the causes of mortality (Recital 54 in the Preamble).

542. Such processing of data concerning health for reasons of public interest should not result in personal data being processed for other purposes by third parties, such as employers or insurance and banking companies (*see* Recital 54 in the Preamble).

543. There seems to exist an overlap between Article 9.2g and Article 9.2i with regard to the explanations given in the Recitals accompanying both provisions. Obviously, the difference is between substantial public interest (Article 9.2g) and substantial interest (Article 9.2i), but where to draw the line and what the consequences are remains vague.

C. Comply with Member States Further Conditions

544. Member States may maintain or introduce further conditions, including limitations, with regard to the processing of genetic data, biometric data or data concerning health (Article 9.4). However, this should not hamper the free flow of personal data within the Union when those conditions apply to cross-border processing of such data (*see* Recital 53 in the Preamble). A consequence of Article 9.4 might be that in the area of health, the GDPR will not be applied in the same manner in each Member State. It may also mean that variations in the implementation of the GDPR may arise within one Member State, in particular where regional legislation applies.[529]

528. *OJ* 2008, L 354.

529. J. Hansen et al., *Assessment of the EU Member States' Rules on Health Data in the Light of the GDPR* 26 (European Commission 2021).

III. Rights of the Data Subject

A. The Right to the Protection of Personal Data

545. The GDPR protects fundamental rights and freedoms of natural persons and, in particular, their right to the protection of personal data (Article 1.2). The right to the protection of personal data concerning him or her is also provided for in Article 8.1 of the Charter of Fundamental Rights of the EU (*see* paragraph 239). Such data must be processed fairly for specified purposes and on the basis of the consent of the person concerned or some other legitimate basis laid down by law. Everyone has the right of access to data which has been collected concerning him or her and the right to have it rectified (Article 8.2). Compliance with these rules shall be subject to control by an independent authority (Article 8.3).

B. Information to Be Provided Where Personal Data Are Collected from the Data Subject

546. Where personal data relating to a data subject are collected from the data subject, the controller has, at the time when personal data are obtained, to provide the data subject with all of the following information: the identity and the contact details of the controller and, where applicable, of the controller's representative; the contact details of the data protection officer, where applicable; the purposes of the processing for which the personal data are intended as well as the legal basis for the processing; the recipients or categories of recipients of the personal data if any (Article 13.1a, b, c and e).

547. In addition to this information, the controller has, at the time when personal data are obtained, to provide the data subject with the following further information necessary to ensure fair and transparent processing: the period for which the personal data will be stored, or if that is not possible, the criteria used to determine that period; the existence of the right to request from the controller access to and rectification or erasure of personal data or restriction of processing concerning the data subject or to object to processing as well as the right to data portability; where the processing is based on Article 9.2a, the existence of the right to withdraw consent at any time, without affecting the lawfulness of processing based on consent before its withdrawal; the right to lodge a complaint with a supervisory authority; whether the provision of personal data is a statutory or contractual requirement, or a requirement necessary to enter into a contract, as well as whether the data subject is obliged to provide the personal data and of the possible consequences of failure to provide such data; the existence of automated decision-making, including profiling, referred to in Article 22(1) and (4) and, at least in those cases, meaningful information about the logic involved, as well as the significance and the envisaged consequences of such processing for the data subject (Article 13.2.).

548. Where the controller intends to further process the personal data for a purpose other than that for which the personal data were collected, the controller has to provide the data subject prior to that further processing with information on that other purpose and with any further relevant information as referred to in Article 13.2. (Article 13.3.).

549. Article 13.1., 2 and 3 do not apply where and insofar as the data subject already has the information (Article 13.4.).

C. The Right of Access by the Data Subject

550. The data subject has the right to obtain from the controller confirmation as to whether or not personal data concerning him or her are being processed, and, where that is the case, access to the personal data and the following information: the purposes of the processing; the categories of personal data concerned; the recipients or categories of recipient to whom the personal data have been or will be disclosed, in particular recipients in third countries or international organizations; where possible, the envisaged period for which the personal data will be stored, or, if not possible, the criteria used to determine that period; the existence of the right to request from the controller rectification or erasure of personal data or restriction of processing of personal data concerning the data subject or to object to such processing; the right to lodge a complaint with a supervisory authority; where the personal data are not collected from the data subject, any available information as to their source; the existence of automated decision-making, including profiling, referred to in Article 22.1. and 22.4. and, at least in those cases, meaningful information about the logic involved, as well as the significance and the envisaged consequences of such processing for the data subject (Article 15.1.). The European Commission received a complaint concerning the interplay between the right of access, as guaranteed under Article 8 of the Charter of Fundamental Rights and Article 15 and the Irish Data Protection Regulations 1989. The complaint concerned whether the mandatory requirement, under the Health Regulations, to consult with a health practitioner before the release of personal health data to a data subject contravened the right of access under data protection law. As part of the complaint process, the Commission liaised with the Irish authorities for further information, and in particular, their plans to revise the Regulations. The Commission was informed that Irish authorities are progressing with new Health Regulations as a matter of priority, which will take account of the requirements of the GDPR and that they will include a review of the mandatory consultation with a health practitioner.[530]

551. The controller provides a copy of the personal data undergoing processing. For any further copies requested by the data subject, the controller may charge a reasonable fee based on administrative costs (*see also* Article 12.5. and below, paragraph 575). Where the data subject makes the request by electronic means, and

530. Answer given by Mr Reynders on behalf of the European Commission to a written Parliamentary question of C. MacManus, Access to Health Records for Mother and Baby Home Survivors, 9 Feb. 2022, E-005638/2021.

unless otherwise requested by the data subject, the information is provided in a commonly used electronic form (Article 15.3.). It must be pointed out that neither the wording of Article 12.5 of the GDPR nor that of Article 15.1. and 15.3. thereof make the provision, free of charge, of a first copy of personal data conditional upon data subjects putting forward reasons to justify their requests. Therefore, those provisions do not give the controller the possibility of demanding that reasons be given for the request for access submitted by the data subject. The first sentence of Article 15.3. of the GDPR must be interpreted as meaning that, in the context of a doctor-patient relationship, the right to obtain a copy of personal data undergoing processing means that the data subject must be given a faithful and intelligible reproduction of all those data. That right entails the right to obtain a full copy of the documents included in his or her medical records and containing, *inter alia*, those data if the provision of such a copy is essential in order to enable the data subject to verify how accurate and exhaustive those data are, as well as to ensure they are intelligible. Regarding data relating to the health of the data subject, that right includes, in any event, the right to obtain a copy of the data in his or her medical records containing information such as diagnoses, examination results, assessments by treating physicians and any treatment or interventions provided to him or her.[531] The right to obtain a copy as referred to in Article 15.3. should not adversely affect the rights and freedoms of others (Article 15.4.).

552. A data subject has the right of access to personal data which have been collected concerning him or her, and to exercise that right easily and at reasonable intervals, in order to be aware of, and verify, the lawfulness of the processing. According to Recital 63 in the Preamble, this right includes the right for data subjects to have access to data concerning their health, for example, the data in their medical records containing information, such as diagnoses, examination results, assessments by treating physicians and any treatment or interventions provided.

D. Right to Rectification

553. The data subject has the right to obtain from the controller without undue delay the rectification of inaccurate personal data concerning him or her. Taking into account the purposes of the processing, the data subject has the right to have incomplete personal data completed, including by means of providing a supplementary statement (Article 16).

554. The controller has to communicate any rectification to each recipient to whom the personal data have been disclosed unless this proves impossible or involves disproportionate effort. The controller has to inform the data subject about those recipients if the data subject requests it (Article 19).

531. CJEU *FT v. DW*, Case C-307/22, ECLI:EU:C:2023:811, paras 38 and 79; 31 *European Journal of Health Law* 111–121 (2024).

E. *Restricted Right to Erasure of Personal Data Regarding Health or Genetic Data ('Right to Be Forgotten')*

555. The data subject has the right to obtain from the controller the erasure of personal data concerning him or her without undue delay, and the controller has the obligation to erase personal data without undue delay where one of the following grounds applies:[532]

(a) the personal data are no longer necessary in relation to the purposes for which they were collected or otherwise processed;
(b) the data subject withdraws consent on which the processing is based according to Article 9.2a and where there is no other legal ground for the processing;
(c) the data subject objects to the processing pursuant to Article 21.1. and there are no overriding legitimate grounds for the processing or the data subject objects to the processing pursuant to Article 21.2.;
(d) the personal data have been unlawfully processed;
(e) the personal data have to be erased for compliance with a legal obligation in Union or Member State law to which the controller is subject;
(f) the personal data have been collected in relation to the offer of information society services referred to in Article 8(1).

556. However, the right to erasure does not apply to the extent that processing of data regarding health and genetic data is necessary for reasons of public health in accordance with Article 9.2h (processing is necessary for health-related purposes), with Article 9.2i (processing is necessary for reasons of public interest in the area of public health) as well as Article 9.3 (processing under the responsibility of a professional subject to the obligation of professional secrecy) (Article 17.3c). A proposal for a Directive on consumer credits aimed at ensuring a high and consistent level of consumer protection, including for vulnerable consumers, and at fostering the internal market for consumer credit. The proposal referred in a recital to European Banking Authority Guidelines on information to be considered for the assessment of consumer creditworthiness and pointed out that such assessments should be based on information on the financial and economic situation of the consumer, while health data, including cancer data, should not be used (Recital 47).[533] The Commission plans to design a first draft of an EU Code of Conduct and to discuss it with

532. *See* H. Nys, 'Towards a Human Right "to Be Forgotten Online"?', 18 *European Journal of Health Law* 469–475 (2011); CJEU, *Commission Nationale de l'Informatique (CNIL)*, Case C-507/17, ECLI:EU:C:2019:772, para. 46: 'Article 17 of that regulation, which specifically governs the "right to erasure", also referred to, in the heading of that article, as the "right to be forgotten".' G. Christou & I. Rashild, 'Interest group lobbying in the European Union: Privacy, Data Protection and the Right to Be Forgotten', 19 *Comparative European Politics* 380–400 (2021); J. Emaus, 'Introduction to the Case Note on the Right to Be Forgotten', 30 *European Review of Private Law* 235–240 (2022).

533. Answer by Mr Reynders on behalf of the European Commission to a written priority Parliamentary question of D. Clune, The Consumer Credit Directive and Cancer Survivors' Right to Be Forgotten, 17 Aug. 2021, P-003587/2021; in the same sense, answer by Mrs Kyriakides and Mrs McGuinness on behalf of the European Commission to a written Parliamentary question of A. Clocca, Cancer survivor's right to be forgotten, 8 Jun. 2022, E-0001012/2022.

Member States, health and patient organizations and the financial industry as a part of implementation of Europe's Beating Cancer Plan.[534]

557. More in general, the right to erasure is not applicable, also with regard to data regarding health and genetic data, to the extent that their processing is necessary for exercising the right of freedom of expression and information and for the establishment, exercise or defence of legal claims (Article 17.3a and e).

558. On the other hand, the right to erasure is applicable if data regarding health or genetic data have been processed with the explicit consent of the data subject based on Article 9.2a.

559. The controller has to communicate any erasure of personal data to each recipient to whom the personal data have been disclosed unless this proves impossible or involves disproportionate effort. The controller has to inform the data subject about those recipients if the data subject requests it (Article 19).

F. Right to Restriction of Processing

560. Restriction of processing means the marking of stored personal data with the aim of limiting their processing in the future (Article 4(4)).

561. The data subject has the right to obtain from the controller restriction of processing where one of the following applies:

(a) the accuracy of the personal data is contested by the data subject for a period, enabling the controller to verify the accuracy of the personal data;
(b) the processing is unlawful, and the data subject opposes the erasure of the personal data and requests the restriction of their use instead;
(c) the controller no longer needs the personal data for the purposes of the processing, but they are required by the data subject for the establishment, exercise or defence of legal claims;
(d) the data subject has objected to processing pursuant to Article 21.1. pending the verification of whether the legitimate grounds of the controller override those of the data subject (Article 18.1.).

562. Where processing has been restricted, the personal data should, with the exception of storage, only be processed with the data subject's consent or for the establishment, exercise or defence of legal claims or for the protection of the rights

534. Answer given by Ms Kyriakides on behalf of the European Commission to a written Parliamentary question of Ch. Gemma a.o., Cancer survivors' right to be forgotten versus discrimination in access to insurance or social security services and loans, 22 Jul. 2022, E-002010/2022; Answer given by Ms Kyriakides on behalf of the European Commission to a written Parliamentary question of E. De Blasis a.o., Right to be forgotten: a fundamental right for European citizens, 8 Sep. 2023, E-002193/2023.

of another natural or legal person or for reasons of important public interest of the Union or of a Member State. (Article 18.2.). A data subject who has obtained a restriction of processing has to be informed by the controller before the restriction of processing is lifted (Article 18.3.).

563. The controller has to communicate any restriction of processing to each recipient to whom the personal data have been disclosed unless this proves impossible or involves disproportionate effort. The controller has to inform the data subject about those recipients if the data subject requests it (Article 19).

564. Methods by which to restrict the processing of personal data could include, *inter alia*, temporarily moving the selected data to another processing system, making the selected personal data unavailable to users, or temporarily removing published data from a website. In automated filing systems, the restriction of processing should, in principle, be ensured by technical means in such a manner that the personal data are not subject to further processing operations and cannot be changed. The fact that the processing of personal data is restricted should be clearly indicated in the system (*see* Recital 67 in the Preamble).

G. Restricted Right to Portability of Data Regarding Health or Genetic Data

565. The data subject has the right to receive the personal data concerning him or her, which he or she has provided to a controller, in a structured, commonly used and machine-readable format and has the right to transmit those data to another controller without hindrance from the controller to which the personal data have been provided when the processing is carried out by automated means. This new right formalized by the GDPR is an implementation of the right of access.[535] When it concerns data regarding health or generic data, this so-called right to portability only applies when these data have been processed upon explicit consent (*see* Article 9.2a) (Article 20.1.) and not in the other situations mentioned in Article 9.2a (*see also* Recital 68 in the Preamble: 'It should not apply where processing is based on a legal ground other than consent').

566. In exercising his or her right to data portability, the data subject has the right to have the personal data transmitted directly from one controller to another, where technically feasible (Article 20.2.). The right to portability of data may not adversely affect the rights and freedoms of others (Article 20.4.).

535. J. Herveg & A. Altavilla, 'Introducing Key Elements Regarding Access to Personal Data for Scientific Research in the Perspective of Developing Innovative Medicines', 27 *European Journal of Health Law* 198–199 (2020), Special issue: Innovative medicine and research: ethical, legal and regulatory issues.

H. Right Not to Be Subject to Automated Individual Decision-Making, Including Profiling

567. The data subject has the right not to be subject to a decision based solely on automated processing, including profiling, which produces legal effects concerning him or her or similarly significantly affects him or her (Article 22.1.).[536] Profiling means any form of automated processing of personal data consisting of the use of personal data to evaluate certain personal aspects relating to a natural person, in particular, to analyse or predict aspects concerning that natural person's performance at work, economic situation, health, personal preferences, interests, reliability, behaviour, location or movements (Article 4(4)). However, the data subject may be subject to such a decision when it is based on, *inter alia*, the data subject's explicit consent (Article 22.2.). However, data regarding health and genetic data are excluded from this possibility unless the decision is based on such data regarding health or genetic data processed after the explicit consent of the data subject (*see* Article 9.2a) or the processing of which is necessary for reasons of substantial public interest (*see* Article 9.2g) (Article 22.3.).

I. Right to Transparent Information and Communication Concerning Rights of the Data Subject

568. The controller takes appropriate measures to provide any information referred to in Articles 13 and 14 and any communication under Articles 15–22 and 34 relating to processing the data subject in a concise, transparent, intelligible and easily accessible form, using clear and plain language, in particular for any information addressed specifically to a child. The information is provided in writing or by other means, including, where appropriate, by electronic means. When requested by the data subject, the information may be provided orally, provided that the identity of the data subject is proven by other means (Article 12.1.). The controller facilitates the exercise of the data subject rights under Articles 15–22 (Article 12.2.).

569. The controller provides information on action taken on a request under Articles 15–22 to the data subject without undue delay and, in any event, within one month of receipt of the request. That period may be extended by two further months where necessary, taking into account the complexity and number of the requests. The controller informs the data subject of any such extension within one month of receipt of the request, together with the reasons for the delay. Where the data subject makes the request by electronic form means, the information has to be provided by electronic means where possible, unless otherwise requested by the data subject

536. *See* Art. 29 Data Protection Party, *Guidelines on automated individual decision making and profiling for the purposes of Regulation 2016/679*, 3 Oct. 2017, WP251. Rev.01; P. Guarda, '"OK Google, Am I Sick?" Artificial Intelligence, E-health and Data Protection Regulation', *Biolaw Journal* 368–371 (2019); L. Tosini, 'The Right to Object to Automated Individual Decisions: Resolving the Ambiguity of Article 22 (1) of the General Data Protection Regulation', 11 *International Data Privacy Law* 33–43 (2021).

(Article 12.3.). If the controller does not take action on the request of the data subject, he has to inform the data subject without delay and, at the latest, within one month of receipt of the request of the reasons for not taking action and the possibility of lodging a complaint with a supervisory authority and seeking a judicial remedy (Article 12.4.).

J. Right to Lodge a Complaint and to an Effective Judicial Remedy

570. Without prejudice to any other administrative or judicial remedy, every data subject has the right to lodge a complaint with a supervisory authority, in particular in the Member State of his or her habitual residence, place of work or place of the alleged infringement if the data subject considers that the processing of personal data relating to him or her infringes the GDPR. The supervisory authority with which the complaint has been lodged has to inform the complainant of the progress and the outcome of the complaint, including the possibility of a judicial remedy pursuant to Article 78 (Article 77).

571. Without prejudice to any other administrative or non-judicial remedy, each data subject has the right to an effective judicial remedy where the supervisory authority which is competent does not handle a complaint or does not inform the data subject within three months of the progress or outcome of the complaint lodged pursuant to Article 77. Proceedings against a supervisory authority are to be brought before the courts of the Member State where the supervisory authority is established (Article 78.2. and 78.3.).

572. Without prejudice to any available administrative or non-judicial remedy, including the right to lodge a complaint with a supervisory authority pursuant to Article 77, each data subject has the right to an effective judicial remedy against a controller or a processor where he or she considers that his or her rights under the GDPR have been infringed as a result of the processing of his or her personal data in non-compliance with the GDPR. Such proceedings are to be brought before the courts of the Member State where the controller or processor has an establishment. Alternatively, such proceedings may be brought before the courts of the Member State where the data subject has his or her habitual residence, unless the controller or processor is a public authority of a Member State acting in the exercise of its public powers (Article 79).

K. Right to Be Represented

573. The data subject has the right to mandate a not-for-profit body, organization or association which has been properly constituted in accordance with the law of a Member State, has statutory objectives which are in the public interest, and is active in the field of the protection of data subjects' rights and freedoms with regard to the protection of their personal data to lodge the complaint on his or her behalf, to exercise the rights referred to in Articles 77, 78 and 79 on his or her behalf, and to exercise the right to receive compensation referred to in Article 82 on his or her behalf where provided for by Member State law (Article 80.1.).

L. Right to Compensation and Liability

574. Any person who has suffered material or non-material damage as a result of an infringement of the GDPR has the right to receive compensation from the controller or processor for the damage suffered. Any controller involved in processing is liable for the damage caused by processing which infringes on the GDPR. A processor is liable for the damage caused by processing only where it has not complied with obligations of the GDPR specifically directed to processors or where it has acted outside or contrary to lawful instructions of the controller. A controller or processor is exempt from liability if it proves that it is not in any way responsible for the event giving rise to the damage. Where more than one controller or processor, or both a controller and a processor, are involved in the same processing and where they are responsible for any damage caused by processing, each controller or processor is held liable for the entire damage in order to ensure effective compensation of the data subject (Article 82.1–4).

IV. Modalities for the Exercise of the Rights of the Data Subject

575. Information provided under Articles 13 and 14 and any communication and any actions taken under Articles 15–22 and 34 are provided free of charge (*see also* Article 15.3., above paragraph 550). Where requests from a data subject are manifestly unfounded or excessive, in particular because of their repetitive character, the controller may either charge a reasonable fee taking into account the administrative costs of providing the information or communication or taking the action requested, or refuse to act on the request. The controller bears the burden of demonstrating the manifestly unfounded or excessive character of the request (Article 12.5.).

576. Where the controller has reasonable doubts concerning the identity of the natural person making the request referred to in Articles 15–21, the controller may request the provision of additional information necessary to confirm the identity of the data subject (Article 12.6.).

577. The information to be provided to data subjects pursuant to Articles 13 and 14 may be provided in combination with standardized icons in order to give in an easily visible, intelligible and clearly legible manner a meaningful overview of the intended processing. Where the icons are presented electronically, they have to be machine-readable (Article 12.7.). The Commission is empowered to adopt delegated acts in accordance with Article 92 for the purpose of determining the information to be presented by the icons and the procedures for providing standardized icons (Article 12.8.).

V. Data Protection by Design and by Default

578. Taking into account the state of the art, the cost of implementation and the nature, scope, context and purposes of processing, as well as the risks of varying likelihood and severity for rights and freedoms of natural persons posed by the processing, the controller implements, both at the time of the determination of the means for processing and at the time of the processing itself, appropriate technical and organizational measures, such as pseudonymization, which are designed to implement data protection principles, such as data minimization, in an effective manner and to integrate the necessary safeguards into the processing in order to meet the requirements of this Regulation and protect the rights of data subjects (Article 25.1.).

579. Pseudonymization means the processing of personal data in such a manner that the personal data can no longer be attributed to a specific data subject without the use of additional information, provided that such additional information is kept separately and is subject to technical and organizational measures to ensure that the personal data are not attributed to an identified or identifiable natural person (Article 4(5)). The likelihood and severity of the risk to the rights and freedoms of the data subject should be determined by reference to the nature, scope, context and purposes of the processing. Risk should be evaluated on the basis of an objective assessment, by which it is established whether data processing operations involve a risk or a high risk (*see* Recital 76 in the Preamble).

580. The controller has to implement appropriate technical and organizational measures to ensure that, by default, only personal data which are necessary for each specific purpose of the processing are processed. That obligation applies to the amount of personal data collected, the extent of their processing, the period of their storage and their accessibility. In particular, such measures have to ensure that by default, personal data are not made accessible without the individual's intervention to an indefinite number of natural persons (Article 25.2.).

VI. Communication of a Personal Data Breach to the Data Subject

581. Personal data breach means a breach of security leading to accidental or unlawful destruction, loss, alteration, or unauthorized disclosure of, or access to, personal data transmitted, stored, or otherwise processed (Article 4(12)).

582. When the personal data breach is likely to result in a high risk to the rights and freedoms of natural persons, the controller has to communicate the personal data breach to the data subject without undue delay (Article 34.1.). This communication to the data subject describes in clear and plain language the nature of the personal data breach and contains at least the following information and measures: the name and contact details of the data protection officer or other contact points where more information can be obtained, the likely consequences of the personal data breach and the measures taken or proposed to be taken by the controller to address the personal data breach, including, where appropriate, measures to mitigate its possible adverse effects (Article 34.2.).

583. The communication to the data subject is not required if any of the following conditions are met: (a) the controller has implemented appropriate technical and organizational protection measures, and those measures were applied to the personal data affected by the personal data breach, in particular, those that render the personal data unintelligible to any person who is not authorized to access it, such as encryption; (b) the controller has taken subsequent measures which ensure that the high risk to the rights and freedoms of data subjects is no longer likely to materialize; (c) it would involve disproportionate effort. In such a case, there has instead to be a public communication or similar measure whereby the data subjects are informed in an equally effective manner (Article 34.3.).

VII. Data Protection Impact Assessment

584. Directive 95/46/EC provided for a general obligation to notify the processing of personal data to the supervisory authorities. While that obligation produced administrative and financial burdens, it did not, in all cases, contribute to improving the protection of personal data. Such indiscriminate general notification obligations have, therefore, been abolished and replaced by effective procedures and mechanisms which focus instead on those types of processing operations which are likely to result in a high risk to the rights and freedoms of natural persons by virtue of their nature, scope, context and purposes. Such types of processing operations may be those which in particular involve using new technologies, or are of a new kind and where no data protection impact assessment has been carried out before by the controller, or where they become necessary in the light of the time that has elapsed since the initial processing (*see* Recital 89 in the Preamble).

585. Where a type of processing, in particular, using new technologies and taking into account the nature, scope, context and purposes of the processing, is likely to result in a high risk to the rights and freedoms of natural persons, the controller has, prior to the processing, to carry out an assessment of the impact of the envisaged processing operations on the protection of personal data. A single assessment may address a set of similar processing operations that present similar high risks (Article 35.1.).

VIII. Designation of a Data Protection Officer When Data Regarding Health or Genetic Data Are Processed on a Large Scale

586. The controller and the processor have to designate a data protection officer in any case where the core activities of the controller or the processor consist of processing large-scale data regarding health or genetic data (Article 37.1c). Large-scale processing operations aim to process a considerable amount of personal data at regional, national or supranational levels and which could affect a large number of data subjects and are likely to result in a high risk. The processing of personal data is not considered to be on a large scale if the processing concerns personal data from patients by an individual physician or other healthcare professional. In such cases, a data protection officer is not mandatory (analogues to Recital 91 of the Preamble).

§3. Scientific Research with Data Concerning Health or Genetic Data[537]

I. Introduction

587. Historically, personal data concerning health were collected from physical experimentation, such as clinical trials that were performed on a select group of subjects.[538] The informed consent for the experiment also covered the collection and use of these data for research purposes. Technological developments in the late twentieth and early twenty-first century have made possible forms of medical research on pre-existing data. The first source of such data involves the re-use of data from previous experiments. The second source is biobanks and related depositories of health data, while the third one consists of the use of electronic health records.[539]

588. Recital 157 in the Preamble to the GDPR recognizes the importance of the use of pre-existing data concerning research purposes: 'By coupling information from registries, researchers can obtain new knowledge of great value with regard to widespread medical conditions, such as cardiovascular disease, cancer and depression. Research results obtained through registries provide solid, high-quality knowledge which can provide the basis for the formulation and implementation of knowledge-based policy, improve the quality of life for a number of people and improve the efficiency of social services.'

589. While the GDPR is, in general, directly applicable in the Member States, this is not the case when it concerns research with personal data: 'In order to facilitate scientific research, personal data can be processed for scientific research purposes, subject to appropriate conditions and safeguards set out in Union or Member State law.'[540] More specifically, EU law in this regard is not expected in the short term. It is up to the Member States to define more elaborated rules. Some authors assume 'that most Member States will leave their present state of the law intact in

537. G. Comandè & G. Schneider, 'Differential Data Protection Regimes in Data-Driven Research: Why the GDPR is More Research-Friendly than You Think', 23 *German Law Journal* 559–596 (2022).
538. *Supra* n. 523, 349.
539. *Supra* n. 523, 350–351; A. Altavilla et al., 'The Secondary Use of Paediatric Data under GDPR: Looking for New Safeguards for Research', 3 *European Pharmaceutical Law Review* 156–164 (2019).
540. The Welcome Trust, *Implementing the General Data Protection Regulation 2016/679 to Maintain a Competitive Environment for Research in Europe*, September 2016.

this respect as that was part of the political compromise'.[541] Nevertheless, the GDPR sets a frame that has to be respected by the Member States. It does not provide approval from an ethics committee.[542]

Although the GDPR establishes a scientific research regime, it does not define what scientific research is.[543] For the purposes of the GDPR, the processing of personal data for scientific research purposes should be interpreted in a broad manner, including, for example, technological development and demonstration, fundamental research, applied research and privately funded research. In addition, it should take into account the Union's objective under Article 179(1) TFEU of achieving a European Research Area. Scientific research purposes should also include studies conducted in the public interest in the area of public health (*see* Recital 159 in the Preamble). The importance of scientific research is further reflected in Article 5.1b that assumes for further processing not to be considered incompatible when the purpose is, among others, scientific research.[544] A definition of scientific research is, however, not included in the Regulation: 'a lacuna which creates a considerable degree of legal uncertainty'.[545]

II. Research after Anonymization of the Data

590. The principles of data protection do not apply to anonymous information, namely information which does not relate to an identified or identifiable natural person or to personal data rendered anonymous in such a manner that the data subject is not or no longer identifiable (Recital 26 in the Preamble).[546] Where the purposes of the research can be fulfilled by further processing that does not permit or no longer permits the identification of data subjects, those purposes have to be fulfilled in that manner according to Article 89.1. The GDPR does not require absolute anonymity, however, because it is almost impossible to achieve this, especially in the case of genetic data.[547] According to Recital 26 in the Preamble, to determine whether a natural person is identifiable, an account should be taken of all the means reasonably likely to be used, such as singling out, either by the controller or by another person, to identify the natural person directly or indirectly. To ascertain

541. *Supra* n. 490, 59 and 62.

542. M. Donelly & M. Donagh, 'Health Research, Consent and the GDPR Exemption', 26 *European Journal of Health Law* 97–119 (2019).

543. S. Slokenberga, *Setting the Foundations: Individual Rights, Public Interest and Biobanking, in GDPR and Biobanking. Individual Rights, Public Interest and Research Regulation Across Europe* 20 (S. Slokenberga, O. Tzortzatou & J. Reichel eds, Springer 2021).

544. A. Altavilla et al., 'The Secondary Use of Paediatric Data under GDPR: Looking for New Safeguards for Research', 3 *European Pharmaceutical Law Review* 156–164 (2019); C. Barbosa, *The Processing of Personal Data for Scientific Research Purposes in Medicine. Some aspects of the General Data Protection Regulation, in Deep Diving into Data Protection* 398–401 (J. Herveg ed., Larcier 2021).

545. G. Verhenneman et al., 'How GDPR Enhances Transparency and Fosters Pseudonymisation in Academic Medical Research', 27 *European Journal of Health Law* 38 (2020).

546. *Supra* n. 517, 105–120.

547. N. Savage, 'The Myth of Anonymity', 537 *Nature* 70–72 (2016); M. Mostert, et al., 'Big Data in Medical Research and EU Data Protection Law: Challenges to the Consent or Anonymise Approach', 24 *European Journal of Human Genetics* 956–960 (2016); *supra* n. 412, 50.

whether means are reasonably likely to be used to identify the natural person, account should be taken of all objective factors, such as the costs of and the amount of time required for identification, taking into consideration the available technology at the time of the processing and technological developments.

591. Article 89.1. is directly applicable and does not need implementation in the law of the Member States.

III. Appropriate Safeguards for the Rights and Freedoms of the Data Subject

592. Processing for scientific research purposes is subject to appropriate safeguards, in accordance with the GDPR, for the rights and freedoms of the data subject. Those measures have to ensure that technical and organizational measures are in place, particularly to ensure respect for the principle of data minimization. Those measures may include pseudonymization provided that the purposes can be fulfilled in that manner (Article 89.1.). Pseudonymization is defined as the process through which data 'can no longer be attributed to a specific data subject without the use of additional information, provided that such additional information is kept separately and is subject to technical and organizational measures to ensure that the personal data are not attributed to an identified of identifiable natural person' (Article 4.5). The Regulation explicitly defines data that have undergone pseudonymization as personal data, thus falling under its scope.[548]

593. Where personal data are processed for scientific research purposes, Union or Member State law may provide for derogations from the rights referred to in Articles 15 (right of access), 16 (right to rectification), 18 (right to restriction of processing) and 21 (right to object), subject to the conditions and safeguards referred to Article 89.1., in so far as such rights are likely to render impossible or seriously impair the achievement of the specific purposes, and such derogations are necessary for the fulfilment of those purposes (Article 89.2.). Derogations or exceptions from the right to information are not allowed at all when personal data are collected from the data subject himself (Article 13).[549]

IV. Explicit Consent

594. If the purposes of the research cannot be fulfilled by making use of anonymous data concerning health or genetic data, a first possibility is a research with the explicit consent of the data subject, in as much that the prohibition to process such

548. M. Shabani & L. Marelli, *Re-identifiability of Genomic Data and the GDPR*, e48316 Embo Reports 1 (24 May 2019).
549. M. Mostert, et al., 'From Privacy to Data Protection in the EU: Implications for Big Data Health Research', 25 *European Journal of Health Law* 51 (2018); J. Reichel, 'The GDPR and Processing of Personal Data for Research Purposes: What about Case Law?', 27 *European Public Law* 171–177 (2021).

data is lifted in the Member State concerned (Article 9.1 and 2, a). Article 9.2a requires 'one or more specific purposes'. Informed consent for participation in research should not be confused with informed consent for data processing. According to Verhenneman et al., informed consent should be discouraged as a legal basis for the processing of data for research purposes because the subject has no real choice: patients cannot take part in a study when they do not give consent to the processing of their data. Also, the European Commission recommended against informed consent as the preferable legal ground for the processing of personal data in the context of scientific research.[550]

V. Processing for Research Purposes Is in the Public Interest or Has a Legitimate Interest

595. An alternative for explicit consent is offered by Article 9.2g that allows processing of data regarding health of genetic data when this is necessary for reasons of substantial public interest (*see* paragraph 526). With regard to research, this legal basis may only be used when national or European law applicable to the research organization recognizes research as its task. Article 6.3 indeed requires that tasks carried out in the public interest are laid down in national law. The possibility to qualify research as public interest allows the exclusion of a right to opt-out (Article 21.6.). Where a public interest provision is lacking, it has to be proven that the research serves a legitimate interest. When relying on this legal basis, the right of the data subject to object to the processing must be acknowledged (Article 21.1.).[551]

596. According to some authors, Article 9.2h provides for an exemption in the context of so-called diagnostic research in medical care.[552] They do not explain what this means. Neither Article 9.2h nor Recital 53 refers to this kind of research, however.

§4. The European Health Data Space

597. On 3 May 2022, the European Commission published the proposal for a Regulation of the European Parliament and of the Council on the European Health Data Space (EHDS).[553] The aim of this Regulation is to establish the EHDS in order

550. *Supra* n. 476, 47; E.S. Dove & J. Chen, 'Should Consent for Data Processing be Privileged in Health Research? A Comparative Analysis', 10 *International Data Privacy Law* 119–121 (2020).
551. *Supra* n. 476, 48.
552. M. Timmers et al., 'Will the EU Data Protection Regulation 2016/679 Inhibit Critical Care Research?', 27 *Medical Law Review* 71 (2019).
553. COM(2022) 197 final; L. Marelli et al., 'The European health data space: Too big to succeed?', 135 *Health Policy* 104861 (2023); A. Kiseleva & I. de Miguel Beriain, 'What Will Become of Our Health Data When We Die? The European Health Data Space might Have an Answer', 7 *European Pharmaceutical Law Review* 16–28 (2023); P. Terzis et al., 'Interoperability and Governance in the European Health Data Space Regulation', 23 *Medical Law International* 368–376 (2023); J. van de

to improve access to and control by natural persons over their personal electronic health data in the context of healthcare (primary use of electronic health data), as well as for other purposes that would benefit the society such as research, innovation, policymaking, patient safety, personalized medicine, official statistics or regulatory activities (secondary use of electronic health data) (Recital 1)

598. Primary use of electronic health data means the processing of personal electronic health data for the provision of health services to assess, maintain or restore the state of health of the natural person to whom that data relates, including the prescription, dispensation and provision of medicinal products and medical devices, as well as for relevant social security, administrative or reimbursement services (Article 2.2.d).

599. The European Parliament supported the proposal for an EHDS with 516 votes in favour compared to 95 votes against. The proposal is based on the Union's competences under Articles 16 and 114 TFEU. The EHDS proposal foresees strong safeguards for the privacy of patients. Pseudonymised personal data to be made available for secondary use will only be processed in secure processing environments and in accordance with Articles 6 and 9 GDPR. Thus, to give an example, a public health authority would rely on its 'task carried out in the public interest' (Article 6(1)(e) GDPR) assigned by Union or Member State law, and the processing of health data would be 'necessary for reasons of public interest in the area of public health', based on Union law. The EHDS regulation will provide the appropriate safeguards to meet the conditions of Article 9(2)(i) GDPR.[554]

600. The EHDS will be the framework for implementing the EEHRxF, a digital format for health data to achieve secure, interoperable, cross-border access and exchange in the EU.[555]

I. Rights of Natural Persons and Access and Transmission of Personal Electronic Health Data for Primary Use

601. Natural persons have the right to access their personal electronic health data processed in the context of primary use of electronic health data immediately, free of charge and in an easily readable, consolidated and accessible form and to receive an electronic copy (Article 3.1 and 3.2). In accordance with Article 23 GDPR, Member States may restrict the scope of this right whenever necessary for the protection of the natural person based on patient safety and ethics by delaying their access to their personal electronic health data for a limited period of time until a health professional can properly communicate and explain to the natural person

Gronden & M. Veenbrink, 'EHDS and Free Movement of Patients: What EU Intervention is Needed?', 31 *European Journal of Health Law* 249–283 (2024).

554. Answer given by Ms Kyriakides on behalf of the European Commission to a written Parliamentary question of H.Vilimsky and G.Mayer, European Health Data Space, 23 Feb. 2024, E-003623/2023.

555. Answer given by Mr Breton on behalf of the European Commission to a written Parliamentary question of D. Charanzová, Emergency health information card, 19 Jan.2024, E-003414/2023.

information that can have a significant impact on his or her health (Article 3.3). Natural persons may insert their electronic health data in their own EHR or in that of natural persons whose health information they can access through electronic health data access services or applications linked to these services. That information shall be marked as inserted by the natural person or by his or her representative (Article 3.6).

602. Natural persons have the right to give access to or request a data holder from the health or social security sector to transmit their electronic health data to a data recipient of their choice from the health or social security sector immediately, free of charge and without hindrance from the data holder or from the manufacturers of the systems used by that holder (Article 3.8). Notwithstanding Article 6.1d GDPR, natural persons have the right to restrict access of health professionals to all or part of their electronic health data. Member States shall establish the rules and specific safeguards regarding such restriction mechanisms (Article 3.9). Natural persons have the right to obtain information on the healthcare providers and health professionals that have accessed their electronic health data in the context of healthcare. The information has to be provided immediately and free of charge through electronic health data access services (Article 3.10.).

II. Access by Health Professionals

603. Where they process data in an electronic format, health professionals have access to the electronic health data of natural persons under their treatment, irrespective of the Member State of affiliation and the Member State of treatment (Article 4.1a). They ensure that the personal electronic health data of the natural persons they treat are updated with information related to the health services provided (Article 4.1b). Where access to electronic health data has been restricted by the natural person, the healthcare provider or health professionals shall not be informed of the content of the electronic health data without prior authorization by the natural person, including where the provider or professional is informed of the existence and nature of the restricted electronic health data. In cases where processing is necessary in order to protect the vital interests of the data subject or of another natural person, the healthcare provider or health professional may get access to the restricted electronic health data. Following such access, the healthcare provider or health professional shall inform the data holder and the natural person concerned or his/her guardians that access to electronic health data has been granted. Member States' law may add additional safeguards (Article 4.4).

Chapter 8. Transplantation of Organs

604. Directive 2010/53/EU of the European Parliament and of the Council of 7 July 2010 on standards of quality and safety of human organs intended for transplantation (the Organs Directive)[556] also has legal consequences for the legal position of the patient who receives an organ and his physician/his medical team.

605. The legal basis of the Organs Directive is Article 168.4a TFEU which states: 'By way of derogation from Article 2.5 and Article 6a and in accordance with Article 4.2k, the European Parliament and the Council, acting in accordance with the ordinary legislative procedure and after consulting the Economic and Social Committee and the Committee of the Regions, shall contribute to the achievement of the objectives referred to in this article through adopting in order to meet common safety concerns:(a) measures setting high standards of quality and safety of organs and substances of human origin, blood and blood derivatives; these measures shall not prevent any Member State from maintaining or introducing more stringent protective measures.' However, according to Article 168.7, 'the measures referred to in paragraph 4(a) shall not affect national provisions on the donation or medical use of organs and blood'. Recital 8 in the Preamble of the Organs Directive adds that this is also the case for 'the surgical act of transplantation itself'. Regulating this medical act of transplanting an organ thus has remained the competence of the Member States.

606. However, this Recital 8 continues as follows: 'In view of the objective of reducing the associated risks of the transplanted organs, it is necessary to include in the scope of this Directive certain provisions concerning transplantation and, in particular, provisions aimed at addressing unintended and unexpected situations occurring during the transplantation that might affect the quality and safety of organs.'

607. The Organs Directive applies 'to … the transplantation of organs intended for transplantation' (Article 2.1). Where such organs are used for research purposes, the Directive only applies where they are intended for transplantation into the human body (Article 2.2). Organ means a differentiated part of the human body, formed by different tissues, that maintains its structure, vascularization and capacity to develop physiological functions with a significant level of autonomy. A part of an organ is also considered to be an organ if its function is to be used for the same purpose as the entire organ in the human body, maintaining the requirements of structure and vascularization (Article 3h). Transplantation means a process intended to restore certain functions of the human body by transferring an organ from a donor to a recipient (Article 3q). Recipient means a person who receives a transplant of an organ (Article 3m).

556. Originally referred to as Directive 2010/45, *OJ* 2010, L 207, corrected in *OJ* 2010, L 243.

608. According to Recital 5 in the Preamble, transplantation is carried out by hospitals or professionals falling under different jurisdictions, and there are significant differences in quality and safety requirements between Member States. There is, therefore, a need for common quality and safety standards for the procurement, transport and use of organs at the Union level. Such standards would facilitate exchanges of organs to the benefit of thousands of European patients in need of this type of therapy each year. Union legislation has to ensure that organs comply with recognized standards of quality and safety. Such standards would help to reassure the public that organs procured in another Member State carry the same basic quality and safety guarantees as those obtained in their own country.

609. Member States have to ensure that transplantation takes place in, or is carried out by, transplantation centres that comply with the rules laid down in the Organs Directive (Article 9.1). Transplantation centre means a healthcare establishment, a team or a unit of a hospital or any other body which undertakes the transplantation of organs and is authorized to do so by the competent authority under the regulatory framework in the Member State concerned (Article 3r). The transplantation centre has to verify before proceeding to transplantation that the organ and donor characterization are completed and recorded in accordance with Article 7 and the Annex and that the conditions of preservation and transport of shipped organs have been maintained (Article 9.3a and b).

610. The risk-benefit ratio is a fundamental aspect of organ transplantation. Owing to the shortage of organs and the inherent life-threatening nature of diseases leading to the need for organs for transplantation, the overall benefits of organ transplantation are high, and more risks are accepted than with blood or most tissues and cell-based treatments. The clinician plays an important role in this context by deciding whether or not organs are suitable for transplantation. The Directive sets out the information required to make that assessment (*see* Recital 11 in the Preamble).

611. Member States have to ensure that all procured organs and donors thereof are characterized before transplantation through the collection of the information set out in the Annex. The information specified in Part A of the Annex contains a set of minimum data which has to be collected for each donation. Information specified in Part B of the Annex contains a set of complementary data to be collected based on the decision of the medical team, taking into account the availability of such information and the particular circumstances of the case (Article 7.1).

612. However, if, according to a risk-benefit analysis in a particular case, including in life-threatening emergencies, the expected benefits for the recipient outweigh the risks posed by incomplete data, an organ may be considered for transplantation even where not all of the minimum data specified in Part A of the Annex are available (Article 7.2). In those particular cases, the medical team should assess the particular risk posed to the potential recipient by the lack of information and by not proceeding with transplantation of the organ in question. Where a complete characterization of an organ, according to Part A of the Annex, is not possible in time or due to particular circumstances, the organ may be considered for transplantation where non-transplantation might pose a greater risk to the potential recipient (*see* Recital 13 in the Preamble).

613. Member States have to ensure that all organs transplanted on their territory can be traced from the donor to the recipient and vice versa in order to safeguard the health of recipients (Article 10.1.). Where organs are exchanged between Member States, those Member States have to transmit the necessary information to ensure the traceability of organs, in conformity with the procedures established by the Commission pursuant to Article 29 (Article 10.4.; *see* Commission Implementing Directive 2012/25/EU of 9 October 2012 laying down information procedures for the exchange, between the Member States, of human organs intended for transplantation).[557]

614. The fundamental right to protection of personal data has to be protected fully and effectively in all organ transplantation activities, in conformity with Union provisions on the protection of personal data (Article 17.2h; *see also* Article 16 in this regard).

557. *OJ* 2012, L 275.

Chapter 9. Clinical Use of Tissues and Cells of Human Origin for Human Application

615. Member States have to ensure that healthcare personnel directly involved in the chain from donation to the transplantation or disposal of organs are suitably qualified or trained and competent to perform their tasks and are provided with the relevant training, as referred to in Article 4.3 (Article 12).

616. The clinical use of tissues and cells of human origin for human application is regulated by Directive 2004/23/EC of the European Parliament and of the Council of 31 March 2004 on setting standards of quality and safety for the donation, procurement, testing, processing, preservation, storage and distribution of human tissues and cells (the Tissues and Cells Directive).[558]

617. Cells mean individual human cells or a collection of human cells when not bound by any form of connective tissue (Article 3a). Tissue means all constituent parts of the human body formed by cells (Article 3b). Human application means the use of tissues or cells on or in a human recipient and extracorporeal applications (Article 3l).

618. The Tissues and Cells Directive *respects* fundamental rights, *observes* the principles reflected in the Charter of Fundamental Rights of the EU and *takes into account*, as appropriate, the Convention on Human RRights and Biomedicine. Neither the Charter nor the Convention makes express provision for harmonization or prevents Member States from introducing more stringent requirements in their legislation (Recital 22 in the Preamble, italics added; *see also* Article 4.2).

619. Member States have to take all necessary measures to ensure that all data, including genetic information, collated within the scope of the Directive and to which third parties have access, have been rendered anonymous so that neither donors nor recipients remain identifiable (Article 14.1.). Member States have to take all necessary measures to ensure that the identity of the recipient(s) is not disclosed to the donor or his family without prejudice to legislation in force in the Member States on the conditions for disclosure, notably in the case of gametes donation (Article 14.3.).

620. Member States take all necessary measures to ensure that any promotion and publicity activities in support of the donation of human tissues and cells comply with guidelines or legislative provisions laid down by the Member States. Such guidelines or legislative provisions include appropriate restrictions or prohibitions on advertising the need for human tissues and cells with a view to offering financial gain or comparable advantage (Article 12.2.).

558. *OJ* 2004, L 102; M. Martens & L. Arifagic, 'First Assessment of the SOHO Proposal for a New Legislation of Blood, Tissues and Cells (the SOHO Protocol)', 6 *European Pharmaceutical Law Review* 53–72 (2023).

621. The European Parliament adopted on 24 April 2024 a new Regulation, proposed by the European Commission in July 2022, that will replace Directive 2004/23.[559] It provides a holistic approach to the regulation of substances of human origin. The new rules notably include better protection of recipients and donors of substances of human origin.

Donation and collection systems need to be aligned with local healthcare systems. Donor registration requires regular follow-up to ensure candidate donors remain fit for donation when a call arrives. This will also require ad-hoc medical investigations and acts to be performed in healthcare facilities close to the donor in order to collect haematopoetic stem cells. Therefore, full harmonization across all Member States would not be appropriate.[560]

559. Proposal for a Regulation of the European Parliament and of the Council on standards of quality and safety for substances of human origin intended for human application and repealing Directives 2002/98/EC and 2004/23.

560. Answer given by Ms Kyriakides on behalf of the European Commission on a written Parliamentary question of P. Arimont, Harmonisation of conditions for stem cell donation in Europe, 7 Dec. 2023, E-002833/2023.

Chapter 10. Rights of the Medical Examinee

622. A medical examinee is a person subjected to a medical examination, the results of which are not directly relevant to him or herself but to a third person.[561] An example of such a medical examination is the (pre-) employment or recruitment medical examination in EU institutions.[562] A medical officer's opinion is a measure paving the way for the decision at issue, and the applicant is accordingly not entitled to contest it directly. It follows that the claims directed against that opinion must be rejected as inadmissible. A pre-recruitment medical examination must, if it is not to be completely pointless, necessarily include a clinical examination and any supplementary biological tests ordered by the medical officer.[563]

623. EU law does not provide for a comprehensive legal framework of the rights of the medical examinee. However, secondary law sources offer some guidance.[564]

§1. Rights of the Living Organ Donor

624. Donor means a person who donates one or several organs (Article 3c Organs Directive). Donation means donating organs for transplantation (Article 3e Organs Directive).

625. Member States ensure that living donors are selected on the basis of their health and medical history by suitably qualified or trained and competent professionals. Such assessments may provide for the exclusion of persons whose donation could present unacceptable health risks (Article 15.2.).

626. Pre-transplant evaluation of potential donors is an essential part of organ transplantation. That evaluation has to provide enough information for the transplantation centre to undertake a proper risk-benefit analysis. It is necessary to identify and document the risks and characteristics of the organ in order to allow its allocation to a suitable recipient. Information from a potential donor's medical history, physical examination and complementary tests have to be collected for the adequate characterization of the organ and the donor (*see* Recital 12 in the Preamble to the Organs Directive). Donor characterization means the collection of the relevant information on the characteristics of the donor needed to evaluate his/her suitability for organ donation in order to undertake a proper risk assessment, minimize the risks for the recipient, and optimize organ allocation (Article 3f). Organ

561. S. Defloor, 'The Legal Protection of the Medically Examined Applicant for Insurance', 29 *Medicine and Law* 183–192 (2010).
562. A. Hendriks & J. Gevers, '(Pre-)Employment Medical Examinations and the Law, with Particular Reference to the European Union', 1 *European Journal of Health Law* 229–264 (1994).
563. EU Civil Service Tribunal, Case F-46/09, *V. and EDPS*, ECLI:EU:F:2011:101, paras 60 and 77.
564. K. Sein & G. Splindler, 'GDPR and Processing Health Data in Insurance Relationships: the Role of Statutory Legal Basis', 6 *European Pharmaceutical Law Review* 98–116 (2022).

characterization means the collection of the relevant information on the characteristics of the organ needed to evaluate its suitability in order to undertake a proper risk assessment, minimize the risks for the recipient, and optimize organ allocation (Article 3h).

627. To obtain an accurate, reliable and objective history, the medical team has to perform an interview with the living donor, during which the team should properly inform him or her about the potential risks and consequences of donation (*see* Recital 12 in the Preamble).

628. Living donors face risks linked both to testing to ascertain their suitability as a donor and to the procedure to obtain the organ. Complications may be medical, surgical, social, financial or psychological. The level of risk depends, in particular, on the type of organ to be donated. Therefore, living donations need to be performed in a manner that minimizes the physical, psychological and social risk to the individual donor and the recipient and does not jeopardize the public's trust in the healthcare community. The potential living donor has to be able to take an independent decision on the basis of all the relevant information and should be informed in advance as to the purpose and nature of the donation, as well as the consequences and risks. In this context, and to guarantee respect for the principles governing donation, the highest possible protection of living donors should be ensured. It should also be noted that some Member States are signatories to the Convention on Human Rights and Biomedicine of the Council of Europe and its additional protocol on Transplantation of Organs and Tissues of Human Origin. Complete information, a proper evaluation, and an adequate follow-up are internationally recognized measures aimed at protecting the living donors and also contributing to ensuring the quality and safety of organs (*see* Recital 23 in the Preamble).

629. Member States have to ensure that donations of organs from living donors are voluntary and unpaid (Article 13.1.). However, the principle of non-payment does not prevent living donors from receiving compensation, provided it is strictly limited to making good the expenses and loss of income related to the donation. Member States define the conditions under which such compensation may be granted while avoiding any financial incentives or benefits for a potential donor (Article 13.2.). Member States prohibit advertising the availability of organs where such advertising is with a view to seeking financial gain or comparable advantage (Article 13.3.).

630. The procurement of organs has to be carried out only after all requirements relating to consent in force in the Member State concerned have been met (Article 14).

631. Member States have to ensure that the fundamental right to protection of personal data is fully and effectively protected in all organ donation activities, in conformity with Union provisions on the protection of personal data. Member States have to take all necessary measures to ensure that: (a) the data processed are kept confidential and secure. Any unauthorized access to data or systems that make identification of donors possible has to be penalized; (b) donors whose data are processed within the scope of this Directive are not identifiable. Any use of systems or data that makes the identification of donors possible with a view to tracing donors, including medical purposes, has to be penalized in accordance with Article 23 of this Directive; (c) the principles relating to data quality are met (Article 16).

§2. Rights of the Living Donor of Tissue and Cells

632. In order to ensure that the health status of a living donor is not affected by the donation, a prior medical examination should be required (*see* Recital 16 in the Preamble to the Tissues and Cells Directive). The Directive itself does not contain rules regarding this medical examination.

633. A Member State may introduce requirements for voluntary unpaid donation, which include the prohibition or restriction of imports of human tissues and cells, to ensure a high level of health protection, provided that the conditions of the Treaty are met (Article 4.2).

634. Member States endeavour to ensure voluntary and unpaid donations of tissues and cells. Donors may receive compensation, which is strictly limited to making good the expenses and inconveniences related to the donation. In that case, Member States define the conditions under which compensation may be granted (Article 12.1.).

635. Member States take all necessary measures to ensure that any promotion and publicity activities in support of the donation of human tissues and cells comply with guidelines or legislative provisions laid down by the Member States. Such guidelines or legislative provisions include appropriate restrictions or prohibitions on advertising the availability of human tissues and cells with a view to seeking financial gain or comparable advantage (Article 12.2.).

636. The procurement of human tissues or cells is authorized only after all mandatory consent or authorization requirements in force in the Member State concerned have been met. Member States take, in keeping with their national legislation, all necessary measures to ensure that donors, their relatives or any persons granting authorization on behalf of the donors are provided with all appropriate information as referred to in Annex A (Article 13).

637. The person in charge of the donation process ensures that the donor has been properly informed of at least those aspects relating to the donation and procurement process outlined in paragraph 3 of Annex A. Information must be given prior to the procurement (paragraph 1 of Annex A). The information must be given by a trained person who is able to transmit it in an appropriate and clear manner, using terms that are easily understood by the donor (paragraph 2 of Annex A). The information must cover: the purpose and nature of the procurement; its consequences and risks; analytical tests, if they are performed; recording and protection of donor data, medical confidentiality; therapeutic purpose and potential benefits and information on the applicable safeguards intended to protect the donor (paragraph 3 of Annex A). The donor must be informed that he/she has the right to receive the confirmed results of the analytical tests, clearly explained (paragraph 4 of Annex A). Information must be given on the necessity for requiring the applicable mandatory consent, certification and authorization in order for the tissue and/or cell procurement to be carried out (paragraph 5 of Annex A).

638. Member States take all necessary measures to ensure that all data, including genetic information, collated within the scope of the Directive and to which third parties have access, have been rendered anonymous so that neither donors nor recipients remain identifiable (Article 14.1.). Member States take all necessary measures to ensure that the identity of the donor is not disclosed to the recipient(s) or his family, without prejudice to legislation in force in the Member States on the conditions for disclosure, notably in the case of gametes donation (Article 14.3.).

§3. Rights of the Donor of Blood

639. Directive 2002/98/EC of the European Parliament and of the Council of 27 January 2003 sets standards of quality and safety for the collection, testing, processing, storage and distribution of human blood and blood components and amending Directive 2001/83/EC (the Blood Directive).[565]

640. The Blood Directive applies to the collection and testing of human blood and blood components, whatever their intended purpose, and to their processing, storage and distribution when intended for transfusion (Article 2.1). It does not apply to blood stem cells (Article 2.4). The organization of the supply of blood and blood components for transfusion remains, however, under the responsibility of each Member State, as do the medical decisions on the appropriate use of these therapies.[566]

641. Blood means whole blood collected from a donor and processed either for transfusion or for further manufacturing (Article 3a). Blood component means a therapeutic constituent of blood (red cells, white cells, platelets, plasma) that can be prepared by various methods (Article 3b).

642. Member States have to ensure that all prospective donors of blood or blood components in the Community are provided with information referred to in Article

565. *OJ* 2003, L 33.
566. Answer given by Ms Kyriakides on behalf of the European Commission to a written Parliamentary question of L. Nikolaou-Alavanos, Criminal unavailability of blood transfusions for patients and severe blood shortages in hospital blood transfusion units, 23 Apr. 2024, E-000523/2024.

29b (Article 16) (Article 29b refers to information to be provided to donors). Member States have to ensure that blood establishments provide prospective donors of blood or blood components with the information set out in Part A of Annex II (Article 2 of Commission Directive 2004/33/EC of 22 March 2004 implementing Directive 2002/98 as regards certain technical requirements for blood and blood components).[567] According to paragraph 2 of Part A of this Annex, this information concerns the reasons for requiring an examination, health and medical history, and the testing of donations and the significance of 'informed consent'. Paragraph 6 of this Annex requires information on the option for donors to change their mind about donating prior to proceeding further or the possibility of withdrawing or self-deferring at any time during the donation process without any undue embarrassment or discomfort.

643. Member States have to take all necessary measures to ensure that, upon agreement of a willingness to commence the donation of blood or blood components, all donors in the Union provide the information referred to in Article 29c to the blood establishment (Article 17). The information referred to in Article 29c includes the identity, health history and the signature of the donor. This information is further elaborated in Article 3 and Part B of Annex II of Commission Directive 2004/33/EC of 22 March 2004, implementing Directive 2002/98 as regards certain technical requirements for blood and blood components.

644. Blood establishments have to ensure that there are evaluation procedures in place for all donors of blood and blood components and that the criteria for donation referred to in Article 29(d) are met. These eligibility criteria are further elaborated in Article 4 and Annex III of Commission Directive 2004/33/EC of 22 March 2004, implementing Directive 2002/98 as regards certain technical requirements for blood and blood components. The results of the donor evaluation and testing procedures have to be documented, and any relevant abnormal findings have to be reported to the donor (Article 18). When abnormal findings are reported to the donor, relevant counselling is also provided (*see* Recital 19 in the Preamble).

645. An examination of the donor, including an interview, has to be carried out before any donation of blood or blood components. A qualified health professional has to be responsible, in particular, for giving to and gathering from donors the information which is necessary to assess their eligibility to donate and, on the basis thereof, to assess the eligibility of donors (Article 19).

646. Member States take all necessary measures to ensure that all data, including genetic information, collated within the scope of the Directive to which third parties have access have been rendered anonymous so that the donor is no longer identifiable (Article 24).

567. *OJ* 2004, L 95.

Part VI. Beginning and End-of-Life Issues in EU Law

Chapter 1. Beginning of Life

§1. Definition of the Legal Term 'Person' or 'Individual'

647. Directive 2004/23/EC (the Tissues and Cells Directive) does not interfere with provisions of Member States defining the legal term 'person' or 'individual' (*see* Recital 12 in the Preamble to this Directive). In the absence of the agreement of Member States as to the legal status of a human being at the prenatal stage and the absence of delegating competence to the Union to determine the status, Member States retain the full competence within this scope.[568] The General Data Protection Directive left unanswered the protection of prenatally obtained genetic data.[569]

§2. Protection of the Human Body

648. The human body, at the various stages of its formation and development, and the simple discovery of one of its elements, including the sequence or partial sequence of a gene, cannot constitute patentable inventions (Article 5.1 Directive 98/44 of the European Parliament and of the Council of 6 July 1998 on the legal protection of biotechnological inventions, the Biotech Patent Directive).

649. If an invention is based on biological material of human origin or if it uses such material and where a patent application is filed, the person from whose body the material is taken must have had an opportunity to express free and informed consent thereto, in accordance with national law (*see* Recital 26 in the Preamble of the Biotech Patent Directive). According to Advocate General Jacobs, it is not clear from the wording of this Recital in the various language versions whether the consent must relate to the filing of the patent application or to the taking of the material from the donor.[570] According to the Advocate General, it is, of course, desirable that no element of human origin should be taken from a person without their consent.

568. M. Safjan (ed.), *Medical Law. Cases and Commentaries* 160 (Warszawa: Wolters Kluwer 2012).
569. K. Pormeister & L. Drozdzowski, 'Protecting the Genetic Data of the Unborn Children: A Critical Analysis', *EDPL* 53–64 (2018).
570. Opinion AG Jacobs in, Case C-377/98, *Netherlands v. Parliament and Council*, ECLI-:EU:C:2001:329, para. 209.

That principle is expressed at the forefront of the Charter of Fundamental Rights of the EU; it is also enshrined in Chapter II of the Convention on Human Rights and Biomedicine. However, in his view, patent law is not the appropriate framework for the imposition and monitoring of a requirement of consent to all potential uses of human material.[571]

§3. Definition and Protection of the Human Embryo

650. 'On the basis of Article 6.1 ['inventions shall be considered unpatentable where their commercial exploitation would be contrary to *ordre public* or morality; however, exploitation shall not be deemed to be so contrary merely because it is prohibited by law or regulation'], the following, in particular, shall be considered unpatentable: ... uses of human embryos for industrial or commercial purposes' (Article 6.2c Biotech Patent Directive).

651. The text of this Directive does not define human embryo, nor does it contain any reference to national laws as regards the meaning to be applied to those terms. It, therefore, follows that it must be regarded, for the purposes of the application of the Directive, as designating an autonomous concept of EU Law which must be interpreted in a uniform manner throughout the territory of the Union.[572] According to van Leeuwen, the Court 'as such has effectively harmonised what constitutes a human embryo under EU law (and) essentially imposed one ethical position on the Member States'.[573]

652. As regards the meaning to be given to the concept of 'human embryo' set out in Article 6.2c, the CJEU pointed out that, although the definition of human embryo is a very sensitive social issue in many Member States, marked by their multiple traditions and value systems, it was not called upon to broach questions of a medical or ethical nature, but must restrict itself to a legal interpretation of the relevant provisions of the Directive.[574] The meaning and scope of terms for which EU law provides no definition must be determined by considering, *inter alia*, the context in which they occur and the purposes of the rules of which they form part.[575] The context and aim of the Directive show that the EU legislature intended to exclude any possibility of patentability where respect for human dignity could thereby be affected. It follows that the concept of 'human embryo' within the meaning of Article 6.2c of the Directive must be understood in a wide sense.[576]

---

571. *Ibid.*, paras 210–211.

572. CJEU, *Brüstle v. Greenpeace*, Case C-34/10, ECLI:EU:C:2011:669, para. 26; *see* S.H.E. Harmon, G. Laurie & A. Courtney, 'Case Comment. Dignity, Plurality and Patentability: The Unfinished Story of *Brüstle v. Greenpeace*', 38 *European Law Review* 92–106 (2013).

573. B. van Leeuwen, 'Euthanasia and the Ethics of Free Movement Law: The Principle of Recognition in the Internal Market', 19 *German Law Journal* 1422–1423 (2018).

574. CJEU, *Brüstle v. Greenpeace*, Case C-34/10, ECLI:EU:C:2011:669, para. 30.

575. *Ibid.*, para. 31.

576. *Ibid.*, para. 34; CJEU, *International Stem Cell Corporation,* Case C-364/13, ECLI:C:2014:2451, para. 24.

653. Accordingly, any human ovum must, as soon as fertilized, be regarded as a 'human embryo' within the meaning and for the purposes of the application of Article 6.2c of the Directive, since that fertilization is such as to commence the process of development of a human being.[577] That classification must also apply to a non-fertilized human ovum into which the cell nucleus from a mature human cell has been transplanted and a non-fertilized human ovum whose division and further development have been stimulated by parthenogenesis. Although those organisms have not, strictly speaking, been the object of fertilization, due to the effect of the technique used to obtain them, they are, as is apparent from the written observations presented to the Court, capable of commencing the process of development of a human being just as an embryo created by fertilization of an ovum can do so.[578]

654. As regards stem cells obtained from a human embryo at the blastocyst stage, it was for the referring court to ascertain, in the light of scientific developments, whether they are capable of commencing the process of development of a human being and, therefore, are included within the concept of 'human embryo' within the meaning and for the purposes of the application of Article 6.2c of the Directive. In the ruling issued by the German *Bundesgerichtshof* after the preliminary reference to the CJEU, the German Court found certain non-viable organisms developing from unviable in vitro fertilization oocytes not to be embryos in light of the judgment of the CJEU, as they are not capable of commencing the process of development of a human being.[579]

655. In *International Stem Cell Corporation,* the CJEU clarified that it follows from the judgment in *Brüstle* that a non-fertilized human ovum must be classified as a 'human embryo', within the meaning of Article 6.2c of the Directive, *in so far as that organism is 'capable of commencing the process of development of a human being'* (italics added).[580] Consequently, where a non-fertilized human ovum does not fulfil that condition, the mere fact that that organism commences a process of development is not sufficient for it to be regarded as a 'human embryo', within the meaning and for the purposes of the application of the Directive.[581] By contrast, where such an ovum does have the inherent capacity to develop into a human being, it should, in light of Article 6.2c, be treated in the same way as a fertilized human ovum at all stages of its development.[582]

656. It was for the referring court to determine whether or not, in the light of knowledge which is sufficiently tried and tested by international medical science,

---

577. CJEU, *Brüstle v. Greenpeace*, Case C-34/10, ECLI:EU:C:2011:669, para. 35.
578. *Ibid.*, paras 36 and 26.
579. Opinion AG Cruz Vallanon, in Case C-364/13, *International Stem Cell Corporation* ECLI:C:2014:2104, para. 58; J. Mansnérus, 'Patentability of Parthenogenic Stem Cells: *International Stem Cell Corporation v. Comptroller General of Patents*', 23 *European Journal of Health Law* 267–286 (2015); S. Slokenberga, T. Minssen & A. Nordberg (eds), 'Special Issue: Genome Editing, Health Innovation and Regulation', 29 *European Journal of Health Law* 327–619.
580. CJEU, *International Stem Cell Corporation,* Case C-364/13, ECLI:C:2014:2451, para. 27.
581. *Ibid.*, para. 29.
582. *Ibid.*, para. 30.

human parthenotes, such as those which were the subjects of the applications for registration in the case in the main proceedings, have the inherent capacity of developing into a human being. If the referring court were to find that those parthenotes do not have such a capacity, it should infer from this that they do not constitute 'human embryos' within the meaning of Article 6.2c.

657. In response to the question: 'would the Commission consider revising existing rules inhibiting research on gene editing, such as the current ban on funding of research intended to modify the heritable genes of humans', Mr Moedas, on behalf of the Commission answered: 'Under Horizon 2020, research intended to modify the genetic heritage of human beings that could make such changes heritable, or intended to create human embryos solely for the purpose of research or for the purpose of stem cells procurement is not eligible for funding. Furthermore, the modifications to the subject's germ line genetic identity are prohibited under the EU clinical trials legislation … . The current approach to avoid the inheritance of genetic diseases such as Huntington's disease is preimplantation genetic diagnosis. This approach, legal in 17 Member States and permitted in most of the remaining Member States for certain medical indications, remains the most robust method. The field of genome editing of non-heritable cells to treat and/or cure diseases is funded in Horizon 2020 … . In preparing the next Framework Programme for Research and Innovation, consideration will be given to ensure that all the research and innovation activities carried out comply with ethical principles and relevant national, EU and international legislation.'[583] Article 90 of the Clinical Trials Regulation 536/2014 states that: 'No gene therapy clinical trials may be carried out which result in modifications of the subject's germ line genetic identity.' mRNA COVID-19 vaccines are not considered gene therapies. mRNA COVID-19 vaccines are classified and regulated as biotechnology medicinal products and are subject to requirements of the EU pharmaceutical legislation.[584]

§4. In Vitro Fertilization and the Beginning of a Pregnancy

658. The TEU and the TFEU do not give the EU powers to adopt legislation on harmonization of national substantive laws on assisted human reproduction, including surrogacy. It falls within the competence of individual Member States to regulate this matter. Member States have to ensure that fundamental rights are effectively respected and protected in accordance with their national legislation and international human rights obligations.[585] The EU's competence in the field of reproductive medicine is limited to setting quality and safety standards for human

583. Question for written answer by F. Ries on 14 Feb. 2018; answer given on 19 Mar. 2018, P-000932/2018.

584. Answer given by Ms Kyriakides on behalf of the European Commission to a written Parliamentary question, of V. Joron, Lobbies calling for mRNA vaccines not to be classified as gene therapy, 9 Apr. 2024, E-000355/2024.

585. Answer given by Mr Reynders on behalf of the European Commission to a written Parliamentary question of S. Baldassarre a.o., 'Men having babies' surrogacy conference, 11 May 2022,

tissues and cells intended for human application.[586] The European Parliament adopted on 24 April 2024 a new Regulation for the regulation of substances of human origin. The new rules notably will include better protection of children born from medically assisted procreation.

Allowing gene-editing technologies in in vitro fertilization is a national decision. In case a Member State would allow such technique, it needs to comply with EU requirements on safety and quality as laid down in Directive 2001/23/EC.[587]

659. The Austrian *Oberster Gerichtshof* asked the CJEU, in essence, whether Council Directive 92/85 of 19 October 1992 on the introduction of measures to encourage improvements in the safety and health at work of pregnant workers and workers who have recently given birth or are breastfeeding[588] and, in particular, the prohibition of dismissal of pregnant workers provided for in Article 10.1. of that Directive must be interpreted as extending to a worker who is undergoing in vitro fertilization treatment where, on the date she is given notice of her dismissal, her ova have already been fertilized by her partner's sperm cells, so that in vitro fertilized ova exist, but those ova have not yet been transferred into her uterus.[589]

660. According to the CJEU, it is apparent, both from the wording of Article 10 of Directive 92/85 and from the primary objective pursued by that Directive, that to benefit from the protection against dismissal granted by that Article, the pregnancy in question must have begun. In that regard, it pointed out that although, as the Austrian Government observed, artificial fertilization and viable cell treatment is a very sensitive social issue in many Member States, marked by their multiple traditions and value systems, the Court is not called upon to broach questions of a medical or ethical nature, but must restrict itself to a legal interpretation of the relevant provisions of Directive 92/85 taking account of the wording, the broad logic and the objectives of that Directive.

661. It is clear, as has moreover been pointed out by the Austrian Government, that it is the earliest possible date in a pregnancy which must be chosen to ensure the safety and protection of pregnant workers. However, even allowing, in regard to in vitro fertilization, that the date is that of the transfer of the fertilized ova into the woman's uterus, it cannot be accepted, for reasons connected with the principle of legal certainty, that the protection established by Article 10 of Directive 92/85 may be extended to a worker when, on the date she was given notice of her dismissal, the in vitro fertilized ova had not yet been transferred into her uterus. As is apparent from the observations submitted to the Court and from paragraphs 43–45 of the

---

E.005063/2021; same answer given by Ms Dali on behalf of the European Commission to a written question of I. Tavaglieri and S. Baldassarre, Surrogacy fair in Milan: treating human life as a mere commodity, 25 May 2022, E-000941/2022.

586. Answer by Ms Kyriakides on behalf of the European Commission to a written Parliamentary question of S. Spurek, IVF reimbursement guarantee, 20 Feb. 2020, E-004374/2019.
587. Answer by Mr Andriukaitis on behalf of the European Commission to a written Parliamentary question of M. Benova, Human gene editing, 29 Jan. 2019, P-006073/2018.
588. *OJ* 1992, L 348.
589. CJEU, *S. Mayr,* Case C-506/06, ECLI:EU:C:2008:119, para. 29.

opinion of the Advocate General, before their transfer into the uterus of the woman concerned, those ova may, in certain Member States, be kept for an indeterminate period. The Austrian legislation provides, in that regard, that the fertilized ova may be kept for a maximum period of ten years. Therefore, applying for the protection against dismissal laid down in Article 10 of Directive 92/85 in favour of a female worker before the transfer of the fertilized ova could have the effect of granting the benefit of that protection even where that transfer is postponed, for whatever reason, for a number of years or even where such transfer is definitively abandoned, the in vitro fertilization having been carried out merely by way of precaution.[590]

§5. Gametes Donation for Reproduction

662. Member States have to take all necessary measures to ensure that the identity of a donor is not disclosed to the recipient(s) or his family, without prejudice to legislation in force in the Member States on the conditions for disclosure, notably in the case of gametes donation (Article 14.3. Tissues and Cells Directive). As a general principle, the identity of the recipient(s) should not be disclosed to the donor or his/her family and vice versa, without prejudice to legislation in force in the Member States on the conditions of disclosure, which could authorize in exceptional cases, notably in the case of gametes donation, the lifting of donor anonymity (*see* Recital 29 in the Preamble to the Tissues and Cells Directive).

663. The Tissues and Cells Directive does not affect the decisions of the Member States prohibiting, among others, the donation or use of any specific type of human tissues or cells or cells from any specified source, including where those decisions also concern imports of the same type of human tissues or cells (Article 4.3).

664. The TEU and the TFEU do not give the EU powers to adopt legislation on harmonization of national laws on assisted human reproduction, including surrogacy.[591] In this respect, the EU may only regulate quality and safety aspects regarding tissues and cells (Article 168, 4a TFEU). It is for the Member States to regulate this matter in the light of their social and cultural traditions and to ensure that fundamental rights are effectively respected and protected in accordance with their national legislation and international human rights obligations.[592]

590. *Ibid.*, paras 38–43.

591. Answer given by Ms Dali on behalf of the European Commission to the written Parliamentary question of J. Wisniewska and M. de la Pisa Carrion, Surrogacy in the EU, 15 Mar. 2021, E-000209/2021.

592. Answer given by Mr Reynders on behalf of the European Commission to the written Parliamentary question of A. Panza et al., Désir d'enfant (Desire of a child), 5 Nov. 2021, E-004271/2021; answer given by Mr Reynders on behalf of the European Commission to a written Parliamentary question of L. Ferrara, Problems in services for the voluntary termination of pregnancy in certain regions of Italy, 27 Aug. 2021, E-003434/2021.

§6. VOLUNTARY TERMINATION OF PREGNANCY

665. According to Article 60 of the EEC Treaty (now Article 57 TFEU), services are to be considered to be 'services' within the meaning of the Treaty where they are normally provided for remuneration, in so far as they are not governed by the provisions relating to the freedom of movement for goods, capital or persons. Intend (d) of the second paragraph of Article 60 expressly stated that activities of the professions fall within the definition of services. It must be held that termination of pregnancy, as lawfully practised in several Member States, is a medical activity which is normally provided for remuneration and may be carried out as part of a professional activity. In any event, the CJEU had already held in the judgment of *Luisi and Carbone*[593] that medical activities fall within the scope of Article 60 of the Treaty.[594]

666. The *Society for the Protection of Unborn Children Ireland* (SPUC) maintained that the provision of abortion could not be regarded as being a service on the grounds that it is grossly immoral and involves the destruction of the life of a human being, namely the unborn child. Whatever the merits of those arguments on the moral plane, it was not for the CJEU to substitute its assessment for that of the legislature in those Member States where these activities are practised legally. Accordingly, medical termination of pregnancy, performed in accordance with the law of the State in which it is carried out, constitutes a service within the meaning of the Treaty.[595]

667. This judgment has caused serious political repercussions. It was a direct reason why the Member States supplemented the Treaty of Maastricht with the additional Protocol No. 17 guaranteeing that: 'Nothing in the Treaty on European Union or in the Treaties establishing the European Communities or in the Treaties or Acts modifying or supplementing those Treaties shall affect the application in Ireland of Article 40.3.3. of the Constitution of Ireland.'[596]

668. A Dutch member of the European Parliament raised different questions to the Council concerning a ship with doctors on board that sailed from the Netherlands in the direction of Ireland in order to offer Irish women the opportunity to have abortions. The ship was sailing under a Dutch flag, and the abortions would be carried out in international waters. One of the questions raised was, 'how does this initiative stand in relation to European Community law, relevant case-law and international public law'. The Council replied that it was 'not competent to give an answer to the questions raised since it is an internal affair of a Member State'.[597]

---

593. CJEU, *Luisi and Carbone*, joint Cases C-282/82 and C-26/83, ECLI:EU:C:1984:35.
594. CJEU 4 Oct. 1991, C-159/90, *The Society for the Protection of Unborn Children Ireland (SPUC) and S. Grogan and Others*, ECLI:EU:C:1991:378, paras 17–18.
595. *Ibid.*, paras 19–21. According to Advocate General van Gerven 'there can in my view be no doubt that the medical termination of pregnancy which if they are normally provided for remuneration constitute services' (I-4707 para. 9).
596. *Supra* n. 568, 139.
597. *OJ* 2002, C 40 E, 120.

During his speech to the Parliament on 19 January 2022, the President of the French Republic, Emmanuel Macron, announced that he would like to see the right to abortion included in the Charter of Fundamental Rights. A member of the Parliament asked how the Council Presidency planned to achieve the unanimity needed in order to revise the Charter of Fundamental Rights. The Council replied that it had not discussed this question and that any discussion regarding abortion and its potential inclusion in the Charter of Fundamental Rights would pay special attention to all the pertinent political and legal elements.[598]

669. In an answer to another question, Mr Dalli, on behalf of the Commission, admitted that 'unsafe abortions, not carried out by qualified medical personnel, clearly represent a health risk for women'. But he also repeated that 'considering the ethical, social and cultural dimensions of abortions, it is for Member States to develop and implement their policies and legal frameworks'. He added that the Commission does not have the intention to complement national health policies in this respect.[599] Legislative powers in this area lie within the exclusive competence of the Member States. Member States must respect fundamental rights binding them by virtue of their commitments under international law, including the right to private life under Article 8 of the ECHR. Data related to pregnancies are data related to health that can only be processed under certain circumstances, e.g., when necessary for the 'provision of health or social care or treatment' and subject to certain safeguards, like obligations of professional secrecy. Access to the health record has to be in line with the purpose of the record, i.e., to provide medical treatment.[600]

670. In yet another answer to a written question, Mr Borg, on behalf of the Commission, acknowledged the differences in the EU Member States' national policies and laws with regard to abortion. And he repeated that 'as such the EU has no competences on abortion policy at national level and can therefore not interfere in Member States' policies in this area'.[601] With regard to the reimbursement of termination of pregnancy under the Cross-Border Care Directive, the Commission referred to Recital 7 in the Preamble that states: 'This Directive respects and is without prejudice to the freedom of each Member State to decide what type of healthcare it considers appropriate. No provision of this Directive should be interpreted in such a way as to undermine the fundamental ethical choices of Member States.'[602] Article

598. Anonymous reply to a written Parliamentary question of N. Colin-Oesterlé, Inclusion of the right to abortion in the Charter of Fundamental Rights, 12 Dec. 2022, E-002301/2022.

599. *OJ* 2013, C 240 E, 183.

600. Answer given by Mr Reynders on behalf of the European Commission to a written Parliamentary question of R. Biedron & S. Rafaela, Register of Pregnancies in Poland, 17 Feb. 2022, E-005342/2021.

601. *OJ* 2014, C 286/136; *see also* the answer given by Mr Andriukaitis on behalf of the European Commission to the written Parliamentary question of S. in 't Veld, Safe abortion at risk in Europe, 27 Nov. 2018, E-005023/2018 and to the written Parliamentary question of J. Meuthen, Late-term pregnancies and Art. 2 of the TEU, 25 Mar. 2019, E-000296/2019 and the answer given by Ms Kyriakides on behalf of the European Commission to the written Parliamentary question of I-H. Kloc, Situation of persons with Down's syndrome, 16 Sep. 2020, E-003055/2020.

602. Answer given by Ms Kyriakides on behalf of the European Commission to the written Parliamentary question of S. Spurek, Right to safe termination of pregnancy on demand in connection with

11.1. of this Directive provides that a pharmacist may refuse to dispense a product that was prescribed in another Member State for 'ethical reasons' if he has this right and also if the prescription had been issued in the Member State of affiliation. Sovig rightly states that 'it is noteworthy that a similar limitation is not stipulated for medical personnel that experience similar reasons of conscience in situations of medical treatment'.[603]

671. In response to the question: 'What is the Commission's position on misuse of the conscience clause, which can result in the breach of the patient's right to healthcare?' the Commission answered: 'Member States must respect fundamental rights binding them by virtue of their commitments under international law, including the right to private life under Article 8 and the right to freedom of thought, conscience, and religion under Article 9 of the European Convention of Human Rights and the manner in which competing rights need to be balanced against each other.'[604]

672. On 11 April 2024, the European Parliament adopted a resolution on including the right to abortion in the EU Fundamental Rights Charter. The resolution urges the European Council to launch a Convention for the revision of the Treaties, as requested in its resolutions of 9 June 2022 and 22 November 2023, and to adopt its proposal included in its resolution of 22 November 2023 to add sexual and reproductive healthcare and the right to safe and legal abortion to the Charter and amend it as follows: 'Article 3: Right to the integrity of the person and to bodily autonomy: 2a. Everyone has the right to bodily autonomy, to free, informed, full and universal access to sexual and reproductive health and rights, and to all related healthcare services without discrimination, including access to safe and legal abortion.'

§7. Forced Sterilization

673. Forced sterilization is a grave violation of fundamental rights, such as the right to human dignity, the right to integrity of the person, prohibition of torture or inhuman or degrading treatment and the right to private and family life, as enshrined in Article 2 TEU and in the Charter of Fundamental Rights of the European Union.

The Convention on the Rights of Persons with Disabilities – to which all Member States and the EU are State Parties – requires to ensure freedom from torture or cruel, inhuman or degrading treatment or punishment as well as freedom from exploitation, violence and abuse for persons with disabilities on an equal basis with others.

---

cross-border healthcare in the EU, 10 Jan. 2020, E-003619/2019. *See* A. Mulligan, 'The Right to Travel for Abortion Services: A Case Study in Irish "Cross-Border Reproductive Care"', 22 *European Journal of Health Law* 239–266 (2015); I. Tucak & A. Blagojevic, 'COVID-19 Pandemic and the Protection of Abortion', *EU Comparative Law Issues and Challenges* 853–877 (2021).

603. *Supra* n. 359, 39.

604. Answer given by Ms Dali to a written Parliamentary question on behalf of the European Commission to the written Parliamentary question of R. Biedroń, Addressing misuse of the conscience clause leading to denial of the right to abortion, 21 Jun. 2023, E-001198/2023/rev.

The Commission encourages all Member States to ratify the Istanbul Convention that requires criminalizing forced sterilization.[605] The EU has acceded to the Convention in June 2023. Furthermore, the Commission has proposed a Directive on violence against women and domestic violence. While it does not criminalize forced sterilization, the measures for victim support and protection do apply to any type of violence criminalized at the national level.[606]

605. Answer by Ms Dalli on behalf of the European Commission to a written Parliamentary question of G. Da Re, Call for action by the Commission to condemn forced sterilization of people with disabilities, 12 Jan. 2023, E-003249/2022.

606. Answer given by Ms Dali on behalf of the European Commission to a written Parliamentary question of J. Gusmao, 11 Sep. 2023, E-001857/2023. *See* for the proposed Directive, Com (2012) 105 final.

Chapter 2. End of Life

§1 The Deceased Organ Donor

674. Donor means a person who donates one or several organs, whether donation occurs during a lifetime or after death (Article 3d Organs Directive). Internationally recognized principles guiding practices in organ donation and transplantation include, *inter alia*, the certification or the confirmation of death in accordance with national provisions before the procurement of organs from deceased persons (*see* Recital 20 in the Preamble to the Organs Directive).

675. Member States ensure that donations of organs from deceased donors are voluntary and unpaid (Article 13.1.). Member States prohibit advertising the availability of organs where such advertising is with a view to seeking financial gain or comparable advantage (Article 13.3.).

676. The procurement of organs may be carried out only after all requirements relating to consent, authorization or absence of any objection in force in the Member State concerned have been met (Article 14). Several models of consent to donation coexist in the Union, including opting-in systems in which consent to organ donation has to be explicitly obtained and opting-out systems in which donation can take place unless there is evidence of any objection to donation. In order to enable individuals to express their wishes in this regard, some Member States have developed specific registries where citizens record them. The Organs Directive is without prejudice to the broad diversity of the systems of consent already in place in the Member States. In addition, by means of its Action Plan on Organ Donation and Transplantation, the Commission aims to increase public awareness of organ donation and, in particular, to develop mechanisms to facilitate the identification of organ donors across Europe (*see* Recital 21 in the Preamble).

§2. The Deceased Cells and Tissue Donor

677. Donor means every human source, whether living or deceased, of human cells or tissues (Article 3c Tissues and Cells Directive).

678. The procurement of human tissues or cells from a deceased donor is authorized only after all mandatory consent or authorization requirements in force in the Member State concerned have been met. Member States have to take, in keeping with their national legislation, all necessary measures to ensure that donors, their relatives or any persons granting authorization on behalf of the deceased donors are provided with all appropriate information as referred to in Annex B (Article 13). All information must be given, and all necessary consents and authorizations must be obtained in accordance with the legislation in force in the Member States (paragraph 1 of Annex B). The confirmed results of the donor's evaluation must be communicated and clearly explained to the relevant persons in accordance with the legislation in the Member States (paragraph 2 of Annex B).

679. Member States have to take all necessary measures to ensure that all data, including genetic information, collated within the scope of the Directive and to which third parties have access, have been rendered anonymous so that neither donors nor recipients remain identifiable (Article 14).

§3. ADVANCE DIRECTIVES

680. In a written question to the Commission, it was stated that in the EU, the entirely sensible procedure of drawing up an advance directive or advance statement concerning future medical care is governed, if at all, by national law. This was followed by this question: 'Does the Commission plan to create a uniform legal framework for such procedures or to take other harmonisation measures with a view to offering members of the public better guarantees that their wishes will be taken into account outside their own countries as well?' On behalf of the Commission, Mr Kyprianou answered as follows: 'there are no existing EU rules regulating issues of advance directives or advance statements. According to Article 152 of the EC Treaty, the organisation and delivery of healthcare is primarily the responsibility of the Member States. The Commission is not aware of any issues regarding patient orders or precaution orders which would be directly related to the cross-border mobility of patients'.[607] The European Parliament expressly urged, in its Resolution of 1 June 2017 on the protection of vulnerable adults, the Member States to promote self-determination for adults by introducing, in their national laws, 'mandates in anticipation of incapacity', drawing on the principles set out in the Recommendation of the Council of Europe concerning continuing powers of attorney and advance directives for incapacity. The Commission supports such developments of national laws. The Commission is reflecting on further actions to promote self-determination for adults.[608]

§4. EUTHANASIA

681. In answering a written Parliamentary question on whether the approval of what erroneously is called 'child euthanasia' by the Belgian Parliament is 'contrary to the EU's Charter of Fundamental Rights, particularly Article 2 (the right to life) and Article 24 (the rights of the child)', Mr Hahn on behalf of the Commission has given the following answer: 'Legal rules governing euthanasia – whether applied to

607. *OJ* 2006, C 327.
608. Answer given by Mr Reynders on behalf of the European Commission to a written Parliamentary question of A. Schwaab, Cross-border recognition of lasting powers of attorney, 10 Mar. 2020, E-000060/2020.

children or not – do not fall within the boundaries of Union competences.'[609] The Commission does not hold an overview of the current legal situation of euthanasia in the Member States.[610]

§5. Patients in a Vegetative State

682. In her answer to a parliamentary question on the Commission's position on the creation and maintenance of multilingual information portals at the EU level related to the care of patients in a vegetative state, Ms Kyriakides answered that according to Article 168, TFEU putting in place portals with information on advice and support for specific health conditions within a country falls under this Member State competence.[611]

609. *OJ* 2014, C 365, 15. Exactly the same answer has been given by Mrs Reding to a similar question, *OJ* 2014, C 405. Regarding euthanasia on mature minors in Belgium, *see supra* n. 413, 129–130; L. Bovens, 'Child Euthanasia: Should We Just Not Talk About It?', 41 *Journal of Medical Ethics* 630–634 (2015).
610. Answer given by Mr Andriukaitis on behalf of the European Commission to a written Parliamentary question of A. Miranda, 11 Jun. 2019, E-001801/2019.
611. Answer given by Ms Kyriakides on behalf of the European Commission to a written Parliamentary question of R. Haider, Caring for patients in a vegetative state, 7 Dec. 2023, E-003582/2023.

Selected Bibliography

Altavilla, A. 'Safe, Innovative and Accessible Medicines in Europe: A Renewed Strategy for Patients and the Pharmaceutical Sector'. *European Journal of Health Law* 25 (2018): 133–156.

Altavilla, A., et al. 'The Secondary Use of Paediatric Data under GDPR: Looking for New Safeguards for Research'. *European Pharmaceutical Law Review* 3 (2019): 156–164.

Axmin, M. *Access to Cross-Border Healthcare for Older Persons in the European Union*. Lund: Lund University, 2020.

Axmin, M. 'Access to Cross-Border Healthcare in the Light of Religious Freedom. Commentary on the Case C-243/19'. *European Journal of Health Law* 28 (2021): 185–196.

Baeten, R. *Was the Exclusion of Health Care from the Services Directive a Pyrrhic Victory? A Proportionality Test on Regulation of Health Professions.* OSE Opinion Paper No. 18 April 2017.

Baeten, R. 'Healthcare Regulation: An Obstacle to Cross-Border Trade in Services? On the Muffled Application of the EU Single Market Strategy'. In *Social Policy in the EU: State of Play,* edited by Vanhercke, B., Sabato, S. & Bouqet, D. Brussels: European Trade Union Institute and European Social Observatory, 2017.

Barbosa, C., 'The Processing of Personal Data for Scientific Research Purposes in Medicine. Some Aspects of the General Data Protection Regulation'. In *Deep Diving into Data Protection*, edited by J. Herveg. Brussels: Larcier, 2021.

Berki, G. *Free Movement of Patients in the EU: A Patient's Perspective.* Cambridge: Intersentia, 2018.

Berki, G. 'Patient Mobility in the EU: A Playground for All of Us?'. *Belgisch Tijdschrift voor Sociale Zekerheid (Belgian Journal on Social Security)* (2019): 65–79.

Bioy, X. 'Le droit fondamental à l'accès aux soins en Europe. Vers un standard de conciliation entre libertés économiques et droits du patient'. *Revue des Affaires Européennes* (2011): 495–506.

Bongers, L. *Moving Towards European Convergence in Classical Individual Patient's Rights. Can the New Individual Patients' Rights to Information under Article 6 (3) of Directive 2011/24/EU contribute?*. Doctoral thesis, University of Maastricht, 2022, 363 p.

Bovens, L. 'Child Euthanasia: Should We Just Not Talk about It?'. *Journal of Medical Ethics* 41 (2015): 630–634.

Selected Bibliography

Busby, H., T. Hervey & A. Mohr. 'Ethical EU Law? The Influence of the European Group on Ethics in Science and New Technologies'. *European Law Review* 33 (2008): 803–842.

Büyüksagis, S. 'L'arrêt Sanofi. La responsabilité du fait des produits défectueux appliquée aux vaccins, une responsabilité objective basée sur des presomptions'. *Journal de droit européen* (2017): 395–397.

Chassang, G. 'What about Post-Mortem Digital Privacy and Personal Health Data Protection?'. In *Deep Diving into Data Protection,* edited by J. Herveg. Brussels: Larcier, 2021.

Christou, G. & I. Rashild. 'Interest Group Lobbying in the European Union: Privacy, Data Protection and the Right to Be Forgotten'. *Comparative European Politics* 19 (2021): 380–400.

Cloatre, E. 'Regulating Alternative Healing in France, and the Problem of "Non-Medicine"'. *Medical Law Review* 27 (2019): 189–214.

Cloatre, E. & F. Salvini Ramas. 'The Regulation of Acupuncture in France and the United Kingdom: Shifts and Fragmentation in Contrasting Healthcare Systems'. *Medical Law International* 19 (2019): 235–257.

Comandè, G. & G. Schneider. 'Differential Data Protection Regimes in Data-Driven Research: Why the GDPR is More Research-Friendly Than You Think'. *German Law Journal* 23 (2022): 559–596.

Daniel, E. 'La liberté de circulation des professionels face aux exigences linguistiques'. *Revue des Affaires Européennes* (2016): 371–379.

Davies, G. 'Legislating for Patients' Rights'. In *Health Care and EU Law*, edited by J.W. van de Gronden et al. The Hague: Asser Press, 2011.

Defloor, S. 'The Legal Protection of the Medically Examined Applicant for Insurance'. *Medicine and Law* 29 (2010): 183–192.

De Grove-Valdeyron, N. 'La Directive sur les droits des patients en matière de soins de santé transfrontaliers. Véritable statut juridique européen du patient ou simple clarification d'un régime de mobilité?'. *Revue Trimestrielle de Droit Européen* 47 (2011): 299–327.

De Grove-Valdeyron, N. 'De l'espace européen de la santé en ligne à l'espace européen des données de la santé: le numérique au service de la construction d'une Union Européenne de la santé' ['From the European E-health Space to the European Health Data Space: Digital Technology for the Construction of a European Health Union']. *Revue des Affaires Européennes/Law and European Affairs* (2021): 335–347.

De La Rosa, S. 'The Directive on Cross-Border Healthcare or the Art of Codifying Complex Case Law'. *Common Market Law Review* 49 (2012): 15–46.

Delnoij, D. & W. Sauter. 'Patient Information under the EU Patients' Rights Directive'. *European Journal of Public Health* 21 (2011): 271–272.

de Miguel Beriain, I., et al. 'What Can We Do with the Data of Deceased People? A Normative Proposal'. *European Review of Private Law* 29 (2021): 785–806.

de Miguel Beriain, I., et.al. 'An EU Comparative Analysis of the Regulation of Clinical Trials Supervising Bodies in the Aftermath of Regulation 536/2014'. *European Public Law* 26 (2020): 307–330.

den Exter, A. (ed.). *European Health Law.* Antwerp: Maklu, 2017.

den Exter, A. (ed.). *Cross-Border Health Care and European Union Law.* Rotterdam: Erasmus University Press, 2017.

den Exter, A. 'Case Note. Medical Professionals as Digital Marketeers and the Advertising Ban'. *Journal of Medical Law and Ethics* 5 (2017): 115–122.

de Ruijter, A. 'Mapping the Institutional Consolidation of EU Human Health Expertise'. *Comparative European Politics* 15 (2017): 370–393.

de Ruijter, A. *EU Health Law and Policy: The Expansion of EU Power in Public Health and Health Care.* Oxford: Oxford University Press, 2019.

Devetzi, S. & J. McHale. 'Health and Long-Term Care Benefits and the Proposed Revised Coordination Regulation: A Brave New World or Much Ado About Nothing?'. *European Journal of Social Security* 22 (2020): 180–195.

De Vries, S.A. 'De Europese patiëntenrechtenrichtlijn: van privileges naar rechten voor alle patiënten in Europa'. *Nederlands Tijdschrift voor Europees Recht* (2011): 215–224.

Donelly, M. & M. Donagh. 'Health Research, Consent and the GDPR Exemption'. *European Journal of Health Law* 26 (2019): 97–119.

Dove, E.S. & J. Chen. 'Should Consent for Data Processing Be Privileged in Health Research? A Comparative Analysis'. *International Data Privacy Law* 10 (2020): 117–131.

Drventic, U. 'The Protection of Adults in the EU'. *EU and Comparative Law Issues and Challenges* (2019): 804–829.

Dubouis, L. 'La directive n° 2011/24 relative à l'application des droits des patients en matière des soins de santé'. *Revue de Droit Sanitaire et Social* (2011): 1059–1070.

Dubuis, A. *Les droits du patient en droit de l'Union européenne.* Brussels: Bruylant, 2017.

Duguet, A.-M. & J. Herveg. 'Safeguards and Derogations Relating to Processing for Scientific Purposes: Article 89 Analysis for Biobank Review'. In *GDPR and Biobanking. Individual Rights, Public Interest and Research Regulation Across Europe*, edited by S. Slokenberga, O. Tzortzatou & J. Reichel. Cham: Springer, 2021.

Emaus, J. 'Introduction to the Case Note on the Right to be Forgotten', *European Review of Private Law* 30 (2022): 235–240.

Ernst, G. & K. Stöger. 'Give Due Consideration … Some Thoughts on Member States' Obligations Under Article 13 of the HTA Regulation', *European Journal of Health Law* 31 (2024): 171–186.

Faltus, T. & I. Miguel Berlain. 'The EU Legal Framework on Clinical Trials Directed to Therapeutic Germline Gene Alteration: A Critical and Systematic Analysis'. *Medical Law International* 23 (2023): 44–69.

Flear, M.L. 'The EU Clinical Trials Regulation: Key Priorities, Purposes and Aims and the Implications for Public Health', *Journal of Medical Ethics* 42 (2016): 192–198.

Fartunova-Michel, M. & B. Nabli. *Droit de l'Union Europeénne de la Bioéthique.* Brussels: Bruylant, 2021.

Florea, M. 'Withdrawal of Consent for Processing Personal Data in Biomedical Research'. *International Data Privacy Law* 13 (2023): 107–122.

Selected Bibliography

Gaspari, E. 'Sponsoring a Clinical Trial: Pharmaceutical Companies' Liability under the Scrutiny of the Italian Supreme Court'. *European Pharmaceutical Law Review* 5 (2021): 98–101.

Gennet, E., R. Andorno & B. Elger. 'Does the New EU Regulation on Clinical Trials Adequately Protect Vulnerable Research Participants'. *Health Policy* 119 (2015): 925–931.

Gevers, S. 'Health Law in Europe: From the Present to the Future'. *European Journal of Health Law* 15 (2008): 261–272.

Guarda, P. '"OK Google, Am I Sick?" Artificial Intelligence, E-health and Data Protection Regulation'. *Biolaw Journal* (2019): 368–371.

Hansen, J., et al. *Assessment of the EU Member States' Rules on Health Data in the Light of the GDPR*. Brussels: European Commission, 2021.

Harbinja, E. 'Posthumus Medical Data Donation: The Case for a Legal Framework'. In *The Ethics of Medical Data Donation*, edited by J. Krutzinna & L. Floridi. Cham: Springer, 2019.

Harmon, S.H.E., G. Laurie & A. Courtney. 'Case Comment. Dignity, Plurality and Patentability: The Unfinished Story of Brüstle v Greenpeace'. *European Law Review* 38 (2013): 92–106.

Hendriks, A. & J. Gevers. '(Pre-)employment Medical Examinations and the Law, with Particular Reference to the European Union'. *European Journal of Health Law* 1 (1994): 229–264.

Hendriks, A. 'Editorial. High-Quality of Care Throughout Europe – But Do We Speak the Same Language?'. *European Journal of Health Law* 23 (2016): 1–4.

Hennette-Vauchez, S. 'Biomedicine and EU Law: Unlikely Encounters?'. *Legal Issues of Economic Integration* 38 (2011): 5–31.

Herringa, J. & J. Dute. 'The Proposed EU-Regulation on Clinical Trials on Medicinal Products'. *European Journal of Health Law* 20 (2013): 347–362.

Herveg, J. & A. Altavilla. 'Introducing Key Elements Regarding Access to Personal Data for Scientific Research in the Perspective of Developing Innovative Medicines'. *European Journal of Health Law* 27 (2020): 195–212, Special Issue: Innovative Medicine and Research: Ethical, Legal and Regulatory Issues.

Hervey, T. 'EU Law and National Health Policies: Problem or Opportunity?'. *Health Economics, Policy and Law* 2 (2007): 1–6.

Hervey, T. 'Cooperation Between Healthcare Authorities in the Proposed Directive on Patients' Rights in Cross-Border Healthcare'. In *Health Care and EU Law*, edited by J.W. van de Gronden et al. The Hague: Asser Press, 2011.

Hervey T.K. & J.V. McHale. *European Union Health Law. Themes and Implications.* Cambridge: Cambridge University Press, 2015.

Hervey, T.K. 'Telling Stories About European Union Health Law: The Emergence of a New Field of Law', *Comparative European Politics* 15 (2017): 352–369.

Hervey, T.K. 'Patient Mobility, Solidarity and Equal Access'. In *Cross-Border Health Care and European Union Law*, edited by A. Den Exter. Rotterdam: Erasmus University Press, 2017.

Hervey, T. & S. Sheldon. 'Abortion by Telemedicine in the European Union'. *International Journal of Gynecology & Obstetrics* 145 (2018): 125–128.

Hervey, T. & A. De Ruijter. 'The Dynamic Potential of European Union Health Law'. *European Journal of Risk Regulation* 11 (2020): 726–735.

Heselhaus, S. 'Human Dignity in Europe'. In *Handbook of Human Dignity in Europe*, edited by P. Becchi & K. Mathis. Cham: Springer Nature Switzerland, 2019.

Kalokairinou, L., H. Howard & P. Borry. 'Current Developments in the Regulation of Direct-to-Consumer Genetic Testing in Europe'. *Medical Law International* 15 (2015): 97–123.

Kalokairinou, L., et al. 'Legislation of Direct-to-Consumer Genetic Testing in Europe: A Fragmented Regulatory Landscape'. *Journal of Community Genetics* 8, published online 18 November 2017.

Kierkegaard, P. 'Electronic Health Record: Wiring Europe's Healthcare'. *Computer Law & Security Review* 27 (2011): 503–515.

Kiseleva, A & P. De Hert. 'Creating a European Health Data Space: Obstacles in Four Key Legal Areas'. *European Pharmaceutical Law Review* 5 (2021): 21–36.

Kiseleva, A & I. de Miguel Beriain. 'What Will Become of Our Health Data When We Die? The European Health Data Space Might Have an Answer'. *European Pharmaceutical Law Review* 7 (2023): 16–28.

Klesta, L. 'Le patient est-il un consommmateur?'. *European Journal of Consumer Law-Revue Européenne de Droit de la Consommation* (2010): 225–234.

Kortese, L. 'Exploring Professional Recognition in the EU: A Legal Perspective'. *Journal of International Mobility* (2016): 43–58.

Laurie, G. 'Editorial. The European Association of Health Law: Addressing Unmet Needs in Policy, Practice and Research'. *European Journal of Health Law* 15 (2008): 251–259.

Leenen, H.J.J. 'Patients' Rights in Europe'. *Health Policy* 8 (1987): 33–38.

Leenen, H.J.J. 'Editorial. The European Journal of Health Law: A New Publication'. *European Journal of Health Law* 1 (1994): 1–3.

Legemaate, J. 'Patients' Rights Relating to Patient Safety'. In *Direito Da Saudo. Estudos em Homenagem ao Prof. Doutor Guilherme de Oliveira*, edited by Loureiro, J., Pereira, A.D. & Barbosa, C. (Coord.). Coimbra: Almedina, 2016.

Legido-Quigley, H., et al. 'Cross-Border Healthcare in Europe: Clarifying Patients' Rights'. *British Medical Journal* 342 (2011): 364–367.

Lindstad, S. & K.R. Ludvigsen. 'When is the Processing of Data from Medical Implants Lawful? The Legal Grounds for Processing Health-Related Data from ICT Implantable Medical Devices for Treatment Purposes under EU Data Protection Law', *Medical Law Review* 31 (2023): 317–339.

Long, W. & F. Blythe. 'Continued Uncertainty for the GDPR and Clinical Trials'. *European Pharmaceutical Law Review* 3 (2019): 82–85.

Mansnérus, J. 'Patentability of Parthenogenic Stem Cells: International Stem Cell Corporation v. Comptroller General of Patents'. *European Journal of Health Law* 22 (2015): 267–286.

Marelli, L., et al. 'The European Health Data Space: Too Big to Succeed?'. *Health Policy* 135 (2023): 104861.

Martens, M. & L. Arifagic. 'First Assessment of the SOHO Proposal for a New Legislation of Blood, Tissues and Cells (the SOHO Protocol)'. *European Pharmaceutical Law Review* 6 (2023): 53–72.

McHale, J. 'Fundamental Rights and Healthcare'. In *Health Systems Governance in Europe: The Role of EU Law and Policy*, edited by E. Mossialos, et al. Cambridge: Cambridge University Press, 2010.

McHale, J.V. 'Reforming the EU Clinical Trials Directive: Streamlining Processes of a Radical "New" Agenda?'. *European Journal of Health Law* 20 (2013): 363–381.

McHale, J.V. 'Health Law, Brexit and Medical Devices: A Question of Legal Regulation and Patient Safety'. *Medical Law International* 18 (2018): 195–215.

McMillan, C. 'Rethinking the Regulation of Digital Contraception under the Medical Devices Regime'. *Medical Law International* 23 (2023): 3–25.

Michalowicz, A. 'How to Protect Information About Our Mental States? A Few Remarks on Processing of Mental Data Under the GDPR'. *European Journal of Consumer Law* (2023): 127–143.

Michalowski, S. 'Right to the Integrity of the Person'. In *The EU Charter of Fundamental Rights: A Commentary*, edited by S. Peers, et al. London: Hart Publishing, 2014.

Michel, V. 'Entre logique économique et sanitaire: la conception des droits des patients en matière de soins de santé transfrontaliers'. *Revue des Affaires Européens* (2011): 507–518.

Misheva, K. & M. Ampovska. 'The Legal Aspects of Telehealth'. *EU and Comparative Issues and Challenges* (2022): 393–409.

Misic Radanovic, N. & I. Vukusic. 'Causation in Medical Malpractice'. *EU Comparative Law Issues and Challenges* (2020): 771–797.

Morton, A.J.B. 'European Health Care Systems and the Emerging Influence of European Union Competition Policy'. *Journal of Health Politics, Policy and Law* 46 (2021): 467–486.

Mostert, M., et al. 'Big Data in Medical Research and EU Data Protection Law: Challenges to the Consent or Anonymise Approach'. *European Journal of Human Genetics* 24 (2016): 956–960.

Mostert, M., et al. 'From Privacy to Data Protection in the EU: Implications for Big Data Health Research'. *European Journal of Health Law* 25 (2018): 43–55.

Mulligan, A. 'The Right to Travel for Abortion Services: A Case Study in Irish "Cross-Border Reproductive Care"'. *European Journal of Health Law* 22 (2015): 239–266.

Nordeng, Z. & F. Veggeland. 'The Implementation of European Union (EU) Rules on Cross-Border Care: Moving Towards Convergence'. *Health Economics, Policy and Law* 15 (2020): 141–159.

Nys, H. 'Medical Law and Health Law: From Co-existence to Symbiosis?'. In 'Health Legislation at the Dawn of the XXIst Century', *International Digest of Health Legislation* 49 (1998), Special Issue: Health Legislation at the Dawn of the XXIst Century, 1–18.

Nys, H. 'Organ Transplantation and the Proposed Directive on Cross Border Care'. *European Journal of Health Law* 17 (2010): 427–431.

Nys, H. 'The Exclusion of Organ Transplantation from the Cross-Border Care Directive: Boundary or Opportunity?'. In *Organ Transplantation: Ethical, Legal and Psychosocial Aspects. Expanding the European Platform*, edited by M.A. Weimar et al. Lengerich: Pabst Science Publishers, 2011.

Nys, H. 'Towards a Human Right "To Be Forgotten Online"?'. *European Journal of Health Law* 18 (2011): 469–475.

Nys, H. 'Editorial. The Right to Informed Choice and the Patients' Rights Directive'. *European Journal of Health Law* 19 (2012): 327–331.

Nys, H. 'New European Rules Regarding the Approval of Clinical Trials, the Role of Ethics Committees and the Protection of Subjects'. *Archives Immunology Experimental Therapy* 30 (2012): 405–414.

Nys, H. 'The Information Rights of the Patient in the European Patients' Rights Directive'. In *Direito Da Saudo. Estudos em Homenagem ao Prof. Doutor Guilherme de Oliveira*, edited by Loureiro, J., Pereira, A.D. & Barbosa, C. (Coord.). Coimbra: Almedina, 2016.

Nys, H. *Medical Law in Belgium.* Alphen aan den Rijn: Wolters Kluwer, 2017.

Nys, H. *Medical Law in the Netherlands.* 2nd edn. Alphen aan de Rijn: Kluwer Law International, 2021.

Nys, H. 'Editorial: the Directive on a Proportionality Test and Healthcare Professions'. *European Journal of Health Law* 26 (2019): 1–3.

Nys, H. *Medical Law in Belgium.* 6th edn. Alphen aan den Rijn: Wolters Kluwer, 2021.

Olsson, J., J. De Smedt & F. De Wispelaere. *Data on Cross-Border Patient Healthcare following Directive 2011/24/EU. Reference Year 2020.* Brussels: European Commission DG Santé, 2021.

Pahlsson, R. 'The VAT Exemption for Health Care: The EU Law and Its Impact on Swedish Law'. *Nordic Tax Journal* (2015): 18–35.

Paju, J. 'Case C-243/19 A v. Veselibas Ministrija'. *Maastricht Journal of European and Comparative Law* 28 (2021): 900–907.

Palm, W. & R. Baeten. 'The Quality and Safety Paradox in the Patients' Rights Directive'. *European Journal of Public Health* 21 (2011): 272–274.

Palm, W., et al. 'Patients' Rights: From Recognition to Implementation'. In *Achieving Person-Centred Health Systems. Evidence, Strategies and Challenges*, edited by E. Nolte et al. Cambridge: Cambridge University Press, 2020.

Patuzzo, S. & E. Pulice. 'Towards a European Code of Medical Ethics: Ethical and Legal Issues'. *Journal of Medical Ethics* 43 (2017): 41–46.

Peeters, M. 'Free Movement of Patients: Directive 2011/24 on the Application of Patients' Rights in Cross-Border Healthcare'. *European Journal of Health Law* 19 (2012): 29–60.

Peeters, M. 'Richtlijn 2011/24 betreffende de toepassing van de rechten van de patiënt bij grensoverschrijdende zorg: impact op de (Belgische) gezondheidszorg'. *Tijdschrift voor Gezondheidsrecht/Revue Droit de la Santé* 17 (2011–2012): 94–112.

Penosa, S., et al. 'The EU General Data Protection Regulation: How Will It Impact the Regulation of Research Biobanks? Setting the Legal Frame in the Mediterranean and Eastern European Area'. *Medical Law International* 18 (2018): 241–255.

Pertek, J., 'Partial Access to the Professions for Which Recognition Is Automatic: Directive 2005/36 Does Not Organise It, but Does Not Prevent It'. *Revue des Affaires Européennes* (2021): 217–221.

Pertini, C. 'What Is the Role of Ethics Committees after Regulation (EU) 536/ 2014?'. *Journal of Medical Ethics* 42 (2016): 186–188.

Pormeister, K. & L. Drozdzowski. 'Protecting the Genetic Data of the Unborn Children: A Critical Analysis'. *EDPL* (2018): 53–64.

Quinn, P. & P. De Hert. 'The European Patients' Rights Directive: A Clarification and Codification of Individual Rights Relating to Cross-Border Healthcare and Novel Initiatives Aimed at Improving Pan-European Healthcare Cooperation'. *Medical Law International* (2012): 1–42.

Quinn, P. 'The Anonymisation of Research Data – A Pyric Victory for Privacy that Should Not Be Pushed Too Hard by the EU Data Protection Framework'. *European Journal of Health Law* 24 (2017): 347–367.

Quinn, P. & G. Malgieri. 'The Difficulty of Defining Sensitive Data – The Concept of Sensitive Data in the EU Data Protection Framework'. *German Law Journal* 22 (2021): 1583–1612.

Reichel, J. 'The GDPR and Processing of Personal Data for Research Purposes: What about Case Law?'. *European Public Law* 27 (2021): 167–189.

Rial-Sebbag, E., G. Chassang & F. Taboulet. 'Quelle gouvernance pour les droits des patients en Europe?'. *Revue des Affaires Européennes* (2011): 549–564.

Rieder, C.M. 'The Application and Interpretation of the EU Charter in the Context of Cross-Border Movement of Patients'. *Columbia Journal of European Law* 22 (2016): 451–482.

Roscam Abbing, H.D.C. 'Rights of Patients in the European Context, Ten Years and After'. *European Journal of Health Law* 11 (2004): 7–16.

Roscam Abbing, H.D.C. 'Editorial. Founding a European Association for Health Law: The Rationale'. *European Journal of Health Law* 13 (2006): 203–207.

Roscam Abbing, H.D.C. 'Problem Doctors and Patients' Rights to Good Quality Care in the European Union'. *European Journal of Health Law* 13 (2006): 301–308.

Roscam Abbing, H.D.C. 'Patients' Rights to Quality of Healthcare: How Satisfactory Are the European Union's Regulatory Policies?'. *European Journal of Health Law* 19 (2012): 415–422.

Roscam Abbing, H.D.C. 'Twenty Years WHO Principles of Patients' Rights in Europe, a Common Framework: Looking Back to the Future'. *European Journal of Health Law* 21 (2014): 323–337.

Roscam Abbing, H.D.C. 'Patients' Rights to Access to Quality of Healthcare Throughout the European Union: The Role of EU Legislation'. In *Direito Da Saudo. Estudos em Homenagem ao Prof. Doutor Guilherme de Oliveira,* edited by Loureiro, J., Pereira, A.D. & Barbosa, C. (Coord.). Coimbra: Almedina, 2016.

Roscam Abbing, H.D.C. 'Editorial. New EU Rules for in Vitro Diagnostic Genetic Tests, a First Step in the Right Direction'. *European Journal of Health Law* 25 (2017): 121–133.

Roscam Abbing, H.D.C. 'Editorial. Human Organs for Transplantation: Self-Sufficiency, a European Perspective'. *European Journal of Health Law* 26 (2019): 87–96.

Safjan, M. (ed.). *Medical Law. Cases and Commentaries.* Warszawa: Wolters Kluwer, 2012.

Sauter, W. *Harmonization in Healthcare: The EU Patients' Rights Directive,* Research Paper Tilec, 2011, no. 06.

Schäfke-Zell, W. 'Revisiting the Definition of Health Data in the Age of Digitalized Health Care'. *International Data Privacy Law* 12 (2022): 33–43.

Schmidt, A.E, et al. 'Cross-Border Healthcare Collaboration in Europe (2007–2017)'. *Health Policy* 126 (2022): 1241–1247.

Shabani, M. & L. Marelli. 'Re-identifiability of Genomic Data and the GDPR'. *Embo Reports* (24 May 2019): e48316.

Shatrov, K. & C.R. Blankart. 'After the Four-Year Transition Period: Is the European Union's Medical Device Regulation of 2017 Likely to Achieve Its Main Goals?' *Health Policy* 126 (2022): 1233–1240.

Shaw, D. & D. Townend. 'Division and Discord in the Clinical Trials Regulation'. *Journal of Medical Ethics* 42 (2016): 729–731.

Sein, K. & G. Splindler. 'GDPR and Processing Health Data in Insurance Relationships: the Role of Statutory Legal Basis'. *European Pharmaceutical Law Review* 6 (2022): 98–116.

Slokenberga, S. 'Direct-to-Consumer Genetic Testing: Changes in the EU Regulatory Landscape'. *European Journal of Health Law* 20 (2015): 463–480.

Slokenberga, S. *European Legal Perspectives on Health-Related Direct-to-Consumer Genetic Testing.* Stockholm: Jure, 2016.

Slokenberga, S. 'Setting the Foundations: Individual Rights, Public Interest and Biobanking'. In *GDPR and Biobanking. Individual Rights, Public Interest and Research Regulation Across Europe*, edited by S. Slokenberga, O. Tzortzatou & J. Reichel. Cham: Springer, 2021.

Slokenberga, S., Minssen, T. & A. Nordberg (eds). 'Special Issue: Genome Editing, Health Innovation and Regulation'. *European Journal of Health Law* 29 (2022): 327–619.

Stuyck, J. 'Arrêt Vanderborght: l'interdiction belge de publicité en matière de soins dentaires à l'épreuve du droit de l'Union europeénne'. *Journal de droit européen* (2017): 324–326.

Taylor, M., et al. 'When the Child Speaks for Herself? The Limits of Parental Consent in Data Protection Law for Health Research'. *Medical Law Review* 26 (2018): 377–382.

Terzis, P., et al. 'Interoperability and Governance in the European Health Data Space Regulation'. *Medical Law International* 23 (2023): 368–376.

Timmers, M., et al. 'Will the EU Data Protection Regulation 2016/679 Inhibit Critical Care Research?'. *Medical Law Review* 27 (2019): 59–78.

Tinière, R. 'L' Europe de la santé à l'épreuve du tourisme médical motivé par les convictions religieuses. The Hypothetical Emergence of a Medical Tourism Founded on Religious Convictions'. *Revue des Affaires Européennes* (2020): 957–962.

Tosini, L. 'The Right to Object to Automated Individual Decisions: Resolving the Ambiguity of Article 22 (1) of the General Data Protection Regulation'. *International Data Privacy Law* 11 (2021): 33–43.

Tucak, I. & A. Blagojevic. 'COVID-19 Pandemic and the Protection of Abortion'. *EU Comparative Law Issues and Challenges* (2021): 853–877.

van de Gronden, J.W. 'Richtlijn Rechten van de patiënt bij grensoverschrijdende gezondheidszorg: veel huiswerk voor de Nederlandse zorgwetgever?'. *SEW* (2011): 373–387.

van de Gronden, J. & M. Veenbrink. 'EHDS and Free Movement of Patients: What EU Intervention is Needed?' *European Journal of Health Law* 31 (2024): 249–283.

van den Bossche, A.M. & P. Ploscar. 'Rights of Dental Patients in the EU – A Legal Assessment'. *Journal of Forensic Odonto-Stomatology* 30, No. 1 (November 2012): 4–11.

van Der Meij, A.P. 'The New Directive on Patients' Rights in Cross-Border Healthcare'. *Maastricht Journal of Comparative and European Law* 18 (2011): 382–392.

van Kolfschooten, H. 'EU Regulation of Artificial Intelligence: Challenges for Patients' Rights'. *Common Market Law Review* 59 (2022): 81–112.

van Leeuwen, B. 'The Doctor, the Patient, and EU Law: The Impact of Free Movement on Quality Standards in the Healthcare Sector'. *European Law Review* 41 (2016): 638–654.

van Leeuwen, B. 'Euthanasia and the Ethics of Free Movement Law: The Principle of Recognition in the Internal Market'. *German Law Journal* 19 (2018): 1417–1436.

Verhenneman, G., et al. 'How GDPR Enhances Transparency and Fosters Pseudonymisation in Academic Medical Research'. *European Journal of Health Law* 27 (2020): 35–57.

Vidalis, T. *The Emergence of Biolaw. The European Experience and the Evolutionary Approach.* Cham: Springer Textbooks in Law, 2022.

Vinck, I., et al. 'Market Introduction of Innovative High Risk Medical Devices: Towards a Recast of the Directive Concerning Medical Devices'. *European Journal of Health Law* 18 (2011): 477–489.

Visser, H. 'Non-therapeutic Research in the EU in Adults Incapable of Giving Consent'. *The Lancet* (2001): 818–819.

Wade, K. 'Defining the Threshold of Permissible Risk for Non-therapeutic Clinical Trials with Children in Europe'. *European Journal of Health Law* 24 (2017): 414–431.

Wested, J., 'The New Regulation of Health Technology Assessment'. *European Pharmaceutical Law Review* 6 (2022): 122–126.

Westra, A.E. 'Ambiguous Articles in the New EU Regulation May Lead to Exploitation of Vulnerable Research Subjects'. *Journal of Medical Ethics* 42 (2016): 189–191.

Zahn, R. 'The Regulation of Healthcare in the European Union: Member States' Discretion or a Widening of EU Law?'. *Femarbel* and *Ottica New Line, Common Market Law Review* 51 (2014): 1521–1538.

Index

The numbers here refer to paragraph numbers.

Active Citizen Network, 270
Asymmetry of information, 234
Autopsy, 26

Blacklist of medical practitioners, 196
Blastocyst stage, 654
Blood establishment, 642–644

Cannabis-based medicinal preparations, 70
Clientèle, 218
Clinical embryologist, 143
Communicable disease, 206, 538
Companion diagnostic, 498, 501, 517, 519
Conclusions on Common values and principles in European Health systems, 10
Confidence, 116, 211, 357
Consumer protection, 114, 115, 117, 123, 126, 128, 227, 556
Contact lenses, 49, 50
Corporate self-regulation, 225
Customer, 49, 51, 76, 92, 112

Dental clinic, 57
Declaration of Helsinki, 268, 461, 495
DNA, 530

European Group on Ethics in Science and New Technologies (EGE), 239
European Health Data Space (EHDS), 360, 597–603
European Health Union, 1, 310
Euthanasia, 26, 681

Fitness certificate, 35

Gene editing, 657, 658
Genetic test, 21, 29, 515–520
Group dental practice, 57
Group practice, 57, 206, 208, 214

Handbook on the Implementation of the Services Directive, 61, 69, 72
Health technology, 47
Helsinki Declaration, 268, 461, 495
Human ovum, 653, 655
Human parthenotes, 656

Insured person, 36, 133, 343

Lay person, 465, 499

Mandatory military service
Clinical trials, 450, 487, 508
Medical contract, 211, 213
Medical masseur-hydrotherapist, 76, 112, 116
Medical skills, 34
Medical prescription, 223
Medical supervision, 61

One-time patient, 206
Ophthalmologist, 49, 50, 200
Optical products, 54, 55
Optician's shop, 50–51, 54, 76
Opting-in, 676
Opting-out, 676
Order forms, 39–40
Ordre public, 650

Participative patient, 235
Passive patient, 235
Patients' rights day, 292, 293
Permanent availability of care, 214
Personal data and emotions, 525
Plastic surgery, 32

Index

Presumption of innocence, 107, 348
Problem doctor, 348
Professional mobility, 121

Recipient of a service, 141
Relaxation, 69
Residential care institutions
  Clinical trials, 450, 487
RNA, 530
Rogue doctor, 348

Sensitive activities, 65
Serious professional malpractice, 126, 128–130
Soft law, 7, 259–265
Speech therapy, 180
Standardized icons, 577
Stem cell bank, 31
Sunglasses, 76
Surrogacy, 658, 664

Taking of blood, 36
Telemedicine, 236
Therapeutic window, 455, 488
Transplantation centre, 609, 626

www.ingramcontent.com/pod-product-compliance
Lightning Source LLC
LaVergne TN
LVHW011121300926
849160LV00008B/463
9789403547282